Advance 1

"Ed Rahill's wonderful *One Mile at a Time* is a compelling, inspirational, heartfelt true story. I recommend this to anyone ready for an excellent memory-building book. Ed's story comes to a dramatic conclusion as he overcomes adversity and a deep personal loss during the running of the last great American road race.

This is a story of a young man on a hero's journey that reminds us of the best cars of 1960s, 1970s, and 1980s."

—Brian O'Shea, Driftwood, Texas

"When I sat down to read *One Mile at a Time*, I expected it to be an adventure story, a story about the great cross-country endurance races that became legendary in the twentieth century. Indeed, it was, but it is so much more. It is a story about love found and love lost, the gratification of making a difference in the lives of people in their time of need. And the deep connections we can have with each other and prior generations. It is also a story of how emotional collapse and heartbreak finally breaks a man. It is a story of what it was like to dwell on the dark side of emotions, and the painful impact on a man as his spirit collapses and his life is filled with hopelessness and a feeling of abandonment.

"Ed finds himself in this state, until one June night, when everything had fallen apart, and he had little hope of putting it back together. He was facing a choice, accept the setbacks and give up, or look deep into who he was, and look to his past, to make a choice in face of seemingly unbeatable odds. To try to rediscover the inner resilience he once had.

"It was a story about growing up and living in the twentieth century, the connections between family, lessons passed on from older generations to deal with adversity in the face of what at times seemed to be impossible odds. *One Mile at a Time* deals with challenges and joys of life, courage to do what one has to do in the face of fear of failure.

"For me as a professional counselor and life coach for clients at their time of deep despair and emotional collapse, I have come to understand how setbacks can emotionally devastate a person. The excitement I felt when I finished this book came from the realization that I had found a story, a true story that I can use to show my patients that life is worth living, with discovering their inner courage, respect for who they are, and the resilience they have within them. I feel for the moment that they can find some inspiration from Ed's story. Yes, it is a story about endurance racing. But it is a true story about a life well-lived."

—Andrew Warnecke, Marietta, Georgia

One Mile at a Time

A Memoir of the Last
Great American Road Race
and the Adventure We Call Life

Edward M. Rahill

Intellectual Property Notice: This document and content is the intellectual property of Edward M. Rahill and not to be copied, distributed, or used as a basis for another document, screenplay without consent.
Copyright June 23, 2022. "One Mile at a Time"
Application No. 1-114630830

This book is the sole copyright of the author. It cannot be reproduced in any form or distributed except through the channels chosen by the author. Excerpts may be used for reviews and the book may be used as the basis of classroom curriculum. For any other permissions or to schedule an author talk contact the author's representative.

info@edrahill.com

© Edward M. Rahill 2024

paperback ISBN — 978-1-954779-85-3
hardcover ISBN — 978-1-954779-86-0

Summary:
Destiny brought Edward Rahill the opportunity to compete in the road race of the century—a challenge he had dreamed of since he was a boy. The race was a turning point that shaped his life. This is a story of family, love and friendships, and triumph over impossible odds.

Contents

Foreword ix
How It Began xi

Chapter 1 How It All Started for Me 1
Chapter 2 Coming into My Own 23
Chapter 3 College Years and Grad School 47
Chapter 4 A Marriage between Friends 69
Chapter 5 Nancy 77
Chapter 6 A Race Too Far 97
Chapter 7 Everyone Gets a Break 123
Chapter 8 If at First You Don't Succeed 149
Chapter 9 God Works through People 159
Chapter 10 It's Time to Get Ready 169
Chapter 11 Strategies for Racing 181
Chapter 12 Gentlemen, Start your Engines 203
Chapter 13 Leaving the Past Behind 215
Chapter 14 A Thousand Miles to Go 237
Chapter 15 Setting Records and Wrecking a Car 265
Chapter 16 And Now the Rest of the Story 297
Epilogue 305

Appendix: News Clippings and Documentation I
Memorable Quotes XXV
About the Author XXX

Foreword

Ed and his drive at the monuments honoring the first transcontinental auto race. Coordinates: 44° 24' 12.9"N, 122° 22' 47.4"W

As I pulled up my Mustang to the monuments on the side of the road, I realized what had just happened. Running parallel to the now-paved US Highway 20 was a near-forgotten road, the original Santiam Wagon Road from over 150 years ago. I had just navigated the sportscar over some twenty miles of gravel, dirt, and stone, with its hairpin turns and steep and dangerous descents. It was similar to the conditions experienced by Dwight Huss and Milford Wigle in their forty-four-day transcontinental run back in

Edward M. Rahill

1905. I found my Mustang ill-equipped to handle the road, but it was perhaps better suited than their Old Scout, the 1904 Oldsmobile curved-dash runabout. It was then I realized my own race in 1984 closed the book on a hundred-year period in American history—one never to be experienced again.

This book chronicles the last documented endurance road race across the continental United States, which found its roots in 1893 and came to a dramatic conclusion in 1984. It was the race that set a new world record, one that thirty-nine years later still stands.

Times have changed, and America has, too. At the beginning of the last century, driving was an adventure, a statement of personal freedom, and a chance to experience the exhilaration of speed. In the twenty-first century, cars have become another utilitarian mode of transport, emphasizing efficiency, regulation, and limiting environmental impact.

In my own way, I have written this as a story of the twentieth century. As we live our lives, we tend to see our actions as individual choices. But that is not always the case. Sometimes the choices we make impact others. They have the potential to change people's lives and even inspire future generations.

This memoir tells the story of my experience growing up in the twentieth century, and how it intersected with American history. It is also a love story about love found and lost. It is a story about America filled with a certain passion, a nation filled with hope and a sense of adventure.

How It Began

The Great Cowboy Race of 1893

The riders wait at the starting gate to begin an epic 1,000-mile journey. (Public domain photograph)

The Great Cowboy Race of 1893 had been conceived as a publicity stunt to help put the town of Chadron, Nebraska on the map. It was never intended to be run. But the press got wind of it. Promoters in Chadron were delighted with the attention, and the story was published widely.

An excellent resource on this event is Richard A. Serrano, *American Endurance: Buffalo Bill, The Great Cowboy Race of 1893, and the Vanishing Wild West* (Washington, DC: Smithsonian Books, 2016).

Endurance horse racing had become a part of the American Western Culture with the start of the Pony Express in 1860. While not a race, the Pony Express highlighted the concept of traveling long distances by horse, across the country, as fast as could be done.

But on this day in 1893, a story was about to be made that was to capture America's fascination with Cross Country Road racing for the next one hundred years.

Hundreds of expected riders dwindled to twenty-five as the race day neared. It was June 13, 1893, and the riders assembled at the starting gate to begin an epic thousand-mile horse race. They gathered in the little Nebraska town to determine who was the best cowboy. Finally, that late spring morning, a single gunshot rang out. The horses leapt to full gallop to the cheers of two thousand spectators.

The contest was supposed to take fourteen days and average fifty-to-seventy-five miles a day—a lot to ask of a team of horses (and their riders). For two weeks, they thundered past angry sheriffs and Humane Society inspectors. Reporters were stationed along the route and reported back by telegraph. Waiting at the finish line was Buffalo Bill Cody, who'd set up his Wild West Show right next to the World's Fair. The winner was to be awarded a gold-plated Colt Forty-Five pistol. Nine riders finished, some traveling up to ninety miles a day. John Berry won, or technically arrived first, but was disqualified for having prior knowledge of the route. Chadron officials declared Joe Gillespie the winner.

Every period has its beginning and its end. The fate of the lone cowboy was sealed with barbed wire and the railroad. However, the uniquely American adventure of running a great contest across the land had only just begun. At the dawn of the twentieth century, a new adventure presented itself. The free spirit of the cowboy would live on.

One Mile at a Time

The First Cross-Continental Race, June 1905

The descent was terrifying. Dwight Huss struggled to control Old Scout, the Oldsmobile that had served his team for almost six weeks. The car began to slide uncontrollably as the downward grade of the gravel road neared 40 percent. When they approached the top of the Cascades Mountain pass, Milford Wigle, a mechanic and Dwight's partner, anticipated a problem with the brakes on the way down. He'd cut down several trees at the top of the pass on Santiam Wagon Road and tied the logs together so Old Scout could drag them behind. But it was even worse than they had feared. In a last-ditch effort to save the car, Wigle leapt out onto the tree trunk cargo to weigh them down and increase the drag.

Old Scout slid close to disaster as they barreled toward a bend in the gravel path. There was nothing to stop them from dropping off the precipice seventy yards ahead. Huss struggled to gain control of the car as she slid closer to the edge. The front wheels were angled to the right, not turning, just plowing through loose dirt. Huss decided to take one more chance. He momentarily turned his wheels into the slide. All four wheels were spinning again. Then, quickly, he turned the front wheels back to the turn. He released the brakes and increased the fuel with the hand accelerator.

The rear wheels were now pushing the car, and the front wheels were steering it again. It had worked. By turning into the slide, Huss had allowed the front wheels to reestablish their traction and turn back toward the curve of the road. It was close and for a moment, both left wheels had been hanging out in space.

Old Scout came to a stop as the road leveled out, and Dwight and Milford were stunned. They had been racing across the continent for forty days; they thought they'd seen the worst of it. The race had started in New York City. They were but four days from winning. The second-place car was to finish four days later. Dwight and Milford soon became heroes to a generation of adventurers. The time to beat for cross-continental road racing was forty-four days.

Edward M. Rahill

They had no idea what they had set in motion. Cross-continental endurance racing was born.

In 1905, Dwight Huss and Milford Wigle, winners of the first transcontinental race, delivered a message in Portland, Oregon. (Public domain)

One Mile at a Time

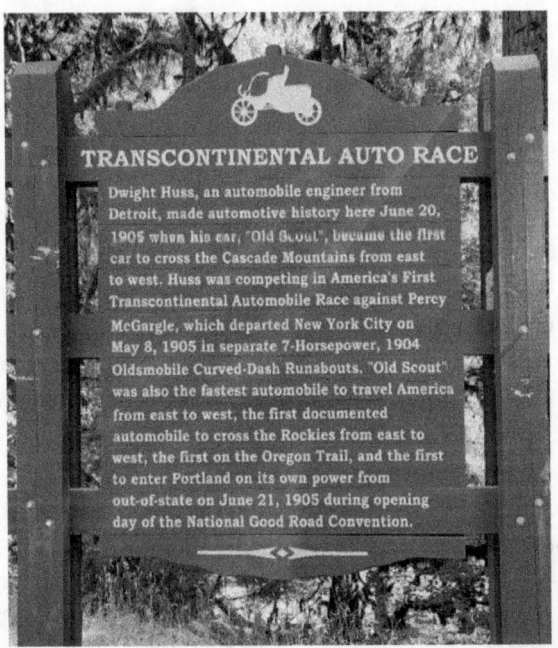

Plaque in Oregon honoring Huss and Wigle's victory in the first transcontinental automobile race, setting the stage for America's fascination for the next eighty years. Photo by the author, July 2023.

Edward M. Rahill

The Nation Came to Know Him as Cannonball Baker

The year was 1933. As Erwin George Baker drove through the farms of New Jersey, he saw the one thing he had been waiting to see since he had left L.A. fifty-one hours earlier. The Empire State Building emerged on the horizon. A few more miles and the outline of a second building became clear—the Chrysler. He'd driven over 2,700 brutal miles, mostly on dirt roads. While the roads had significantly improved since his previous attempt, the conditions were only bearable in larger cities, such as Indianapolis.

As his final cross-country run neared its close, Baker reminisced about his previous transcontinental adventures, which had started in San Diego in May 1914 via motorcycle. In May 1915, at the request of Harry Stutz, founder of the Stutz Motor Company, Baker crossed the country in one of Harry's famed Bearcats. Upon arriving in New York City, a newspaper reporter nicknamed Baker "Cannonball"—a nod to the Cannonball Express, a train famous for its great nonstop distances. The conditions were terrible, and crossing the plains presented dangers hidden beneath tall grass, including a run-in with quicksand that nearly ended his effort. Baker eventually arrived in New York after eleven days, seven hours, and fifteen minutes. In 1916, he again crossed the country in a Cadillac 8 Roadster. Baker covered the distance from L.A. to Times Square in just over a week.

Seventeen years later, he was about to arrive in that city driving a 1933 Graham-Paige model 57 Blue Streak 8 having raced across the U.S. in a little more than two days. At under fifty-four hours, he held the record for thirty-eight years. Later, his race inspired a journalist from an automotive magazine to take the concept of endurance racing to a new level.

One Mile at a Time

Erwin Baker with his 1914 motorcycle and later with a teammate during what is believed to be his 1916 Los Angeles to New York City run. (Public domain)

Edward M. Rahill

Transcontinental road racing is reborn.

Gurney/Yates Win First Cannonball, Polish Racing Hierarchy Finish Close Second
by Brad Niemcek, December 1971

Redondo Beach, Calif., Nov. 17, 1971. Dan Gurney and Brock Yates co-drove a Kirk F. White Ferrari Daytona coupe to a new unofficial record for cross-country vehicular travel here today. In the process, the team outran a field of seven others to win the first official Cannonball Baker Sea to Shining Sea Memorial Trophy Dash.

Yates, center, with his Dodge Challenger and the others from the original Cannonball Run, in 1979. (*Car and Driver* archives)

One Mile at a Time

In grade school, my first spelling mistake was the word apple with one p. I remember briefly engaging the teacher that "aple" was okay because you would pronounce it the same way. I did not get too far with that argument.

I had a good friend in Tinkerbell, the family boxer, and she liked me best. She would try to follow me and kept me company in lonely times. One embarrassing moment was a Sunday morning when we had walked to church. In the middle of Mass during the priest's sermon, there was the dog wandering through the church looking for me.

One day as I was walking home from school, I found her on the side of the road—she had been hit by a car. I remember carrying her lifeless body and crying all the way home. Months later, I wrote about what happened for my school's essay contest. I wrote it myself, and after the teacher accused me of getting extra help with my essay, my mother removed me from school. She later told me that the teacher did not like her because of the divorce.

In third or fourth grade, I had my first experience with bullies. On the walk home from school, I was regularly jumped and beaten up. I remember lying in bed at night and vowing to go down fighting with all my might. After a couple days of the bullies getting torn shirts, broken glasses, and bloody noses, they never touched me again. I wished I had a dad at home like the other boys did. I imagined he could have taught me how to handle these things. I remember thinking, *Life isn't fair. Get used to it.*

In middle school, I had the feeling that the teachers didn't respect me. It was just a feeling, which was confirmed when a guidance counselor met with my mother to tell her I was not college material and should go into the trades. At the time, I was a seventh grader in the eighth-grade science lab. At the teacher's request, I presented a lecture on space-time and the distance between stars. Astronomy was a hobby of mine, and I had a working knowledge of the basics. I can still recall some of the facts I presented that day. *It would take four years, four months, and seven days at the speed of light to reach our closest neighbor, Alpha Centauri. The speed of light is 186,282 miles per second, approximately 16.9 trillion miles a year.*

A year later, to her credit, my mother pulled me out of the local public school and enrolled me in Bishop Fallon High School. This set the stage for success.

She also encouraged me to get a job as soon as I was old enough. I got my working papers at age twelve. My first job was as a stock boy at Loblaws, the local supermarket. Later, I was a paper boy for my mother's paper. I had to get up at 5:15 a.m. Monday through Friday and 6:30 on the weekends. I rode my bike along the route and often crashed in the morning darkness. After all, this was Gardenville, New York, and it snowed a lot. With some of my paper route money, I purchased my first telescope—a 4.25-inch Schmidt reflector. I spent my nights up on the roof gazing at the planets and nebulae.

Another good memory was when my mother took the three of us for horseback riding lessons. We rode for several years as a family. I remember once while riding a trail, something spooked our horses and off they went, first at a canter and then at full gallop. It was a half mile before we stopped with the help of the trainers.

Once I settled down, I started to understand what it was like to gain control of my horse at a high speed. It was a good experience—it helped me overcome the fear of riding fast. I remember the roughness of the trot and the lumbering ride during the canter, but it was the smoothness of her gait at full gallop that impressed me. I would experience this same feeling in a car. I just didn't know it yet.

I stayed with riding another twelve years, gradually changing from English to Western, and I eventually learned how to ride bareback and perform several tricks. My last time on a horse until I reached my thirties was the day I had a terrible fall. The trainer was teaching me to do figure eights around two barrels. I was familiar with barrel racing and was getting proficient at it. But this new technique had me a bit intimidated. I was at a canter while lying on the horse's back, just using my shifting weight to direct the horse around the course. I missed the weight-shift going into the turn, fell, and broke most of my ribs on my right side. My recovery took almost four months.

Life Lessons from My Grandmother

One person who saw how my mother's turmoil affected me was my grandmother. We lived in the back house on her property. Mom would ask me to meet her every day after school. During my formative years, I spent more time with her than with my own mother.

Edward M. Rahill

For some reason, she would call me by my middle name, Michael, or Mick for short.

The message that Mom drove home to me from a young age was that only by providing for my family would I be a good and well-respected man. I understand why she drove this ethic into my being. She had good reason. Mom had lived a hard life.

She had to leave school after fifth grade to work and support her family. Her first job was walking the railroad yards near her house in South Buffalo to gather loose pieces of coal to sell. It was considered a good job. She was able to keep some of the coal to help her family heat the house and cook meals. My great-grandmother (her mother) had been sent to America from Ireland when she was fourteen because her family could no longer provide for her. She landed at Ellis Island and later traveled to a city named Buffalo, never to see her parents or siblings again. She struggled all her life as a maid at a large home on Delaware Avenue.

Later, Mom married and started to live more comfortably—she married and had four children. Her husband—my grandfather, Ed—was always looking for a way to make life better. Ed was a visionary, an entrepreneur. Henry Ford had been expanding into the rural areas of Western New York and was looking for a dealer to sell cars and trucks in the region. My grandfather jumped at the chance and worked with Ford to start the business from scratch. After a year and a half, he was selling and servicing enough vehicles to make ends meet. It was the middle of the Great Depression—1936. Finally, Mom reached a point where she could provide the nurturing and unconditional love, reassurance, and life lessons that young children need—something she never had herself.

But the family suffered a tragedy. My grandfather came down with an acute case of appendicitis, and he did not make it. He died at the age of thirty-seven. Mom had four children under twelve, no husband, a fifth-grade education, and no means of financial support. They had no money saved; it had gone to the dealership, which was their only source of income.

But it got worse. A month later, Ford's regional manager met with Mom to tell her that they had to transfer the franchise to another man; they did not see how she could run it without her husband. Her appeals to Ford in Detroit went unanswered.

Two months after that, a new regional manager stopped by to visit the dealership looking for a new franchisee. Mom prayed that day. After hearing her story, the new regional manager promised to give her a chance—one year, which was all he could cover her for. If she was not meeting the sales target, they would have to give the dealership to someone else. She had some limited experience with the business side, a few visits to customers and dinner discussions with her husband.

Rather than waiting for customers to come to the dealership, she would go door to door, introducing herself and her business. One evening, she was invited inside a home for dinner. She asked for a second serving of blood soup, even though she was totally taken aback that it was real blood—duck blood. The following week, she sold a car to that family. They became lifelong customers.

She never knew if she would make it that first year. She decided to raise chickens for food. Eggs and chicken were household staples for several years. My mother later told me the worst chore she ever had to do was laying the chicken on a wood block and cutting off its head with a small axe. The chicken would run around the yard without a head for ten seconds.

After that difficult year of door-to-door sales and working at the dealership six days a week, my grandmother had made it. She even found a way to increase revenue during the Second World War. She figured out how to convert a few Ford trucks into small buses. She started a bus charter company and contracted with the government to transport workers to and from their factory jobs. She not only earned the right to keep the dealership, but without knowing it, my grandmother became the first woman to own and operate a Ford dealership in the United States. The dealership became the most successful multi-location Ford dealer in Western New York. When I would ask her why she had worked so hard, she would say that she never asked to be put in that position, but she had to provide for her family.

With time, she turned the dealership over to her son and was back where she wanted to be. She got involved in charities, chairing numerous Catholic ones over the years. She served as the chair of the March of Dimes campaign for years. When I was twelve, I attended an awards dinner in her honor. Her faith was deep and her involvement in the church was extensive. She was always looking to help someone in need or tackle an overlooked problem. Of course, I got to know her later in life when her children were grown. Her oldest boy, Joe, had taken over the school bus business, and her youngest son, the dealership. So, I was lucky enough to be imprinted with her life lessons. With her, I found the feeling of "I'm okay."

From my grandmother, I developed my view of the world. I learned what it would take to grow into a respectable man. She would hold up my uncles as role models. Mom wanted me to understand the fleeting nature of our hopes and dreams. She would share her lessons with me regularly. "Life's odds are that everyone will get one opportunity to pursue their dreams; the challenge is recognizing it when you see it."

And along the same theme: "When you get that chance, take it. If you have a dream, chase it. The opportunity might only last for a moment and never present itself again."

Of course, Mom's greatest source of pain was the loss of her husband, a trauma that devastated my mother, who was barely seven years old when her father died. It was a critical moment in her life—a time when a child needs the most attention. My mother's overwhelming feeling of abandonment sprang from the loss of her father. When my grandmother later told me about this, she would say I needed to be strong because she felt that I, at that age, had also suffered abandonment due to my parents' break-up. I promised myself I would not repeat this pattern if I married and had a family of my own.

Mom always had a quick-witted comment. If you stubbed your toe and started to cry, she would say, "Stop whining, your toe is too far away from your head to hurt that much." If you were crying about something else, she would say, "Laugh and the world laughs with you, cry and you're going to cry alone." If she sensed I was procrastinating, she would say, "There are two types of people in the world. People who let life happen to them and people who make things in life happen. It's your choice what type of person you want to be." She would even give me advice about girls. Once she told me, "You're too nice, too accommodating, with the girls—they won't respect you. Make them work for your attention. Some women only want what they think they can't get!"

But the most important lesson was simply the example she set as she faced the trials of her own life. Is there any question why Mom taught me the importance of building a safe and nurturing environment for my loved ones? To provide for them in a way that would allow them to grow to their potential. To protect them from trading their dreams for some form of survival. It was so her future progeny would never have to sacrifice the way she, her children, or my mother did. Mom was asking me to remember the struggle of prior generations and prepare for my future family.

There was a common theme that ran through our after-school talks. She would try to give me advice about enduring difficult times, facing adversity. Mom would leave me with some of her favorite quotes:

"Sometimes a lost cause is the only one worth fighting for."

"Maybe, just maybe, Don Quixote was not crazy in his pursuit of his seemingly impossible quest."

"You will be measured not by the outcome of the struggle, but by the courage with which you handle it."

She would quote Winston Churchill: "Success is not final. Defeat is not fatal. It is the courage to continue that counts."

"Mick, I believe you've been given a gift of insight, ability, an instinctive moral code, and resilience," she told me. At the time, I really did not understand what she was saying. I did not even know what the word resilience meant.

The meaning of her advice only came together over time. I was still young and didn't fully comprehend her wisdom. I believe this was why she repeated the same messages. She would say, "Resilience is special; it is a quality that will serve you well in difficult times."

But what does it mean? I would ask. Am I resilient? She responded, "Resilience is an ability; it is part of your character . . . who you are. The ability to recover and try again," she would say. "It is the will to bounce back, the persistence to keep going on after something bad happens to you. And it takes courage to do that, the courage to dig deep inside and fight through the feelings of loneliness, abandonment, and defeat that will haunt you. I have seen many good people become trapped in these emotions—sometimes for years, some never truly recover."

She paused as if to collect her thoughts and said, "Mick, the most devastating emotion you will ever experience is fear. It will break your will and turn you against everything you believe in.

When that moment comes, force yourself to recall your past and what you believe in. From the past, you will find the courage to reengage in the struggle, it will show you the way. It will help you recover from the emotions that are crippling you; it will set you on the path back to who you are. It is up to you to make the choice to go on. If you make that choice, you will find you're not alone, you see. God helps those who help themselves. This is why I am telling you to pray as if everything depends on God, but also try as if everything depends on you.

Mom stopped there and was quietly staring out the window, lost in thought. I was a bit stunned. I felt overwhelmed, yet the passion she expressed made an impression on me. It made me feel as if she wanted to share a moment in her life when she felt abandoned and alone. In the face of something overwhelming, she did not know if she could go on—yet she did.

I finally asked if she was okay, and she turned to look at me and smiled. "Did I frighten you?" I didn't know how to respond. She smiled and talked about how pleasant the summer weather was. She asked me to come back the next day to visit some of her friends and have lunch.

"Mick, we need to go for a drive."

The next day was Saturday. It was late morning. I knocked at her door. It took a few seconds, but she waved me in. She was on the phone, and she appeared to be comforting a friend. "It's going to work out," she said into the receiver. "I have to go. I'll call you tomorrow to see how it went."

She was looking for her purse and said, "Mick, we need to go for a drive. It's time to continue our talk about life."

The next thing I knew, I was in the passenger seat of her '66 T-Bird, but she was not in the car. I panicked for a second, got out of the car, and found her standing by the driver's side door, waiting for me to open it for her. She was making a point—that I should treat women with respect. I never forgot to open or hold a door for her again.

Finally, we were off to visit a family in South Buffalo. I was amazed by all the people she knew. That day, she was dropping off a few boxes, a gift of a wedding dress for a daughter who was getting married. I later learned that they were a Ukrainian family Mom had sponsored to come to the United States as they had been refugees from World War II. I was starting to learn a pattern to Mom; she always went out of her way to help people in need. She would say it was her way to make a difference.

We finally left and were headed to lunch after a long visit. As we approached a red light, she suddenly stopped talking. There was something going on behind her. Another driver was giving her a hard time. He pulled up next to her at the light. I asked what was going on, and she said he had been cutting off other cars behind her. She said nothing else; she just bit her lip. I knew not to mess with her when she did that! She stepped on the brake and simultaneously pressed the accelerator. The sound of the engine increased in pitch. The T-Bird did not move, but it felt as if it was about to pounce.

The next thing I knew, tires were screeching, and I was thrown back. I felt the rapid acceleration and then the sound—a gripping sound. It was the T-Bird's motor winding through its full power curve as she tore away from the other car. That guy didn't stand a chance. I later learned that Mom's T-Bird had something called a police interceptor motor—it was a special-order car. Why not? It was her dealership!

After that baptism to road racing, we stopped at Schwabl's, a local restaurant, for a late lunch. I ordered beef on weck. Then Mom said she wanted to finish the conversation from the day before. At first, I thought, Here we go again. But this talk was a little different—it was more about me. She started by complimenting me.

> Mick, I think you have a gift to see things differently. You will have insights into situations that no one else does. Some call it intuition. You just know the solution; you don't have to figure it out. A second gift I see in you is empathy. I see it when you're with your cousins—how you interact. You seem to know how they feel or how they will react to something—sometimes before they even realize it themselves. I know this about you because I have it myself. This is where your faith and your personal relationship with God comes in. In all, I have seen these special traits in you: intelligence, empathy, intuition, and resilience of character. But with these gifts will come a burden and a re-

sponsibility. Someday, you will have to decide to act differently from the rest because you know what is right. Don't be afraid to follow that path, other people's lives will be impacted by the decisions you make.

But she drove home the last point. "When faced with another's plight, and you have the opportunity to do something about it, God will leave the decision up to you, because he wants you, not him, to make the choice ... to make a difference. You see, God does not make miracles happen; He works through people who do. In making a choice, just stay open to your soul. From that contemplation, you will come to know what to do—when and how to make a difference."

Much of this was overwhelming to a boy my age. To help me understand, she told me about an experience she had. "Remember when I told you about how it was when your grandfather died, and they were taking the dealership away from me? To this day, I believe that new regional manager was working a small miracle. There is no way he had to do what he did. I saw the compassion in his soul."

We were finishing lunch, and Mom had just asked the waitress for the check. As we were waiting, she looked at me and said, "I know I've shared a lot with you over the last couple of days. But you're getting older now and I was hoping to share with you some of the lessons I have learned in my life.

"Life passes by faster than you realize. And we all need to live our lives to the fullest, because there is no second chance. Sometimes I wish I had two lives, one to learn from and one to live. It is my hope that you may take some of the things I've learned from my experience and use them in yours. I hope you will benefit from some of the lessons I learned." I felt as if she was preparing me for something, a future I did not yet understand.

But there was one more pearl of wisdom she wanted me to have—a reference point to make decisions and stay on the right track. "When you make choices and are unsure what to do, just ask yourself: by following this path, will I be able to say *the world is a better place because I was here?*" Of all the advice Mom gave me, this was the one that stayed with me for the rest of my life.

We don't always appreciate the advice we are given at the time we receive it. I know for me, to some degree, that was true. But because Mom was such an important part of my life then and for the rest of my formative years, I did retain a lot of what she was trying to convey.

Speak softly but carry a big stick.

One summer afternoon when I was a lot boy at the dealership, Mom asked me to drop her car at the dealership for service, where she had left instructions that she needed it delivered to her home by one p.m. Sometime after three p.m. the car had not yet been serviced. A car driven by my cousin with Mom in the passenger seat pulled into the service department and stopped right in the middle of the shop. Mom was never one to flaunt her authority, but she did command respect.

Whenever she felt someone was crossing the line, she would let them know. You could hear a pin drop as she got out of the car. She spoke in a low voice to the service manager, so I didn't hear the complete exchange, but I did hear her last comment: "Don, my son may run this dealership, but let's don't forget: I still own it!"

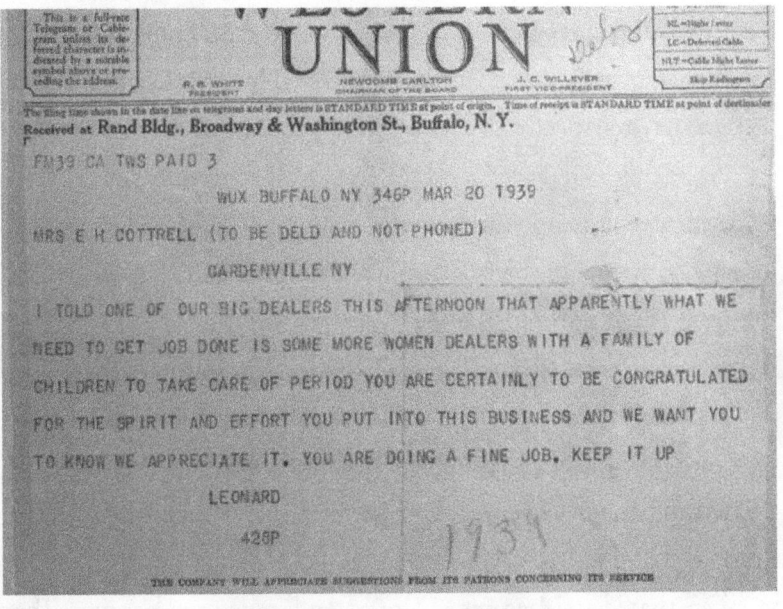

A Western Union telegram from a senior executive at Ford Motor in Detroit congratulating my grandmother on her performance. Notice his subtle humor as he refers to telling "our big dealers" to shape up. This was less than three years after she was first told they were not letting her keep it. (Author's personal collection)

Edward M. Rahill

The Day Road Racing Ignited my Interest

When I was twelve, I was given a part-time job at my uncle's Ford dealership cutting grass. It was a June Saturday in 1966, and I got there at eight a.m. to start my day. As I brought the lawnmower out of storage, one of the salesmen invited me to listen to a broadcast from France on the radio. Everyone was excited as three Fords were one, two, and three in an international road race. Some driver was laps ahead of everyone else. I was captivated by what I heard. Those American cars, specifically Fords, were in a class of their own.

Suddenly, the driver with the long lead started to slow down. I heard several people in the room mumble, "Why is he slowing down? Is there a problem?" After a while, the announcer was describing these Fords in tandem crossing the finish line. Two of them were almost tied, and everyone cheered . Monday, there was a picture in the newspaper of the three Fords crossing the finish line together at the 24 Hours of Le Mans. I heard one salesman say something about someone being robbed of a victory. Years later, I learned that the driver was Ken Miles.

On that day, I became aware of endurance road racing. The only racing I had known before that was on an oval track, which did not appeal to me. But the idea of racing long distances over a real road, braking and accelerating—that did. I tried to visualize what it was like to drive like that. To me, that was what real racing was about.

One Mile at a Time

The finish line of the 1966 24 Hours of Le Mans. Ken Miles had a four-and-a-half-lap (thirty-five-mile) lead over the remaining cars in the race. Ford wanted a tandem finish, and Ken was promised he would be declared a co-winner if he backed off. (Public domain photograph)

Edward M. Rahill

Legend has it this photo captures the moment Shelby told Miles to slow down and wait for the remaining Ford GT40s to catch up. Ford wanted a photo finish and ordered Shelby to make it happen. Ken became deflated but backed off and the remaining GT40s caught up from their thirty-five-mile deficit as they neared the finish line. Ken believed it was to be a photo finish, but he was later declared finishing in second place, because he had a starting position twenty feet ahead of the other driver crossing the line, Bruce McLaren. Photo from Chuck Tannert, "Ford vs. Ferrari: The Real Story Behind the Most Bitter Rivalry in Auto Racing," Forbes Wheels, November 14, 2019. (Getty purchased license)

In his book *Go Like Hell*, A.J. Baime describes how Shelby shed a tear as he spoke about what happened to Ken that day. Shelby supposedly said he should not have asked Ken to slow down. He should have told the car company exec to go to hell.

Chapter 2
Coming into My Own

I was an awkward-looking boy my freshman year, but I still embraced the culture of Bishop Fallon High School. It was a boys college prep, and there, I started to feel I had value and self-worth.

On the first day, I was directed to my homeroom. I was with twenty-four other boys. All of us were looking around, seeking something familiar. One or two recognized each other and started to talk. This set off a commotion of fourteen-year-olds leaving their seats. At that moment, Mr. Battaglia, who would become my cross-country coach, walked into the room and said nothing. The room quieted down for a moment, but the chaos erupted again. I just sat there and looked around, wondering what I'd gotten myself into.

Mr. Battaglia scanned the room. He stopped and approached the biggest boy in class. He picked him up and threw him across the floor the entire length of the room, until the boy was stopped against the wall.

Flustered, he asked, "What'd I do?"

"Nothing," said the teacher. He turned to the whole class. "If I'm willing to do this to him for nothing, consider what I'd do to you if you did something wrong." I had mixed feelings. I was bothered by the chaos and surprised by the teacher's response.

But then he changed his tone. In a calm voice, he asked each of us about ourselves, our families, and why we decided to attend Bishop Fallon. I felt more comfortable after that. Mr. Battaglia had been dealing with boys for two decades. It occurred to me that he had allowed the room to get out of hand because he wanted to set the stage for his first day message. I knew at that moment that the teachers at Fallon understood boys. Perhaps those teachers and my new classmates could help me learn how to become a man.

After a few weeks, two upperclassmen took an interest in me. It turned out one of them, Peter, was close with my cousins. He showed me the ropes and encouraged me to get active in extracurriculars, including sports. I followed him and joined tennis and cross country. I'd never played tennis before, and I wasn't sure what cross country entailed. But I was intrigued, so I joined the team. It took a lot of time and diligence to participate.

Months later, on a cold, gray morning, I was on the city bus, and I'd decided to quit cross country. I was going to tell Mr. Battaglia that day. I arrived and headed toward his office, but I stopped. A feeling of distress and shame came over me. Then I recalled the painful feeling of running miles for practice. I felt defeated, like I would never prove myself. I felt like a quitter, like I wasn't living up to the person I wanted to be. The bell rang, and I went back to my homeroom. I would tell him before practice.

I ran practice that day, and for the first time, I did not finish last. There were two guys, including one upperclassman, behind me. I put the idea of quitting out of my mind and told myself to take it one practice at a time.

The season ended on a high note. In the last race of the season, I found myself in the last hundred yards competing for fifth place. Fifth place was the last position that was recorded in the team score. I ended up finishing seventh. That was when I heard two upperclassmen on the team ask, "Where'd that freshman come from?" I'd found my place at Fallon, and I would no longer be lost in the crowd. I knew I had a place on the team.

In my sophomore year, I was integrated into the school's culture. I started to compete and eventually placed in cross country, and I joined the track team. Academically, I was among the top five in the class. I was no longer the geek I had been freshman year. School started to feel like a place I looked forward to each day; it felt a little like home.

Late in my sophomore year, a sunny May afternoon, it was the last track meet of the year. I was asked to run the quarter mile with two teammates. The meet was against a strong opponent. I'd been running well the previous few weeks, and I was up to the challenge. The gun sounded, and I ran, taking the turns and focusing on each next stride. I came out of the fourth turn, the afternoon sun in my eyes. I maintained my best speed as I zeroed in on the track before me. Suddenly, I had string wrapped around my body as I reached the finish. For a moment, I didn't know what to think. Then it sunk in. I had won my first race as a member of the team.

Junior year was when it all took off. At first, I was assigned the 880-yard event, but after a while, it became clear that I was better suited for the quarter mile. From that point on, I placed in every meet, even against some of the stronger opponents, and I won two races outright. My times slowly improved. I finished with two wins and three second places that year. That summer I doubled my training regimen; I knew I could be good and wanted to give my last year my best effort.

The first time I felt good about myself to a point of embarrassment was at the end of the junior year awards assembly. I was taken by surprise when my name was called for award after award for both academic and athletic performance. I was embarrassed when the priest giving out the awards joked that he hoped we had enough awards left to hand out to others.

I didn't know how to handle the attention. At first, I was surprised and began to get choked up. Then I thought to myself, *This is the time to show you are strong and you can handle your emotions.* I had embraced the stoic mentality that later became my M.O. in the face of sadness or criticism.

The following summer, I got the opportunity to join an organization called VISTA (Volunteers in Service to America). VISTA was founded in 1965 as a domestic version of the Peace Corps. It provides volunteers to nonprofit, faith-based, and community organizations that bring low-income individuals out of poverty.

The goal was to assemble a team to spend the month of June in Appalachia, helping rebuild dilapidated housing in rural West Virginia. I had become aware of the plight facing rural Appalachia from my social studies class.

As our VISTA team traveled into the rural back hills of West Virginia, we saw increasing numbers of decaying homes and barns. Finally, we arrived at a site where a single mother and three children lived. It was a run-down wood-frame and wood-siding structure, resting on a cinderblock foundation. Several windows were cracked, and the house appeared to lean slightly toward the front entrance. It didn't look safe.

The homeowner explained that her house had dropped a few inches the previous week, and she was concerned. We asked if she and her kids could leave the house while my friend Brian and I entered the crawl space through a trapdoor in the floor. It was in rough shape. The joists at the front appeared to have failed. That explained why the front of the house was lower than the back.

When the children entered the home, we felt the floor move. We had just installed a single jack on the center main beam that supported the floor joists. Suddenly, all the joists on the foundation collapsed with a deafening sound of timbers cracking and a boom. All four sides of the home had given way, and the only space that did not collapse was the center section where we'd just installed a support jack. With only a flashlight, Brian and I tried to assess what was left of the crawl space. It took a few seconds, but we realized we had installed the brace just a minute before the collapse. We came that close to being crushed, and we probably would have been killed.

But the danger was not over. The children above us were scared and running toward the door as the rest of foundation gave way. I tried to keep a cool head, and we installed the remaining jacks to raise the floor high enough to get to the trapdoor and escape. Later that day, we were able to get help from a local farmer who used his tractor to lift key sections of the floor so we could get back in and install the remaining support jacks. Our team had several other incidents with other homes, but none as dangerous. It was clear to me that the people living in that region were truly living in poverty—even by late 1960s standards.

Witnessing the conditions in Appalachia had a profound effect on my view of the world. I learned a lot about poverty's systemic causes. The pattern of poverty was obvious; the solutions were not. I felt proud of the work we'd done to improve the lives of the five families whose homes we repaired. But it was obvious that our work was only a temporary fix. Unless a fundamental change was made in the region, things were never going to improve.

The main source of income for those families was public assistance. This made sure they were fed and clothed. But I wondered if that was all there was for them. Public assistance met their needs day to day, but it didn't give them hope to improve their lives. I left West Virginia after my month there, convinced that economic opportunity would be their only way out of poverty. "Give a man a fish, you feed him for a day. Teach a man to fish, you feed him for life."

I returned home to a summer job as a lot boy at Cottrell Ford, my grandmother and uncle's dealership. My day job would be driving the parts truck for the service department. My afternoon and evening job was moving cars, checking in cars on trade, and washing and parking cars in the back lot. Driving all day and working with cars in the evening, I had a lot of opportunities to develop my driving skills. I learned how to drive on the back roads of Gardenville—and I went fast. I also learned I was good at it; one mechanic even told me I had a gift for driving. But instinct was not the same as experience. I didn't yet understand how quickly dangerous situations could arise on the road.

Sometimes I was able to get hold of a late-model car and an occasional Mach 1 from my uncle's dealership. That's where I learned what to expect from a car. The live axles of the cars I drove taught me how to handle a vehicle when she jumped on a rough road and to steer—not just with the steering wheel, but with the brakes and accelerator, too. But the driving skills that stuck with me most were anticipation, quick decision-making, and keeping a cool head. Panic and indecision can kill.

When I think of some of the chances I took as a teenager, I now shiver with fear. But that was how I learned to drive the line and discovered the skill of trail-braking before I even knew what it was. It probably saved me from some serious spinouts in the curves. In high school on Friday nights, I'd go down to the fire roads in South Buffalo with a few friends and try my hand at drag racing, but I did not like the way it felt. Too much like a rocket without real control.

My sister and brother took to this self-taught sport. Somehow my sister had figured out how to blow a 429 cubic-inch engine. My brother was not so lucky; he ran the same roads. Although he did not get seriously hurt, his car was smashed on three sides with a five-inch tree branch embedded in the passenger door. Such was life for a teenager in the rural town of Gardenville. If I had been born a hundred years earlier, I would have been doing the same thing, only instead of a car, it would have been a horse.

Edward M. Rahill

Baptism by Fire

One day, I was driving the parts truck down the road approaching a line of cars. I had just passed the crest of a hill and was heading downhill. The traffic light had turned red. No big deal . . . just step on the brakes and slow down..

No brakes! I was traveling downhill at 60 mph, and I had no brakes.

I panicked. But I quickly refocused. I remember thinking, *Engage the mind, bury the emotions.* First, I tried the emergency brake. Nothing. I was going too fast for the rear drum brakes to engage. That vehicle's brake was designed to hold a car in place rather than serve as a true emergency brake. I was at a loss. I felt totally helpless. But I remembered that my truck was a manual transmission. I grabbed the shifter, hit the clutch, and began steadily downshifting, using my engine to slow down, rear tires screeching with every shift. I was slowing down, but not soon enough.

I had one more idea: to kill the engine. The 351CI V8 engine was now dead, and with the clutch engaged, this meant that the engine would generate more drag. This caused the rear tires to grab.

I pulled the emergency brake again and again. It finally took hold as I struggled to turn the steering wheel away from the other cars. The vehicle had lost power steering when I shut down the engine. I pulled to the right with all my strength and guided the truck into a tight space between the cars and the rail, avoiding plowing into the car in front of me by a couple feet. I stopped right there.

From this experience, I learned how to divert my anxiety and stay engaged—to not let my emotions to stop me from searching for solutions, no matter how bad it got. There was always time for that after the crisis. It saved me more than once in my driving and racing experiences.

I had another great learning experience one summer day when twenty cars were delivered to the dealership's back lot. Every week, we'd receive a shipment of cars, and it was my job to park them in an orderly line to make it easy for salesmen to walk out and see the cars. On that day, the new cars were dropped off from the transports far from the dealership, and my job was to bring them in. It was a giant empty mall parking lot, laid out so you could drive it like a road course. I decided to put each car I picked up through its paces, tracing the edges of the empty lot. I approached 70-plus mph on sections of this short course and trail-braked into the turns.

I loved the feeling of driving each car to its limit. I could feel when each one could go faster or when I needed to back off. It was the first time I understood that to drive fast you needed to become one with the car, know her limits, and intuit when she could do more. I would enter the last turn throttle-steering through the curve. The final leg was a straightaway where I would bring each car to her maximum speed for the distance, then bring her to a stop.

Each subsequent trip was smoother. I was becoming more controlled, almost flowing with the car. The key was to glide it, not jerk the car though the course. The smoother the car ran through the course, the better I learned that a car could talk to me in many ways. I was learning to feel what she was experiencing.

Edward M. Rahill

I parked the last car and began to walk toward the dealership. When I got back, the entire service department was laughing, clapping, and pointing to the line of cars I had just parked. Even I was amazed. There was a row of twenty cars in almost perfect alignment. I had raced each of them through that course, and I had been able to bring each one to a stop within inches of the next. That day, I understood what that mechanic meant when he said I had a gift for driving.

Working at the dealership is one of my fondest memories. In the early evening, when I started my second shift detailing and washing cars in the shop, several of the mechanics would bring their cars in. Every night the shop was filled with teasing and banter. Thanks to the guys, I learned a lot about how cars worked and how to modify them. But what I remember most is the music. Motown's Four Tops, the Temptations, and Smokey Robinson filled the air. We also heard the Ronettes, the Crystals, Beach Boys, Jan and Dean, the Detroit Wheels, the Righteous Brothers, Elvis, Steppenwolf, the Rolling Stones, the Who, and many others. Steppenwolf's "Born to be Wild" was a big hit among the guys.

When you watch documentaries about the 1960s, you get the impression that it was all war protests, Beatles, drugs, and Woodstock. That may have been the focus of the East Coast media and the big-city college crowd. But it was not our experience, at least not for most of us in flyover country. Yes, we had guys who'd been in the service, but it was what their brothers and fathers had done before. Our lives focused on friends and family, football, baseball, girls, and cars. Life was good.

That summer, once or twice a week after work, I would take my grandmother's car out for gas and drive the roads for an hour, just listening to the radio. It was a T-Bird with a 429 cubic-inch motor—she could fly. It was a gift for a seventeen-year-old to hone his driving skills with a car pumping out almost 400 horsepower. I would find an open road and just let her run. I just loved the feeling of the car and the way she changed as the speed increased. Then there was the sound that I'd first heard as a boy—one of the most captivating sounds I have ever heard. It was an American V8 winding toward redline. The car and music just made the drive a special time. I was a teenage boy who was wound up, and the nightly drives would settle me down. I could come home and finally sleep. I never thought the experience would count for much in my future.

Gardenville was a rural town—cornfields and strawberry farms all around. One day, I was driving a Mustang from the dealership with my sister Anne, listening to the radio and having fun. I started to run that backroad like a track. I hit the turns and started to slide through them, much like drift-racing today. Suddenly, there he was. A Gardenville cop was on me, and I had to pull over. Anne and I were taken by surprise because we had never seen a patrol on these roads before. The officer took me apart in a lecture. At first, I was intimidated. Was I about to be arrested? But then his tone changed.

"Son," he said, "I know who you are and we all in town know you can handle your car. It's the old lady driving a Dodge coming around the corner I fear for. She will be driving over the line—not your fault—and you won't be able to stop in time. That's why I am asking you to think about what you're doing. It's the other driver who doesn't have your skills who I'm worried about."

I was stunned! He let me go. He just wanted to "teach, serve, and protect," values that some in police leadership positions have since forgotten. I still think about his lesson: it's not about how good you are, it's about considering what others on the road are thinking before you can drive safely. He gave me a memorable piece of advice: "If you are causing another driver to hit his brakes, you are not driving like a pro." His lecture changed my approach for the rest of my driving future. It also was the foundation for a winning brake-and-go strategy later in life. There isn't a year that goes by that I do not remember his words.

In my senior year, I found myself around underclassmen who looked to me for wisdom. I encouraged them during practice and shouted words of support during their races. For the first time, I realized I was a leader in my peers' eyes. I was shocked to be elected captain of the cross-country team by my teammates. But I feared I would not live up to their expectations.

The second shock came when I was called to a pre-season meeting for the track team. I was informed that I'd been elected co-captain. That hit me even harder. Cross country is a smaller sport; the guys got to know me, and I could rationalize how I got to be captain. But track and field was different. Athletes from all major sports—football, basketball, and tennis—participated as part of their spring practice. Getting elected by this group was akin to being elected by the school at large. I remember being grateful and a bit embarrassed, unsure how to act. But I soon found that all they wanted was for me to be the same guy I'd been the year before, helping bring the younger guys along and encouraging everyone when things were not going their way.

A *Buffalo Courier-Express* article on Fallon's track program. After a losing record the prior year, Pat (half mile) and I (quarter mile) were undefeated, and that started to turn heads in the high school sporting news community.

Edward M. Rahill

Four Proms

It was early spring when I received a call from Mom.

"Mick, I'm asking for a favor," she started. "Some friends of mine have a granddaughter who doesn't have a date to her senior prom." My older cousins had warned me about this type of call, but I was still a bit terrified. Mom did not usually "make requests" on matters like this.

"I want you to be her date," she asserted. I didn't have a chance to ask questions. She went on. "Now, you can have my car, and I will pay for your tux and give you some money so you can go out with her friends afterwards. I told my friends you'd be calling her this week. Get a pencil and write this down." She gave me the number and told me her name was Sarah.

That was it. My mother was standing next to me listening in. "Try to make the best of it," she said and smiled, "because this will not be the last time." I had a moment of panic—ask out a girl I didn't know and go to a prom where I knew no one?

But everything changed the night I drove over to pick her up. At the door, I was greeted by her parents. They were gracious and asked if they could help with some of the expenses that night. I thanked them and said it was already taken care of. I handed the flower for her dress to her mother. Finally, Sarah came down the stairs; she looked at her parents, then at me. I realized that she was as terrified as I was. A hug and pictures from her parents, and we were off.

When we arrived, she was shy and nervous. We tentatively approached her classmates. It was awkward for a moment, so I immediately introduced myself to her classmates' dates and asked about them. I cracked a few jokes about how uncomfortable the tux was. That was all it took. The classmates huddled with her and there was laughter—she was being accepted. The awkwardness was gone.

The next day, late in the afternoon, Mom called. She thanked me and said she'd just gotten off the phone with her friend. Sarah had been beaming when she came home and told her mother it was the best time she'd had in a long time.

The word was getting around to Mom's friends about me, and I got three more calls that year and went to three more proms. The calls continued into the next year and once more in my freshman year of college. The terrified feeling I had after that first call had been replaced with a sense of pride. I was there for someone who just needed my time for an evening. I just had to be relaxed and gracious toward her friends and everything was going to be okay.

At that time, for many teenage girls, to not go to the prom could give them low self-confidence for the long haul. All I had to do was be present and remember that the night was not about me, it was about her. It felt good to know I could help each of those teenage girls face a tough emotional event. Mom was right: I may have been given the opportunity, but it was my choice to make a difference.

Edward M. Rahill

You will be measured not by the outcome of the struggle, but by your courage and the way you handle it.

In my mind, car racing is intertwined with running. I grew into the man I am today with racing. I embodied Mom's lesson of courage in the face of struggle in my last New York State regional all-Catholic track meet. It was the last race of the season at the end of my senior year. I was undefeated in the quarter mile. But that didn't matter; I hadn't qualified for the championship quarter-mile race because the qualification rules were based on race times, and wins alone did not count. I had won every race that year, but my victories were on the South Buffalo cinder track, making my times slower than what the other runners had accomplished on a tarpaulin track. I could see how difficult it was for my coach to break the news to me. He had asked me to run the mile on the only tarp track we had competed on to see what I could do, not knowing I was losing the opportunity to compete later in the season.

Demoralized, my head wasn't really in the race. This would be the last competitive race I would run after years of getting up at five a.m. just to get in a few extra miles before school. And now it was over. If I had qualified for the 440, I would be a shoo-in for a trip to the finals, given that I'd already beaten several of the runners in that race. For now, the only race my coach could get me into was the mile relay because team members were selected by the coach from runners who didn't qualify for other events. I didn't want to run the relay. I saw no purpose in it, and I was feeling sorry for myself. It got worse when one of the runners I'd defeated earlier in the season had just won the regional 440-yard run. He qualified for the New York State Finals.

The sun was low in the late June sky, casting a warm glow on the track and stands. The gun fired for the last race of the meet, and I watched my team fall behind from the start in the mile relay. We were outclassed. Most of us were from the south side of Buffalo, up against the best Western New York had to offer. It was a hopeless situation, and I didn't want to deal with it. I watched as each of my teammates took his turn in sequence—they were uncompetitive; they really didn't stand a chance. Yet they were giving what they had, collapsing in pain at the end of each of their relay legs. Here I was, their team captain, and I wasn't living up to my role. I just wanted to get my final leg over with.

As I stood around waiting my turn, a couple guys from another team were nearby watching. Then one of them said, almost out of pity, "What a bunch of losers." Momentarily stunned, I looked over at them, and my emotions changed from dejection and self-pity to self-awareness. I felt shame, then a welling of anger. I walked away.

I remember muttering under my breath, "They deserve better than this." Then, all I could do was refocus—what had I done? I wasn't encouraging them. I was letting them down. I had to do something about it—anything. I walked back and forth, then back to the track, kicked off my sweats, and prepared for the final leg. It was time to step up. I remember thinking, *The more hopeless the situation, the more important the response.*

Edward M. Rahill

I watched as each of the opposing anchors passed me in sequence, their teams shouting encouragement. They were all on their way to the first turn and ultimately the finish line. I began to breathe deeply and quickly, feeling the adrenaline. The improbable was quickly turning into the impossible, but I didn't care. It wasn't going to change what I was going to do. I was pumping air in and out of my lungs as deeply and quickly as I could. Then I dropped to my knee and prayed to God: *You made me fast. I don't know if it's enough . . . Help me do what I have to do.* It was then I remembered Mom's comment years ago to me: *"God helps those who help themselves."* It was up to me to make a difference.

I looked back at my teammate Ron. I saw the anguish in his eyes as he was stumbling, tripping, struggling to reach me. It seemed like an eternity. He stumbled one more time. I needed to do something. I immediately sprinted back to get closer to him. It might have been against the rules, I may have been out of the box, but no one was paying attention to us anyway—we were that far out of contention.

Rather than begin the baton transfer the way we were trained in a coordinated, synced run, I stood there and waited for him to reach me. I needed to give him a fixed target. His hand was shaking as I grasped the baton with both hands. I turned and exploded. I was off.

I drove my legs as hard and fast as I could, and I looked up to see the other runners heading into the first turn. The back of the pack was at least twenty-five yards ahead, the leader ahead by more. In the back of my mind flashed, *No one can recover from a deficit like this!* I cast out the thought; I knew what I had to do and prayed to God to give me the ability to do it.

Just seconds after I left the start, everything was quiet. I was gliding along a flat synthetic track that made no noise. I just heard my breath and the wind. It felt as if I was driving my body the way I'd drive a car, and I had opened her up, accelerating under full throttle. I was experiencing a runner's high.

In my mind, I was filled with peace and focus. I was doing what I had to, what I'd trained to do, what I needed to do. I knew it was probably the last time I would ever run like that. It was as if in the prior four years of practice and struggle, God was preparing me for this moment. I just remember gliding across the track as if my shoes never completely touched the ground. I was gaining on the pack of runners ahead. I just kept telling myself,

One moment at a time, one stride at a time, one runner at a time.

I saw a runner ahead of me as I entered the first turn of the track. He was in fifth place. I caught up and passed him coming out of the second turn going into the stretch. I was surprised at how easy it was. I was on my way to the midpoint of the race. My pace was at a rate I would employ in my hundred-yard training exercises—not sustainable over 440 yards! I knew this, but I also knew the math: no other strategy had any hope of recovering from where my team was when I started, so it was full throttle—that was how I'd chosen to live those next few moments, all out. I heard some crowd noise beginning at the 220-yard marker as I caught up to the pack.

Edward M. Rahill

I slowed for just a moment; there were four runners ahead of me. The race was half over; I had no time to recover. I knew what to expect. I had expended precious oxygen reserves to get to that point. But my years of conditioning were there for me. I pumped air into my lungs. Then I opened up again, and I was off. That was when I heard something unexpected. Several spectators were shouting from the stands, "Go, Fallon!" Maybe I was not alone as I flew along the track. As I ran, I caught and passed the fourth runner, then the third near the end of the straight. I had never run with so much speed, performance, and endurance—and I knew it. I was gaining on the second-to-last runner, but physical exhaustion was trying to take control of my body as I went into the third turn. I was still pushing, still going after him.

For a flash, with my body showing signs of resistance to the pace, a thought ran across my mind. I could just hold my current position and finish third. I could place. Last place to third, respectable. Even in my diminished physical state, I was still strong enough to hold off any challenges from runners behind me. Just as quickly as that thought entered, it was rejected. That's not who I am. I gave it all I had, and that was how I was going to finish. I momentarily lowered my head and surged.

I caught him in the third turn. He was surprised and trying to fight me off. I had to swing wide to his right, and I was past him. That cost me as I was forced outside and had to cover more distance. My legs started to cramp. My body could no longer remove the lactic residue from my muscles faster than it was building up. There was no longer enough oxygen in my blood to feed the burning muscles in my body, and I could feel the pain in my lungs as I struggled to recycle my blood as fast as I could. The burning was getting worse.

The crowd, who never expected such a spectacle just forty seconds earlier, was on their feet as I caught the lead runner coming off the final turn. I heard shouting and cheering coming from the stands like I'd never heard before. He and I fought for every foot of those last forty yards. Just a few yards from the finish, it was almost like becoming paralyzed. My legs were no longer coordinated; they no longer worked. I was gasping, cramping, stumbling as I came to the finish line, and I fell to the ground. I was unable to get up. I needed to be lifted to regain my footing. I was surrounded by a group congratulating me, but I lost! They seemed excited. Ron, the runner from who I had taken the baton, was there giving me a hug. I went through a series of convulsions as my body reacted as if it was in shock. That ended the celebrations for a while. A few fans from the stands approached me and shook my hand. I was told we had finished second in the mile relay; they told me we lost first place by a few yards. We came from last place to second, missing first by a little more than two yards.

Although it was not an official quarter-mile race, my time was the new school record in the quarter mile. I did it with only my teammates and fans in the stands to see it. If I have any regrets about that day, it was that no one from my family was there to see such a defining moment in my life. When the track meet was over, I hugged my teammates with sadness because that was the last time we'd see each other before we moved on to the next stage of our lives.

A few minutes later, after everything was over, my coach came over and asked if we could talk. It was his first year; he was learning, but he had strong instincts. It was a good conversation; we talked about the year. He said he wished he could have coached me for one more year.

But the thing he said that meant the most was that it took a lot of courage for me to run the race the way I did, and that it was one of the finest performances in the face of adversity he had ever seen. But he wanted to make a bigger point, one that became more important to me later in life. "You showed everybody on this team, especially the underclassmen, that improbable does not mean impossible. Ed, I told the team I wanted them to watch the relay because I wanted them to learn to support their team, win or lose. Some of them didn't want to do it as things started to get bad. I watched the look on your teammates' faces as you started the last leg. I just knew you were good. I was hoping you were going to make an impact I could use to coach on next year. I just didn't know it would be this big. To see the dejection on their faces turn to screaming encouragement within seconds . . . It's what makes coaching worth it."

I didn't know what to say, I really didn't, and I thanked him. I took a bus home realizing my high school years were over. Two months later, I enrolled at the University of Notre Dame. But as I look back on that day, I'm especially proud of living up to what those guys wanted when they voted for me as co-captain. It was not my name listed in the tally sheet that said who placed in the regional all-Catholic meet that June afternoon; it was the Bishop Fallon mile-relay team.

I learned a lesson in life—that sometimes we only discover the true measure of a man by his response when the odds are against him. It was this day I felt I became the man I am today.

The first run of a clandestine race between NYC and LA, and the Cannonball Run was born.

In May 1971, a journalist named Brock Yates had just completed an exploratory race between New York City and Los Angeles. In a nod to my destiny, the first cross-continental race in thirty years was being planned and eventually run in November 1971. Later we would come to know it as the Cannonball Baker Sea to Shining Sea Memorial Trophy Dash. I learned of the event in December of that year from the local sports page. At the time, it captured my interest. My instincts told me I could be good at it, and I even imagined what it might take to win. At the time, I was headed to college, so competing was not in the cards.

But my love of cars was a constant. The summer before college, I put in sixty-hour work weeks to save money. I was working the evening shift as a lot boy. A 1967 Mustang Shelby GT came in for a trade. My job was to wash and prep her for a future sale. As I drove her into the wash bay, I fell in love with the car. I just sat in her for ten minutes as I took it all in. I remember telling myself, *Someday*

Edward M. Rahill

I hope to own one of these. Those cars, especially the GT class, were in my blood.

Early January during Christmas break, I was working at the dealership and was able to secure a 1970 Boss 302 Mustang to drive home after work. I instead drove down to the Southern Tier Expressway to a long section of less-traveled road and opened up the Mustang to see what she could do, but more importantly to test my limits. I wanted to understand how I would react to speed. I brought it up to 110, 120 mph, and that was it. I tested the brakes, and they were not effective. I took my foot off the gas and coasted down to a manageable speed. I had a lot to learn. I was lucky enough and smart enough to know it.

Chapter 3
College Years
and Grad School

I received two letters the same spring day. I had applied to Harvard, Yale, Princeton, and Notre Dame, among other schools. I'd already been accepted to my backup schools but was rejected from Yale and Princeton. Now, here were two letters—one from Harvard and one from Notre Dame.

I opened the Harvard letter first. It said I met all the qualifications to be admitted, but due to the number of applicants, they could not offer me a position in their freshman class. I was asked to contact admissions to confirm my continued interest in attending the school. Should a position open up, they would notify me within thirty days—a waitlist letter.

I opened the second letter. The first line said, "We are pleased to inform you that you have been accepted as a student to the University of Notre Dame." That was it! I knew Notre Dame would be my new home.

I had an invitation from the Notre Dame cross-country coach to try out for the team. But I decided to try out for the football team instead. As I headed to the Stepan Center and the athletic offices on campus, I had a lump in my throat. I'd never played football in my life. As I made my way to the player check-in stations, there was a table set up for freshman scholarship players and a second table for "walk-ons." As I wandered in, I noticed there were about fifteen other guys in the room and a sign-in desk at the front. To my surprise, it was not that difficult to sign up as a walk-on.

The process was straightforward. I was called up to one of four tables where I was briefly interviewed about my sports experience and athletic accomplishments. I had a letter from my track coach vouching for my track-and-field record. Then there was a quick physical evaluation, examining muscle tone, height, and weight. The next thing I knew, I was told to report to the medical center with the scholarship players, where I was given a physical. The doctor asked if I played quarterback. Shocked at the question, I replied, "No, sir, I play cornerback/split end." I was given medical clearance and told to go to a track for a forty-yard timed test. I got into a sprinter's stance. When the gun sounded, I took off. Then, the coaches stopped practice and conferred. I was instructed to run again. They were surprised at my performance in the forty and wanted to confirm it. I was nowhere near as fast as the scholarship athletes, just faster than I looked. They seemed impressed that unlike the other players, I could reproduce my forty times, while the other players' times would degrade as they wore out. After that, we reported to a classroom where the assistant coaches explained what was expected. Later that day, I was informed I made the team on the freshman squad. My assignment would be the practice squad for game day preparation.

Later that month during practice, I had a good moment and an embarrassing one. My one good play: my number was called in the huddle, and I lined up at the split end position. I was scared and in over my head, but I did what I saw the other receivers doing during their rotation. Al Samuels was at quarterback. He reaffirmed the play at the line and hiked the ball. I was to do a sprint then slant. I sprinted seven yards then slanted toward the sideline. As soon as I made my break, I turned and to my amazement, there was the ball, perfectly thrown. I somehow caught it in my hands and pulled it in. I was shocked. No one else knew that that was the first time I had ever caught a football in a real team environment.

Now for the embarrassing moment. At practice, I was assigned to play defensive back. For this play, my position was cornerback. I did not have a clue what I was doing. Suddenly, the ball was snapped and the teammate playing wide receiver raced off the line. Before I knew it, he passed me, and I was trying to cover from behind. Suddenly, the coach's whistle blew. He stopped practice to call everyone together and proceeded to yell that I had just shown, in textbook fashion, how not to cover a receiver. To say I was humiliated is an understatement.

A week later, during practice, I was playing a wide-out position. The ball snapped; I started my route, turned, and the ball was almost there, but high. I leapt to it, felt it touch my hands, and I suddenly cartwheeled to the ground. My left heal was in pain, and I could not get up. I was helped off the field. I had suffered a partial rupture of my Achilles tendon, and that ended my walk-on career with the Fighting Irish. At the end of this story, Coach Murphy told me I probably would not play, but I was welcome to try out in the spring after my recovery, which could take up to six months.

Edward M. Rahill

I thanked him and said, "It's time for me to move on. The chance to practice as part of the team was an honor I will never forget." Some of my fellow players that summer and fall were Tom Clements, Pete Demmerle, Eric Penick, Dave Casper, and Al Samuel. They went on to win the College Football National Championship for the 1973 season.

For the first time in my life, my grades suffered.

In my first three semesters, I barely held a 2.0 GPA and was on the verge of academic probation. I can't tell you why. Perhaps immaturity, or an initial feeling of not belonging. At first, I didn't like most of my classmates. They seemed to come from the upper middle class where they did not have to work for anything. I had to work for everything, including tuition. I even took a job in the evenings in Elkhart, Indiana, at an RV factory making sewage tanks. I also took out student loans each semester.

In classes, it was the first time I ever had significant academic competition. I graduated toward the top of my high school class, but everybody else at Notre Dame did too. I also realized my education was very good and the emphasis on character development was excellent, but I had few options for advanced classes.

When I received my grade on a calculus exam, I was almost shocked. My test had in large red writing *A/D!* And a note: *See me!*

What did that mean? In his office, my professor explained why he was giving me a D even though I'd answered enough questions correctly to get an A. He said, "Ed, this is a calculus class, not a physics class. From your notes, I could construct how you answered each question from your understanding of the science, not the math!"

I was discouraged. I was overwhelmed. I started to attend the morning Mass in my dorm and made evening visits to the grotto, just praying for help to get through each day. I only asked for one day at a time because I could not fathom what it would take beyond that. I wasn't going to give up, but it still felt a little like I was drowning.

Over time, my attitude changed, and I came to understand what the university stood for. I loved it. It embraced everything I believed was true about life, spirituality, and moral character. It scared me to think I may not make it, that I might wash out. But I had been brought up not to give up, and things slowly improved the second semester of my sophomore year.

The university administrators cared that I was having trouble. I met with the assistant dean of the business school twice a week, where he'd give me pep talks about my raw talent, and he reminded me that I wouldn't have been accepted if they did not believe I could make it. I know of no other institution in academia that would put that kind of effort into an academically troubled student.

One day, in my econ class, graded midterms were being returned. I received mine in an envelope. I felt I was a 1.9-GPA student about to receive another blow. I slowly opened the envelope and looked at the grade. It was an A-. I sat there stunned and stared at the front of the room. Things were never the same again. I was going to make it.

Junior year was a complete turnaround for me academically and socially. Getting involved now seemed natural and interacting and dating was becoming more natural. However, I had a terrible crush on one coed, and I acted every bit as awkward as I had back in high school. I hoped that someday I would find the right woman to settle down with, but I knew I wasn't ready. I needed to establish myself first. I was elected to the university Student Life Council, one of only four from the entire student body. I served with eight faculty and administrators to address issues that impacted all aspects of university life. I ran for student body president and lost, but of the 204 residents in my residence hall, 202 voted for me.

Afterward, Fr. Hesburgh, president of the university, spent some time with me. Even though I'd lost the election, he encouraged me to strive to make my abilities a service to mankind. He was giving me advice as to what path to follow when facing difficult decisions. And he had the same advice I had received from my grandmother: "No matter how small the challenge, strive to make a difference, to make the world a better place because you were here."

My grandmother, Mom, left my world but not my life.

Senior year, I was preparing to move on. My grandmother died that year. It hit me extremely hard. She had, in many ways, been like my mother and helped me become the person I needed to be. I was the last one to speak with her at the end.

I was alone with her in the hospital room holding her hand when she said to me, "Why does it hurt so much?" I was at a loss for words. Then I remembered what she would tell me as a child when I would ask her why something sad happened. She would tell me to put that question in my mystery box, and God would answer it when I got to heaven.

So, I said to her, "Mom, put it in your mystery box, and God will answer it when you get to heaven." Although her eyes were closed, I felt her attempt to squeeze my hand, and she smiled. She slipped into a coma and died a few minutes later. I returned to the university, but it was some time before I could get over that loss. But I don't think I've gotten over that loss to this day.

Over the next few months, I reflected on her life. Later, I understood that I owed my Notre Dame experience to her. I was able to pay for college; I took out loans and worked every job I could, including sixty-hour weeks at the dealership during the summer. But that was only two thirds of the cost. She had been directly paying the school the other third. And those summer jobs—she had a hand in getting me the double shifts. Yes, I worked for it, but she

Edward M. Rahill

gave me the opportunities. Later, her memory would continue to play a prominent role in the most significant events in my life.

Notre Dame: Reflections

The Grotto on the Notre Dame Campus, following the passing of President Emeritus Rev. Theodore (Ted) M. Hesburgh, C.S.C. (Photo by University Photographer)

I changed majors several times at Notre Dame, trying to find myself. My academic advisors were patient with me, more than I had been with myself. Because of these changes, and the fact that I had flunked a few courses early in my career, I had to take twenty-one credits in my last semester to graduate in four years. The irony is that the last semester was my best GPA, 3.85. My student years at Notre Dame expanded my horizons. I learned about the world that came before me, and also what I didn't know that I needed to learn. I gained respect and admiration for philosophy, science, and the uniquely human quality of self-awareness.

I entered college an idealist. I saw the world fraught with problems, and I wanted to do something about it. There, I was introduced to such Classical philosophers as Socrates, Plato, Aristotle, Epictetus, and Seneca. I also studied theologians, such as Saint Thomas Aquinas and Thomas More. I learned the concepts behind Stoicism, an ancient Greek school of philosophy that taught that an individual could find virtue, the highest good, based on knowledge; the wise live in harmony with reason that governs nature, and they are indifferent to the vicissitudes of fortune or to pleasure and pain.

Another major philosophical principle I came to embrace at Notre Dame was the role of the individual in society. This was a doctrine of the Roman Catholic Church known as the Principle of Subsidiarity. Subsidiarity argues that all social bodies exist for the sake of the individual. It implies that whatever an individual can do ought not to be taken over by society, and what smaller societies can do, larger societies should not take over. This is why the early Catholic Church was so focused on local parishes: they were close to the people and their individual needs, something a centralized governing body, such as Rome could never do. And it was this principle that influenced Thomas Jefferson as he adopted libertarianism in his vision of the great experiment he saw for America.

I gained respect for these thinkers through the ages, and how they brought humanity the art, literature, culture, philosophy, and enduring principles we once called Western Civilization. An overriding theme in all these foundational principles was morality and character. This gave true meaning to the phrase in Greek philosophy, "A man's character is his destiny."

I learned to see people as individuals and not as a collective, to look at the dignity of the individual who, in the end, is responsible for his or her actions—actions for which they personally answer to God for how they lived their lives. Surrendering our responsibilities to another person, a society, or a government diminishes the person we are.

If you ever visit Notre Dame, take time to visit the Basilica of the Sacred Heart. On the eastern side, there is a modest entrance. Carved above the entrance are the following words: *God, Country, Notre Dame.* These words say it all. God gave us the gift of self-awareness—the ability to grow, think, know, and learn. From its inception, our country has provided an exceptional place for us to grow as individuals, learn with truth, and flourish by following our dreams. Notre Dame belongs with God and country, because the university has been a beacon of light providing knowledge of these principles to past, current, and future generations.

I was tempted to major in the humanities, but my time at the university had given me another perspective. Problems are not just to be discussed; they need to be solved. After two years, I realized it was not enough to care about what is not working right; I needed the skill set to understand what to do about it—problem-solving skills. It was this small epiphany that eventually led to my academic migration from the humanities to economics and finally business and finance. The core of these disciplines was efficiency—finding better a way to do things, not just the classic production/optimization model, but to make the world work better within the rules of economics.

The humanities helped me define my heart—how I felt, what I believed, the direction I should take. Business and economics helped me define my mind—how to do things, understand the reality of the situation, apply reason and logic to problems. As for how to get things done, in one of my management classes, the professor explained how to understand the reality of the situation, how not all desired outcomes are doable. Thinking about how to apply the reality of these facts to a decision, he said, "Reason and logic are your friends in this situation. Perfect is the enemy of good."

Notre Dame gave me a complete education; classes there exposed me to the great minds of philosophy as well as the science of management, both of which have served me well. There, I laid the foundations for how I hoped to live my life. At times, we might take a path chosen by our heart, but we should be honest and not fool ourselves about the implications of our choices. I was going to let my heart set the direction I was to travel, but my head was going to get me there. I just needed to make sure I listened to my heart talk along the way.

I see now that Notre Dame gave me the tools and moral backbone to make a difference in other people's lives. I developed the morals that Fr. Hesburgh asked me to strive for . . . to make the world a better place because I was here.

If there is one thing that college cannot prepare you for, it is the emotional trials that we all someday face in life. We are all naïve to our humanity and how we will respond. I graduated with a new moral code: "Don't give up after a setback, do not go against your values in the face of adversity." At times, I would fall short of this code. But my family, my past, and the university gave me the foundation to find the path back. It is not how far you fall that is a measure of your worth, it is your willingness to find your inner strength and recover that is the measure of a man.

In all, the university gave more to me than I gave back. But that is what makes it, in my mind, one of the finest institutions of higher education in the world today. If you are ever behind a '68 Ford Shelby GT500KR Mustang at a stoplight, and the license plate frame reads, *God, Country, Notre Dame*, it just might be me.

Those guys ran that race again, and I found some new music.

I still remember a *Car and Driver* article detailing the exploits of a group of drivers competing in the 1975 Cannonball run. It captured my imagination, even if I felt it would never happen for me. At the time, I was more focused on graduation and the summer ahead. For the fun of it, I signed up for a three-day race training course at Watkins Glen that summer. It was good to get behind the wheel of a car and push her to the limit, but it was especially good to be reminded of the strategies of driving—when to be aggressive, when to be defensive, when to be patient. Driving in traffic can make us zombies: don't think, just do what the traffic signs tell us. Driving competitively is the law of the jungle.

Every couple years, I'd grab a few days at a track session just to stay fresh. You need to experience speed to understand speed. You need to understand speed to be able to handle it. At the time, I was treating cars and driving as a hobby. I saw my future in a business career. I was going to enter an MBA program in the fall.

Something small but special happened to me in the fall of 1975. It was November 6, and I had returned to Notre Dame to see my friends and attend the Georgia Tech game that year. I got to watch the Rudy Game, when the crowd chanted Rudy and he was carried off the field. But the most memorable part of the day was meeting friends at the senior bar, which was packed, and I heard a new song being played. The song was "Born to Run" by a group led by someone named Bruce Springsteen. Little did I know that his love of cars and stories about life would keep his songs in my life from that time on.

Graduate School

When I graduated from Notre Dame, I was in debt and didn't like the job I was offered at IBM. I needed to pursue graduate school if I ever wanted to fast-track at a company. I enrolled at SUNY Buffalo in the MBA program and got a job selling cars at my uncle's dealership. By becoming a car salesman, I got a demonstrator car to drive. That solved my transportation problem for graduate school.

I had a strong background in economics, marketing, and applied statistics, but after conversations with some of my college professors, I felt my skills were lacking in applied economics, better known as finance. This was my emphasis in my MBA program. I also realized my skills in the application of accounting were lacking and took as many electives in that discipline as I could. I was still drawn to economics, mainly because I had come to believe it was a perfect combination of philosophy and rational thought.

While microeconomics is simply the application of math and statistics to the economic field, macroeconomics is different. In some ways, it resembles theoretical physics in its willingness to speculate. This is because macroeconomics focuses on the relationship of a large group of independent variables. And the effectiveness of macroeconomic models are only as good as the validity of its assumptions. In many ways, macroeconomics is a study of human behaviors and interactions measured in currency. This is why the Nobel Prize committee awards the prize in economics as a social science.

After six months, I had saved enough to buy a used Ford Galaxy 500 and got a part-time job at the Carborundum Company in Niagara Falls in marketing for the high-temperature insulation division. I had a Regents scholarship at the University of Buffalo and only needed to cover gas and incidentals. The job basically turned into a telemarketing position, and I did not object. I needed the work. (As a point of note, yes, I did blow the engine in my Galaxy 500 on the Niagara Expressway. No, my driving habits had not changed.)

One Friday morning, Scott, my boss, asked me to come into his office. He had just returned from corporate downtown. We got along well, and I could see he was pondering something.

"We're facing the shutdown of the major product line of our division, basically closing the operation," he explained. The company was going to announce the plans Monday. He went on. "I hope to be reassigned, but my department is being eliminated, and I'm sorry, but that will include your position."

Edward M. Rahill

It seemed Carborundum had been making and selling a prefabricated high-temp insulation product using proprietary materials and what the company believed to be a non-patentable assembly process for over seventy-five years. A few years prior, a competitor filed a patent for the product and was suing Carborundum to force them to stop making their primary product line. The lawsuit alleged that the assembly process for our products, which were basically premanufactured blocks, violated their recently filed patent.

Carborundum had been fighting this patent suit for years, and they had a major setback and were about to lose the case. They were going to have to shut down. Hundreds of jobs would be lost.

Scott paused and then said, "We have a few weeks left. I don't believe in going down without a fight. I've been thinking about this. Why don't you spend your remaining time here looking over this patent suit? The law firms have run out of options." Scott was deploying what assets he had left—basically, me—to engage a hopeless situation.

A Gift for Looking at Things Differently

I was facing an impossible problem. I knew nothing about the situation that the company was in; I knew even less about how the law worked.

I decided to begin at the beginning. I gathered all the information on the case and took over a conference room. I studied the topic in depth and interviewed as many people as I could. I reconstructed an understanding of what it was like to work in this industry in the past. I was in over my head.

One supervisor I remember was Ron Stefanik. Ron's entire career was with Carborundum. He had started by sweeping the floors after school. Years later, he was a supervisor at the Niagara Falls operation. He gave me an understanding of the business and the people and an appreciation for the history of his company. This was an old manufacturing process and was developed late in the nineteenth century when the industry was in its infancy.

Ron and several of the old-timers had sworn up and down that there was a preexisting patent, which explained why Carborundum did not file one of their own. The only way to break the case was to establish that a patent had existed prior to our competitor filing theirs. Under the law, you cannot patent a product or idea once it has already been patented.

Over the next week my frustration with this assignment increased. Every path I went down was a dead end. The late-night phone calls with the attorneys were not encouraging as every "bright idea" had come back with "we went down that path before." As I became more deflated, the fact that I was going to be out of work in a few weeks flashed across my mind. Maybe it was time for me to look for a job? Maybe it was time for me to look out for myself.

I would lie awake at night thinking about the problem and my concern that I should just give up and move on. But then the next night I awoke from an unusually deep sleep. As I started to become aware of where I was, I struggled to retain the memory of the dream that was fading in my mind. It was a voice that was drifting away. It was saying, *This is why you are here.* The dream scared me for a minute. Then, with a conscious clarity, I lay awake thinking about the problem. Everything I had learned in the readings and interviews struck a chord. What if I took a different approach? I got to work at 5:30 a.m.

At first, I focused on nineteenth-century high-temperature insulation products but quickly found I was heading down the same path the patent law firms had. Then I noticed something interesting. Back when the industry was young, only a handful of inventors were filing patents for all sorts of ideas and not just for a specific application. What if instead of looking for specific end products with specific applications, I researched patents by the inventor? I looked for inventors who patented processes rather than products—how something was assembled, and not just for one application.

As I categorized each inventor's filings, I discovered a man who had filed several patents, not based on how they were to be used, but on how they were made, because he had envisioned a multiplicity of possible applications. A shiver went down my spine as I went through each of his patents for eleven years. Suddenly, there on the table in front of me was a diagram. I looked at it, and then put it down, paused, and then studied it again. It was a diagram of a manufacturing process, a process we were still following. Could the answer be that easy? Had I discovered the long-lost patent document that would break our competitor's lawsuit?

I sat there for a while, collecting my thoughts. It was time. I went to Scott's office. He was on the phone, and I waited. I knocked, and he gestured one minute. He waved me in and asked how I was doing and seemed subdued. "I think I found something; I think it might be the lost patent." He perked up but was dubious. I handed him the book open to the page of the detail patent filing and registration. As he looked it over, I explained my approach, but he motioned me to stop.

"I don't believe it!" he exclaimed. "After all these years, I don't believe you did it."

I could sense his energy as he studied it. And then we discussed next steps. He asked me to come back to his office at noon. He told me he was setting up a meeting with the Carborundum general counsel. He wanted to confirm my findings with the higher-ups.

The next couple weeks were a blur. I met with some attorneys to explain my findings. They filed a request for a delay in the court's ruling due to new evidence, including a request to meet with the plaintiff's legal team.

After our lawyers presented the patent to our competitor's legal team, the competitor withdrew its case against Carborundum. We had beaten the patent suit. A few weeks later, my boss asked me to come to his office. He told me that the company recognized the contribution I had made. I learned that Carborundum was offering me any position in the company I was qualified for. I chose my first real job as a corporate accountant. To combine those skills with my marketing skills, I believed I had a real future.

Edward M. Rahill

Sometimes, lost causes are the only ones worth fighting for.

I was sitting in my cubicle, packing up to move to my new position at corporate. At that moment, an older employee stopped by. It was Ron Stefanik. He smiled, and I smiled back and asked about his wife and kids.

"I just wanted to stop by and let you know a lot of guys woke up today and had their jobs to go to," he said. "It wasn't even a month ago we gave up hope, awaiting the news of when we were gonna be let go. We thought it was over. I just wanted to say thanks."

I was momentarily stunned. He had just told me that my actions changed his and others' lives. This was when I first realized there was truth to what my grandmother said about what she saw in me.

"But with these gifts will come a burden and a responsibility."

The Western New York region was in the middle of an economic decline that had started a decade before, and it was not going to get better. The two hundred-plus jobs that were saved were jobs that would not have been replaced. When I was working on the problem, the personal stakes for people had never occurred to me.

For a moment, I felt a tinge of fear, the kind of feeling when you just missed a disaster and only became aware of the danger after the fact. It scared me to think what might have happened to

Ron and hundreds of others if I had decided to check out, focus on myself and not put in the extra effort.

I quickly put it out of my mind and continued to pack. But little did I know this would not be the last time I was going to be put in a situation to make a difference—a big difference. The memory of my childhood connection with my past was going to come into play again.

Chapter 4
A Marriage between Friends

It makes no sense to most people: a young man marrying someone who has only a few years to live. Carlene and I were attending the same MBA program at SUNY Buffalo. We were in a few classes together and met while working on a group project. Over time, we got to know each other, and I grew fond of her. We discovered we had a lot in common, and we enjoyed talking about politics, health, and religion—all the things you're not supposed to discuss in casual company.

I would often give her a ride to and from classes. As time passed, she confided that she had cystic fibrosis. People living with the condition seldom reached their late twenties. We started dating and went to a few parties together. We got along great. One time she was ill in the hospital and could not meet a deadline for a paper in her finance class. I gave her a copy of one I'd written for the same class the previous semester. I told her I only got a B, but at least she wouldn't miss the deadline. A week later, she got the paper back with an A. I was a little pissed, but then laughed at the irony.

After graduation, she found a job at a bank in downtown Buffalo, and I was already employed with a company in Niagara Falls. We both had our eye on other opportunities. Carlene hoped to apply to a Ph.D. program, but she later revealed that she was resigned to staying in Buffalo, due to her health.

Edward M. Rahill

I wanted to look outside Western New York after Carborundum was acquired by another firm. I had jumped at an opportunity to join Worthington Compressors in South Buffalo as a financial and operations analyst. With that experience, I hoped to make myself more attractive to opportunities outside the region.

Carlene faced two significant obstacles to pursuing a Ph.D. from a top program: she had reached an age where she was no longer able to stay on her family's health insurance plan, and she needed daily therapy support. Once employed, she would be able to secure benefits, but they would end if she left the job. Her parents were trying to find a way for her to receive daily treatments, but it would be difficult if she left her family home.

It became clear I had feelings for Carlene, that I loved who she was, and I felt empathy for what she was going through. I did a lot of soul searching. It was not passionate love, and she was not someone with whom I envisioned starting a family. But that was not the choice I was faced with. The time we would spend together would be short.

I loved her strength of character. She had a kind and loving heart. Given her illness, I thought she was exceptional. I felt a deep connection with her. I have come to believe that feelings for another person are intuitive; they go beyond reason.

At that point in my young life, I felt I had a choice. I could continue on my own with no real compelling direction, or share my journey with Carlene. I could make a huge difference in her life, at least for a brief period. I would be able to help her if we got married. I took some time to reflect and prayed for courage. It struck me that I was not being asked to sacrifice my life; I was considering a way to make a difference in someone else's, someone whose life would be truly short. And I cared deeply for her.

We sat at a table one afternoon sharing our plans. We discussed how her insurance and physical therapy issues could be solved in a single move: marriage. Carlene was shocked. When I suggested the idea, she responded that she couldn't do that to me. I explained that I wanted to; it was an opportunity for us both in what time was left.

I told her to keep looking for post-graduate opportunities around the country, and that I would step up my efforts to find a new position. If we were lucky, we could land one in the same city. Once married, all her insurance problems would go away.

At times, it was a bit awkward. We were not talking about the things engaged couples normally would, like family. One day, while filling out some of the paperwork prior to getting married, she said, "I'm not going to change my name. I plan on keeping my maiden name." In any other situation, given my traditional Catholic family upbringing where a family was going to be involved, that would have been a huge issue for me. But it didn't even cross my mind; I didn't object. I wasn't thinking about a long-term future.

So, Carlene and I married. I continued to work a full-time job and attend graduate school in the evenings in Western New York, and she had her job at the bank. This went on for a year and a half. I'd been putting out feelers for opportunities around the country, and she had also been applying to a few Ph.D. programs. Her luck materialized much faster than mine.

Edward M. Rahill

One day, she received a letter from Northwestern University's business school requesting more information. She was thrilled. The Kellogg Business School was top notch. Over the next few weeks, she was invited for a meeting with some of the faculty.

I scheduled a couple personal days to travel with her to Chicago. She spent the better part of the day on campus, and that evening, I could tell she was excited. The interviews went well. She said all the body language was positive. I was happy for her. This was what she wanted more than anything.

If I had any misgivings, it was that I didn't see a path for my career at that moment. But as I was performing physical therapy on her that night, my thoughts came back to the fact that our time together was short.

About six months went by, and I received a call from an Atlantic Richfield subsidiary in Waterbury, Connecticut. The recruiter started to make a pitch and asked about my background. I responded, but I knew that the location was not going to work. Waterbury was not Chicago. Halfway into the phone interview, the recruiter explained that ARCO was moving the company's headquarters to Rolling Meadows, Illinois, a suburb of Chicago. I almost dropped the phone.

I was hired after the first interview, and I was finally with a company where I could grow and begin a real career. Carlene was ecstatic, and she let Northwestern know she could start that fall. I was able to provide her with medical coverage, something she could not get as a student.

Life for us was difficult; Carlene needed physical therapy two to three times a day to maintain her ability to breathe. This therapy required me to pound her back and chest to clear her lungs. She was routinely hospitalized, about three to four times a year. But the move to Chicago turned out to be even more of a blessing than we thought. Around that time, expensive but effective advances were being pioneered by the University of Chicago and Northwestern medical schools in the treatment of CF, something that was not available to us in Buffalo. Carlene was about to experience a transformation she had never allowed herself to dream of before.

When We Both Knew the Marriage Should not Have Been

Certain key events in my life have changed my perspective. One such event occurred during one of Carlene's hospitalizations. It hit me hard at the time and is still difficult for me to think about. I had been out of town on business for two days and visited as soon as I returned, and Carlene was upset. She had something to tell me, so I sat down and listened. She told me she had become pregnant. I paused for a moment to process what she had said, and I responded, wondering if it would be a boy or girl. She burst into tears and told me she had already had an abortion. I was devastated—a child of mine was taken before it had a chance to live. I would have done anything to find an alternative. But I never got the chance. I was deeply hurt that I was not even consulted on the decision. Even now, I occasionally wonder what kind of person that baby would be. She decided not to ever let that happen again.

She asked the doctor to perform a tubal ligation to ensure she would never become pregnant again. An hour later, her doctor stopped by and explained the procedure and that he felt it was best given her medical condition. We talked for a while, and I remember her telling me she could never have a child because she didn't want to risk passing on her disease. And she didn't want to risk any health complications that a pregnancy could present.

Carlene and I had never discussed the possibility before. I realize it was because we never thought we'd have a long-term relationship. We had made a choice to share a life during the time she had. But now that was changing. I understood then that it was not really a romantic marriage—a husband-and-wife relationship, a future family—it was a marriage between friends.

As time passed, the breakthroughs in her treatment materialized. The new automated/mechanical percussor equipment allowed her to perform much of her own therapy as many times a day as needed without waiting for a caregiver. This was a significant improvement in her quality of life. She and I talked about our futures and recognized the fork in the road. She wanted to fulfill her dreams of joining the academic world she loved, and I wanted a chance to pursue a business career and pursue a family of my own.

Over the next six months, I expressed my concerns about our relationship and my expectations. I explained that I wanted the opportunity to have a family. We had several difficult discussions. But we finally reached a point where we knew we had to go our separate ways.

It would be approximately eighteen months before Carlene could complete the coursework portion of her doctorate. We would separate, and I agreed that we would stay legally married to provide her financial stability and health insurance while she was still a student. At the time, insurance of an employee was not assignable to an ex-spouse.

We separated, and I moved to Barrington, which was closer to my work at Rolling Meadows, and Carlene focused on her work at Northwestern in Evanston. I gave her financial support during this period, and I never thought much of it. A one-bedroom in Barrington was all I needed. It was a little tight from time to time, but I worked it out.

I know separating was as difficult for Carlene as it was for me. We talked about our hopes for our respective futures and wished each other well. It was important for me to have taken care of her in those eighteen months until she could take over. When the time came, we jointly filed for divorce with no animosity or conflict of any kind. As I look back, I feel at peace because I had been able to stand by my commitment.

Chapter 5
Nancy

One Monday morning, I drove into my new office location, the Continental Towers in Rolling Meadows, Illinois. I parked and started to walk toward Building II, a tall white marble building. As I gazed up at the impressive structure a feeling of fateful transition came over me. I had just turned twenty-nine, and I sensed a change from a time of *preparing* for life, to a time of *participating* in life's adventures.

I remember the first moment I saw her walking to her desk. I felt my heart skip a beat and a tightening in my chest. Nancy was in her late twenties with beautiful blond neck-length hair. She was slender with brown eyes and an infectious smile. I was attracted to her vivacious personality. Her signature look was different combinations of blouses and skirts—graceful and together, a little bit preppy. In the winter, she'd wear slacks and a top.

We both worked at ARCO. I was a senior planning analyst, and Nancy had just started work in accounts payable. To me, she was unattainable; I was very insecure. But from time to time, I would go out of my way to pass her workstation, something a guy does when he's smitten. To my surprise, she'd look up and smile. Finally, one day, I stopped and introduced myself. I was shy and planned to walk away, but she responded and asked me what I did at the company. Over the following weeks, I continued to go out of my way to see her, and to my joy, she seemed interested in talking.

One day, I attended a budget meeting to review the accounting and payables budget. I learned that she was going to be awarded a new position. I knew she'd applied and was hoping to get it. But she believed it was a long shot.

I was obligated not to reveal this information, but somehow, I hoped it could help me progress our relationship beyond hallway conversations. The opportunity came. As I walked past her station toward my desk, we shared a polite hello and a brief chat like always. But this time, something was different. Nancy seemed a little down. I asked what was bothering her, and she confided that she really wanted the position she applied for, but she felt it was not going to happen.

My heart jumped. I remember praying. *God, what do I do? The advice I was given when I was young flashed into my mind. If you have a chance, take it, because this moment may never be there for you again.*

"You're better than you think!" I asserted. "And I bet you're gonna get the job." This began a back-and-forth where I playfully teased her, telling her she should have more faith in herself.

She didn't buy it, responding, "I'll bet you I don't." My heart jumped again. I didn't know where to go with this and prayed, *God, please don't let me blow it.*

Then, with fear in my heart, I took a chance. "Okay, it's a bet." I saw an opening and tried to sound energetic but supportive. "If

I'm right and you get the position, you have to agree to go out to dinner to celebrate."

She paused, smiled, and responded that it was a deal. She then thanked me for helping her feel better. I said, "Good!" As I headed back to my desk, I was overwhelmed and grateful. There must have been somebody upstairs watching out for me, giving me the right words at the right time.

Not to my surprise, but to hers, she received the promotion a week later. I waited to approach her after the commotion and congratulations were over. She looked up at me with a smile and said, "I got the job!"

I congratulated her and reminded her about what I'd told her about being better than she gave herself credit for, and we talked about the position and how she felt.

I mustered up the courage to bring up the bet. I was nervous but didn't show it. In a confident voice, I commented, "You know, you lost the bet." She smiled, and I could tell she remembered the exchange. I then said, "I'd like to take you to dinner this week." It seemed like forever before she responded. I was nervous that she would find an excuse to say no.

The magic words came back from her. "How about tomorrow after work?" So that was the beginning of my relationship with Nancy, whom I consider to this day to be the first love of my life.

We met in the lobby after work, and we drove to a local upscale but warm restaurant. Our table was on the small side, and as we both sat down, we bumped heads. It seemed awkward, but it resulted in us both laughing. This removed all my nervousness, and I could see it did the same for her.

It was like magic; we just clicked. We enjoyed talking to each other, and I could sense she was starting to feel comfortable with me. So, I suggested we try out the seafood place near Crystal Lake that had come up earlier in our conversation. She said she would love to, and that Friday worked best. I walked her to her car, we talked for a few minutes, and then we left. On the way home, I reflected on what had just happened. That evening felt so comfortable and natural, like we'd known each other for some time.

I picked her up for the next date, and over dinner, we just talked without regard for the time. But there was one thing that will stay in my mind forever—standing in her kitchen after bringing her home. She was sitting on her counter in a pink patterned dress with a turquoise shirt. I stopped talking, looked into her eyes, and gently kissed her. Not a moment later, she kissed me back.

As the summer went by, we discussed our plans for Labor Day. Nancy told me she didn't have anything planned, and that perhaps she would take the time to practice her dressage horseback riding. She hoped to enter a show or two that fall. She was tired and wanted to just relax and regroup. She had been putting in overtime coming up to speed on her new position.

That was when I said I felt the same way. I paused to get up my courage. "How about getting a cottage in Galina, just hanging out in the quiet of the trees and hills?"

She paused, but to my joy, I could see she was considering it. "Okay, let's do it!"

I secured a two-bedroom A-frame—this was a stage in our relationship where we were not yet intimate. We made dinner together and talked for a few hours. I could see she was tired and in need of the peace that comes with sleep. We cleaned up, she retired for the evening, and I went for a brief walk.

The next morning, I was up early and took advantage of the light to go for a longer than normal walk and think about Nancy, whether it could really happen between us. I was falling in love with her; I just didn't have the confidence that she felt the same.

When I returned, she was up with a cup of coffee and a book. She liked to read. The day was a blur, but I imagine we drove into town, perhaps went out to dinner. That evening, I could feel something was different. We were beginning to emotionally connect. That night, we became lovers, not just friends.

The next morning, we got up and made coffee. Nancy wanted to sit on the deck. There were no chairs, so we settled down on the wooden planks and talked. I still have an image in my mind of the sun lighting up strands of her hair, glimmering in amber and gold.

She asked me about my previous relationships, and I asked about hers. She grasped my hand, and we intertwined our fingers as we talked. It was her way of telling me she was willing to pursue a serious relationship, not just a casual one. I felt she was looking for me to give her a sign about my intentions. That was not hard to do; I was well on my way to falling in love with her.

Edward M. Rahill

We became a couple.

I lived in the village of Barrington, and Nancy was about four miles away in Barrington Hills, a horse-centric rural area. One Saturday morning, we decided to meet for a late breakfast in the village of Barrington at the Canteen Restaurant. Again, we talked, and after an hour, we walked out to the parking lot.

Nancy stopped for a moment and then said, "Ed, I need to tell you something." She started to tell me she'd been seeing a guy before she met me, and he was serious about her. She explained that she wanted to be in a relationship with one man and that was it. I wasn't surprised; she was a beautiful woman with a magnetic personality. How could she not be pursued by other men? I listened, and I told myself that I needed to show my self-confidence. How I responded could be everything. I felt pretty good about myself. If she had to move on, I knew I had to say I was okay with that. But I really didn't mean it. She had already won my heart, so I paused to find the right words. If she and I were to be, this was it.

"Nancy, the moment I saw you, I knew you were the one for me. But it's your choice, your decision." I was trying to show her my commitment and let her know how I really felt about her. I was making myself vulnerable to a true connection. I wanted to be there for her when she needed me.

She looked away for what seemed like an eternity. Then she said, "Okay, I made my choice. I'm free for dinner tonight, but not before six thirty." She got into her car, smiled, and said, "Don't be late!" After that, we started spending time together most days after work and on weekends. It was natural just to stay with each other every night. Barrington Hills made the most sense because she needed to care for her horse. It was a small cottage, but we didn't care; life was good.

It's hard to describe the next few months. At first, we attempted to hide the relationship from our colleagues at work because dating between employees was sometimes frowned upon by management. We would arrive at separate times and leave the same way. Despite our best efforts, it became obvious that we were a couple.

One day, Angie, who was the secretary for our department, came into a conference room where I was working and made a comment to me about Nancy. Angie was a direct and to-the-point type of person. She could read you like a book, but she had a heart of gold. She said that Nancy seemed to be in a happy mood, and she suspected that Nancy was head over heels in a new relationship. I was surprised. But then Angie paused, looking for a response. I looked at her and said nothing, and the length of her pause started to make me a little uncomfortable. Then she cracked a smile. "It's you, isn't it?"

We spent time with Nancy's sister over Thanksgiving, and we traveled to her parents' house in Clarendon Hills for Christmas Eve. Nancy was Catholic like me, so we decided to attend Mass on Christmas Day. It was a sunny morning, unusually warm. The church was packed, so we had to stand. As we stood there during the service, she reached for my hand, and I held her hand during the Mass. This was the first time in my adult life a woman had ever wanted to hold my hand. It warmed my heart.

I got to know her better, and I began to appreciate her interests. Horses were her passion, and as an experienced rider myself, I agreed to the stable owner's request to exercise some of the other boarding horses that were not getting ridden as much as they should. It was a help to her because all the horses needed exercise.

Her other interest was reading. I introduced her to a few books. One of them was *Atlas Shrugged*. I remember lying in bed upstairs waiting to hear her reaction when she realized the main protagonist in the book was not John Galt, not Hank Rearden, but a woman named Dagny Taggart. I heard a shriek from downstairs. I just smiled and went to sleep. The next day, I got a little, "Why didn't you tell me the book is about Dagny?"

Another special moment was when I waited for her to arrive from Chicago to LaGuardia. She was flying into NYC to spend the weekend with me after I had attended a conference there. We had dinner one night at a special French restaurant on the Upper East Side, and the next day we dined at the Windows of the World restaurant at the top of the World Trade Center. But what was most special was that I surprised her with hard-to-get tickets to the Broadway show *Evita*.

A Profound Connection

I would lie next to her praying to God. *If this is what heaven is like, please take me now.* The feeling of being in love and knowing she loved me too was something I was experiencing for the first time. I had just turned thirty, and she was it.

The chemistry was there from the beginning, but it wasn't long before our lives were interwoven. I did not understand the extent of what it meant to not just be with a person, but to connect in a way that brought our souls together. I don't know if two people could have loved each other more. After we moved in together, we looked forward to the end of the day because we could see each other and share our experiences.

We would often sit down at dinner and just talk. It was special because we seldom planned to such long conversations—they just happened. I'd hear about things that had bothered her or experiences she'd had in the past or about how something that happened that day had made her feel good. She would talk about her need to occasionally drive up to Door County for a short weekend by herself. I can only recall one time early in our relationship, when she took that weekend trip. She said she needed to think. I briefly wondered what was on her mind, but dismissed it. Everyone needs time to reflect, including me.

Sometimes, on a cold winter evening, she'd come into the room, stop, and say, "Let's go somewhere." She just wanted a break from the cabin fever of the cold winter nights. One of our favorite places was the Red Door Tavern in the village. I remember how we'd order two amaretto and coffees while sitting at the end of the bar. It was a fun place—the bartenders and owner would always remember us and take a few moments to catch up.

We'd have conversations about what was important to us, but then we'd turn to the activity around us. Nancy and I enjoyed people watching. We'd laugh about something we saw about the people we watched. The bar patrons were a mix of suburban and country folks, the lighting was warm, and it had a jukebox. I remember Rosanne Cash's songs "Seven Year Ache" and "Hold On" in the background. When "Hold On" started to play, she looked at me, moved to the music, and sang along: "If you want to keep a woman like me, you got to hold on." She then sang the second verse, "If you want to see how good it could be, baby, hold on." She owned my heart. She was playing me the only way a woman I loved could. Those were good times.

For a man in love, the emotion of making love is more powerful than the physical experience. One day, I was sitting at the table having coffee and working on something, and Nancy entered the room with a piece of paper. She said she wanted to show me something. She laid out a calendar of the month of January and said with a tone of playful pride, "We made love every day last month and quite a few times more."

I can't begin to describe how much she filled my life. At work, every time I saw her at her desk or walking down the corridor, it was like the first time I saw her. To me, she was beyond beautiful; it was as if I was living a dream every day.

One lazy Sunday morning after getting in late the night before, she was sitting at the table by the window in her red robe with coffee. She was still sleepy without her makeup on. She looked disheveled, hair all over the place. But to me, she was beautiful. I found the camera and took a few pictures. When she realized what I was doing, she got a little upset, told me to stop, and went to the bathroom mirror. "Oh my God!" she said. "I look like a wreck; you can't keep those pictures. I'm so embarrassed."

Sometimes, it all seemed like a dream, and it was destiny that we met at that moment in our lives. I was no longer thinking and feeling as an individual; she was part of my life. It felt natural, as if it was always meant to be.

For the first time in my life, I felt complete. My longing for a companion had been met. She made me a better man. Everything I did was better because I believed she loved me, and I loved her. I realized that I was not meant to live my life alone. Only the love of a woman and the sense of belonging she brings could truly complete me.

Edward M. Rahill

She was haunted by her secrets.

One night, after some intimate moments, I was holding her. She started to sob. She wrapped her arms around me and said, "Please don't ever leave me." I was taken by surprise. I felt empathy for her and an uplifting of my heart. Her comment made me feel I was loved and needed.

But my overpowering instinct was to comfort her. I remember saying, "That will never happen. Everything's okay." Another time, I walked into the room and found her sitting at a table quietly crying. I stood there for a minute until she became aware of my presence. I just sat down with her, not saying a word.

I found her despondent and crying again. This time it was evening, and it was more than a sob. I wanted to reach out to hold her. I took us from her chair to the floor with my arms around her and her head on my shoulder. I don't know why, but I just started to clumsily recite Springsteen's "Racing in the Street." We just stayed on the floor as I held her. She wept; she never said anything explaining why. Even now when I hear those lyrics, I think of that moment.

> But now there's wrinkles around my baby's eyes
> And she cries herself to sleep at night
> When I come home the house is dark
> She sighs, "Baby did you make it all right?"

One Mile at a Time

One Sunday afternoon, the day before I was scheduled to fly out of town, we were both on the floor cleaning up some spilled coffee, trying to make light of the mess. She suddenly paused, looked at me, and said, "Please just hold me tonight. If anything were to happen, at least I will remember us that way." I did not understand the context of her comment until I recalled that an American Airlines flight had crashed at O'Hare months before. Nancy always felt more than she showed.

There were a few more moments when I sensed her insecurity and sadness. It was as if she was powerless to control it, as if somewhere in her past she had felt abandoned or let down. Or there was a deep apprehension about the future that she chose not to share.

These episodes were rare, but they left a profound impression on me. Later, I found hints of what she was feeling when she'd fall into these emotional states and cry. But all I could do at the time was let her know I felt her sadness. In retrospect, I believe her occasional trips alone to Door County were connected to these moods. I could not put my finger on it, but I sensed her feelings of loss, broken promises, or perhaps lost dreams, a loss of hope, or trauma . . . something like that. I felt like she didn't want to tell me, as if she might be protecting me from something.

Nancy never allowed those dark moods to last long. The next day I would find her vivacious and playful again. Her ability to bounce back just confirmed how special she was. And it didn't take long for her to figure out how to get her way and at the same time, make me feel good about it. When she came home a little late and we'd had something planned, I was frustrated. After she walked in, she began to talk to me in a young girl's voice. "Sorry I'm a little late, but I was at Saks. Want to see what I got? Isn't it pretty?" I was pretty much toast after that. I just forgot why I was irritated.

Caution to the Wind

When our relationship started, I was uncertain about where it could go. Was she real? Was the attention she was showing me genuine? I'd never experienced reciprocity in a relationship that had this much potential. It took me a while to learn to trust. Despite my feelings of insecurity, trust is what I learned with Nancy—for me, that trust was real.

I had never experienced throwing caution to the wind until I fell in love with her. One time, when she had to travel to Louisville for a couple days on business, we talked on the phone every day. One afternoon, she called me at work just to check in. She wasn't feeling well, concerned she had a fever, and wished she had some medication. She had one more day in Louisville before she'd be flying back.

After we hung up, I looked at my watch. It was 4:12 p.m. That meant it was 5:12 in Louisville. I suddenly had an idea to surprise her that night. I started to calculate how improbable it would be to pull it off. I grabbed my jacket, ran to the car, and headed to

O'Hare. There was a 5:20 p.m. flight that landed at 7:31 p.m. Louisville time. I stopped at a drugstore and grabbed anything that looked good for cold and flu and raced to the airport. O'Hare was fifteen minutes away, but there was traffic. I doubted I could make it, but that had never stopped me before. I just couldn't believe my luck! Short-term parking was open, and the ticket line was short. I just made it to the plane as the last passenger was boarding.

In Louisville, I rushed off the plane and grabbed the first cab. I rode downtown to her hotel. I was getting nervous. As I stood at her door, I thought about how crazy I was to even think about doing this. What would she think? I was nuts! I knocked, and my heart was in my throat wondering what I should say. So, I just leaned against the door jam and prepared myself to act like I was a cool, nonchalant, unflappable guy. It felt like forever before she responded.

But after a few seconds, she opened the door and gave me one of those *Oh my God* looks. "What are you doing here?!"

I struggled to keep my cool and started talking as if nothing was unusual, just like it was any other day. "After we hung up and you said how bad you felt and thought you were coming down with something, I just thought, well, there's a drugstore on the corner and O'Hare isn't too far out of my way. Why not pick up some medication on my way?"

She was just standing there staring at me, smiling. I just looked at her, trying not to smile myself and said, "What?"

It must have been thirty seconds before she spoke. "You're crazy!" And to my relief, she again said, "You're crazy!" and we hugged.

I stayed that night, and I got up a couple times to give her something for her cough. I flew back to Chicago the next morning and headed into work and was there by eleven a.m. Looking back, it was not such a crazy idea. We got even closer after that.

When Nancy got the chance, she would leave a note in my shirt pocket or surprise me with something for us to do at the spur of the moment. One special gift was a small book of papers with handwritten coupons that I could exchange when I wanted. One page said, "Good for one hug when you need it." These gestures meant a lot to me because she had taken the time to think of each one. She really knew me well.

Life had become fun for us—playful, kidding around. I relished the simple things like a snowball fight after I made her stand out in the cold to take a couple pictures. I still have one picture where you can almost read her lips as she yelled, "Shoot, I'm freezing!"

One incident she never let me live down was when I was exercising one of the horses at the stable. Nancy was grooming her horse while I had saddled a quarter horse owned by one of the boarders. It was raining, so I was exercising the horse in the indoor arena. I was getting comfortable with the horse. She was on the smaller side. I estimated she weighed a little over 800 pounds and was very quick, even with a 185-pound rider.

The arena wasn't that big, but I thought I'd put her through the paces and started running her at a slow canter doing figure eights. She was able to change direction very quickly. I brought her to a slow gallop and pulled her into the turn. The next thing I knew, I had pulled her down on top of me. She was lying on my left leg and started to get up. If that was not embarrassing enough, Nancy was just standing there laughing her head off. She said, "It serves you right, taking advantage of a filly like that!" I didn't live that one down for a while.

I can still remember when I realized how close we'd become. It was a Saturday, and Nancy, her friend Christy, and I were getting ready to go out together. I walked into the room, and Nancy just stopped, looked at me, and said, "That belt must go. You need to put on something else." Christy laughed at the situation. This is the kind of conversation you would expect between a married couple, and usually after they'd been together for years. I had become Nancy's property, and she wanted my style to fit her taste. I smiled and said okay. I was thinking to myself that our relationship had obviously evolved beyond dating. What made this time so special was that we were living in the moment, enjoying the simple things. It was as if the past was no longer a part of our lives, only the now. But this could not last forever. The past and future are destined to interfere.

One night, after having dinner at the cottage, we spent the evening talking for hours. We talked about what we wanted out of life and started to share our feelings about the future. She confided that she saw her future with a family someday. But the way she said it, I very much felt she was saying she wanted us to have a family. "And I want my first son to be named Ben."

I smiled. "My grandmother advised me that three or five is the best number, otherwise the kids tend to team up against each other."

Edward M. Rahill

She smiled back, and said something like, "That's fine for you to say, but you don't have to carry them for nine months."

As I look back, I still choke up a bit. During our time together, I felt complete, at peace, and was experiencing unconditional love. But it wouldn't last. Eventually, a tough cross-country road race, my career destiny, and my commitment to protect Carlene would challenge our relationship. But for now, I had what I believe was the most complete connection two people could ever have. For the first time in my life, I felt I had found what I'd wanted for years: to share life, almost as one, with another human being. For me, life was as good as I could ever have imagined.

The day I made Nancy stand in the cold to take a picture. You can read her lips: "Shoot!" A snowball fight ensued.

One Mile at a Time

Nancy after one of our long evening talks. I just had to capture the moment.

Chapter 6
A Race Too Far

A passion from my past was reignited one February afternoon when a friend from work sent me a name and a phone number. He had dabbled in performance cars and racing as a hobby and had professional racing in the family.

I called him to get some details. "I was expecting your call," he chuckled. "I thought of you when he told me about an opportunity to participate in a big cross-country race."

I immediately asked if he wanted to do it. "Hell, no, I have a wife and three kids. I run this, and I expect the divorce papers to be waiting for me at the finish line."

Ed Preston was the organizer of this new transcontinental road race, the Michael A. Preston Four Ball Rally. I had wanted to do this type of race since I was twelve years old. I contacted Ed and discussed my interest. After a second call, he sent me an entrance questionnaire, an application, and a liability waiver.

My first instinct was to sign up and do it—not to win, but to learn. There was so much I didn't know about what it took to be competitive. Then I had an idea. Nancy and I could share an adventure, and I'd learn the tricks of the trade. It would be something we could tell our kids about.

Nancy was downstairs with a book. I explained that I wanted to enter a race that required two drivers. I was asking if she would consider running the race with me. After a lot of questions, she said she'd think about it. I was pleased and relieved.

A couple days later, she agreed to do the race. In retrospect, it was not good for our relationship. In fact, I believe it contributed to a series of events that we both regretted. But in that moment, things were good. In fact, I joked with her when she would have a slight misgiving that we'd be able to tell our grandchildren about what we did.

I was excited to finally have the chance to participate in what had become an American tradition. Since I was a child, I had followed the outcome of previous endurance races in Europe and the U.S., but I never thought it would be possible for me. Now, I was about to do what had been a dream even a year ago.

Earlier in the year, I chose to buy a car I was familiar with, one I knew could handle racing conditions. I had acquired this knowledge in my driving baptism days growing up. It was a 1978 Firebird Formula. It was what I could afford, and it was in great shape with a solid suspension. I sized her up to determine if she could possibly run the race. While not technically a racing car, it did have good aerodynamics, and I believed it would be stable in the 120-to-130 mph range. I rebuilt the car from the bottom up. We installed larger sway bars for the suspension and a custom four-bolt main 350-cubic-inch engine with racing heads and a four-barrel Rochester carburetor. I chose the Rochester because it was easy to adjust, something I thought we might need to do during the race.

I had the automatic transmission rebuilt with premium parts. I felt this type of transmission would work well for Nancy. The rear end differential was a 3.42 ratio. While the gear was not sized for a drag race, it did offer better fuel economy and a slightly higher top-end speed than more aggressive gears. Standard brakes were replaced with high-end, four-wheel disc pads and rotors, and she had good aerodynamics. With her design and engine running north of 350 horsepower, I believed she could hold and exceed 130 mph. Finally, I replaced the speedometer gear to convert km/h to mph. While I was busy prepping the car, I realize now that I wasn't paying attention to Nancy's feelings about the race. She would give a happy speech to her friends about this cross-country adventure, but I should have started a deep conversation about how she felt.

In the second week of June 1983, we began our trip to Boston where we would start the race. On the way, we stopped to meet my family in Buffalo. It went well—in fact, it is one of my happiest memories. Nancy met my mother, brother, sister, and father. We spent an entire sunny afternoon making final preparations to the car. We worked as a team, and she was all smiles. We were joking around, and my mother brought out drinks and took pictures.

Getting to know my family was huge for her; it made a statement that we were on our way to making a commitment. She was happy; in her mind, her dreams were coming true. The next day, it was gray and overcast, and we packed up the car. My mother added a few drinks and snacks, and we were off. After leaving my family home, the reality was setting in that we were about to undertake something we really did not understand.

We arrived at the Boston hotel and found fifty other teams from around the world, from as far away as Japan. It was a bit intimidating, and I can only imagine how Nancy must have felt. I met the sponsors to discuss the race while Nancy met a couple of other women on the race teams. One woman she met was Sarah, who, just like us, was in the race with a guy she was dating. They drove a late-model, well-equipped BMW.

We also met Tim Montgomery and his partner Jeff. This was the first time running the rally for them, too. They had dressed as the Blues Brothers in Ray Bans and black suits and ties, and they drove a black classic Cadillac. We immediately hit it off and became friends.

Do we know what we're getting into?

I quickly learned that this road race had become a clandestine hotbed for racers. The previous year's winners were a couple of Manhattan Beach, California, entrepreneurs driving a modified 1979 Mercedes 6.9 liter, and they were there to race again. There were several Porsches, a wicked-looking 934 and 930, four BMWs, and four Ford Panteras. Domestic cars included two four-door Ford sedans, each with characteristics of unmarked patrol cars, and a few Firebirds, Camaros, and Corvettes. For the most part, this was a well-prepared and talented group. There were at least three teams who were professional drivers, and there were a handful entrants who were just there for the adventure. But most of the drivers in the race were good. The international teams, experienced drivers, and semi-pro drivers seemed to dominate.

There was a pre-race dinner when drivers were awarded a starting position at random using a ping-pong ball cage. Finally, they called Ed and Nancy, and we were to start somewhere near the seventeenth spot. That night, I was concentrating on installing a taillight kill switch, which took some time. What I should have been doing was thinking about Nancy and how scared she had become. I let my competitive instincts consume me and was not there to give her a hug when she needed it. I wish I'd spent more time with her before the race. When I thought about it later, I felt an emotional sting of regret.

The next day, our turn to start crept up on us rapidly. Nancy was quiet, the way she was when she was apprehensive, and I was a little nervous too. We finally reached the starting line and were off a few minutes before 10:30 a.m. From the outset, we both felt some tension. It was clear that we were not in for a joyride on an expressway. It did not take long to comprehend that speeding across the country was not going to be a relaxing experience.

From the beginning, I approached this as an opportunity to learn what it would take to competitively run such a race. I had decided I would approach it with a sense of caution. But at times, I felt more competitive than I had planned. I had to discipline myself to stay within my limits. I focused on the route east of the Mississippi River, where traffic congestion and police enforcement were known to pose an extra challenge.

Edward M. Rahill

I knew from my research that a cross-country race could be rough on cars and drivers. I was about to find out how right they were. I was advised by a contestant in the last Cannonball Rally that my skills on a mile-long racetrack wouldn't help me. So, I decided not to push the car or myself until the second part of the race. I felt once we were running the Great Plains in the interior of the continent, I would see what I could do. But there was one factor I always had in mind: Nancy. I had seen some nasty car wrecks in my day, and the thought of putting her in danger just made me to want to back off.

I could tell Nancy was intimidated the first time she took the wheel. I grew up in a semi-rural environment where speed laws were treated as a suggestion. Driving 90-to-100 mph was more common in the southern tier of Western New York than anyone would admit. Nancy's entire driving experience was in suburban Chicago, a place where 55 mph ruled, and traffic enforcement was taken very seriously.

This road race was over 3,000 miles of driving as fast as you could and still dodging cars and trucks, scanning for police patrols, and constantly staying on alert during each four-hour shift. Our lives depended on it. Nancy was a trooper and hung in there, but we each had a degree of tension when it was our turn behind the wheel. While this was normal in a racing environment, it was not fun for her from the start, and we had forty-some hours of nonstop racing to go.

The second stress for Nancy was the car itself. It was a high-performance, small-block Chevy V8, putting out well over 350 horsepower. The sheer sound of the car and its sudden powerful responses to the throttle could shock an inexperienced driver. For me, handling these cars was second nature, but I still had to condition myself. Nancy's car was a four-cylinder four-door, and it was quite docile compared to the Firebird. This car needed to be managed with attention. It was well into her second shift before I felt she had relaxed to some degree.

We were outclassed from the start. My lack of experience with endurance road racing started to show. One of my oversights was our car's lack of range. Three hundred and twenty-five miles was the limit she could run before we needed to fill her up. Our fuel capacity was nowhere close to that of the other cars, so we had to make more fuel stops than the others. That cost us time.

My second rookie move was the route I had chosen. I had studied the miles traveled without any insight into actual driving conditions. This led me to choose a route through Pennsylvania using I-80 rather than the New York State tollway. While it was a shorter route than the upstate New York I-90, not being a toll road, I-80 was fraught with truck traffic and congestion from cities and towns along the way. There were several times when we came to a complete stop, sometimes waiting up to fifteen minutes for some construction delay.

In addition, the highway was dominated by twists and turns as we approached the northern end of the Appalachian range in western Pennsylvania. This was not good planning. It cost us time and energy, and the demanding topography of the route exhausted us. By the time we reached Dayton, Ohio, we were already thirteen-

and-a-half hours into the race and had only traveled a little over 800 miles. Not a good start. Driving I-80 through Pennsylvania was hard, and I could tell she was not enjoying it.

Once into Ohio and on I-70, things got better. The highway had long, straight sections of road, and although the sun had set, I could tell Nancy was becoming more confident. The moment I knew she was settling in was when she had to pass some slower traffic. I felt the car accelerate as she whipped us into the left lane. "This car can sure get out of its own way! I like that!" she said. She was very good at staying aware of what was around her. She hit 100 mph on several occasions when she could tell there was no traffic around.

Outside Chandler, Oklahoma, the Firebird started to drift at speed, and I was concerned and pulled to the side of the road. The tire pressure on the front passenger side was low and showing signs of deflating. Nancy and I headed to the next exit to find a service station. As we drove, I noticed a helicopter hovering over the highway two or three miles ahead. The exit was coming up, and I took it. After driving for about ten minutes, we found a station and asked the service attendant to see if he could expedite a repair. After slipping him twenty bucks, he got to work and found a nail in the tire, and we were out of there forty-five minutes later. We later learned that Chandler was a hotbed for troopers, who had arrested several rally teams that day.

After the tire repair, I started to put the car—and myself—to the test. I was finally able to open her up and test her limits. I noticed the steering was becoming less precise, and she tended to drift at over 130 mph. I determined she was getting a buildup of air pressure under the hood at that speed. This caused me to re-evaluate her limits and think about what could go wrong. I was running a six-year-old car. I would never have forgiven myself if anything happened to Nancy, even if I survived. I decided I would limit my top end to 120-to-125 mph with a preferred run rate of 90 to 110 mph, and I would back off if I sensed anything going wrong.

Another issue was the number of fuel stops we had to make, which became more frequent as we increased our average speed. At speeds above 80 mph, three hundred miles was it. That meant at least ten stops over the two-day run, maybe more, and we lost count. Looking back, for the life of me, I don't understand why I had not considered a second fuel cell—the price you pay for inexperience.

My favorite memory of Nancy in the race was in New Mexico. It was her turn to drive, and she was driving pretty fast. Out of nowhere, a state trooper pulled us over. I secretly wished I had been driving. I wasn't sure how she'd react. I handed her the registration, insurance, and her license from the glove compartment, and we waited until the trooper approached the driver's side window. The trooper was polite, and I sensed his surprise to find a pretty, young blond behind the wheel. Nancy was as cool as anyone.

"Yes, officer, how are you?"

"I'm fine, thank you. Do you know how fast you were driving?"

"Why, no, officer, I was just watching the road, and because the sun was getting in my eyes, I was paying more attention to the cars around me than the speedometer in the car."

What a genius of an answer—wow! Not admitting anything but giving an answer that did not show disrespect. I could tell the trooper did not expect that answer, but then he followed up with, "I was clocking you at least twenty miles over the limit, maybe more."

"I'm so sorry, officer. I just didn't know." I could tell when he started to give her a lecture, he was considering letting her go. That's always a good sign, and true enough, he let her off with a warning. Talk about cool under fire.

A few hours later, we were tired after not really sleeping the night before. Trying to sleep while the other one drove before our four-hour turn really didn't work. Late in the afternoon of our second day, I threw up in a bag after having a little food. I was dehydrated and drank what I could. That is what two days of no sleep, inadequate hydration, and the constant pressure of an endurance race will do to you. It didn't help that were driving for several hours at over 5,000 feet altitude. In retrospect, I was impacted by the altitude more than Nancy was. But by the time we broke down in Albuquerque, we were both shot.

The car was about to have had it with the altitude too. We'd been driving at speed for a few hours and were on a particularly challenging section of road. After climbing for almost ten minutes, we were about to start down a long section with winding turns. I was noticing how intense the sun was and that the temperature seemed unusually high, when suddenly the engine started to sputter and lose power. Then it cut out completely. The car was running between 90 and 100 mph. I asked Nancy to put the transmission into neutral. Losing our engine, power brakes, and power steering was not an insignificant problem. Without handling the car correctly, it could be dangerous. To complicate matters, there was no obvious safe place to pull over. I had wanted to put the car back into drive to take advantage of the drag that a dead engine would provide in helping to slow the car down. Without any idea of when we were going to encounter a breakdown lane, we needed to maintain speed to give us as much range as we could.

In a calm voice, I asked her to try to restart the engine. If that didn't work, we would coast while we looked for a place to safely pull over. Nancy tried to restart the car. It cranked, but nothing. I asked her to pump the gas pedal two times and try again. She engaged the starter, the engine cranked, one cylinder of the eight ignited once, but again, nothing. I was concerned about flooding the engine, so it was time to find somewhere we could pull off the road. I warned her she would soon lose power steering, and it was possible the brakes would have only one or two good pumps. I pointed to the emergency brake near her left foot and said, "That's your backup."

I could tell she was intensely concentrating on handling the car. "Got it, thanks," she said. As we started to lose speed, we passed through a sharp bend in the road and noticed a vegetable stand about 500 or 600 yards ahead, and we were approaching it fast. Not a moment too soon. Nancy was struggling with the steering wheel as the power steering boost was now gone. I reached over and helped her turn the wheel one more time as we prepared to turn off the road. Nancy was standing on the brake pedal, as its power boost was diminished, pushing all the way to the floor with her right leg. And with all her strength, she was standing on the emergency brake with her left. I then asked her to put the car in drive. Suddenly as we approached a few parked cars, the Firebird came to an abrupt stop with the added engine drag and we had slowed enough for the emergency brake to engage and lock up the rear wheels. We had brought the car to an uneventful stop. Nancy and I just looked at each other for a moment and she said, "I think it's your turn to drive."

Because I built the car, I immediately suspected the carburetor or fuel filter. We were at almost 6,000 feet elevation, and I guessed the elevation was causing the fuel mixture to run too rich for the amount of oxygen in the air. That proved to be the case. As Nancy tried to start the engine, nothing. I continued working the air/fuel mixture adjustments on the carburetor. I asked Nancy to try again, and she suddenly fired, and Nancy ran it up to full throttle. It was a quick fix, and the air/fuel flow mixture was now leaned out to compensate for the altitude. The rest of the race was uneventful.

For safety reasons alone, I realized that a car needed to be a late-model year with performance-modified systems to reliably run a race like this. The older the car, the more likely that unanticipated problems could arise. I remember criticizing myself, thinking I should have anticipated significant changes in altitude and its impact on a carburetor. After that last breakdown, I knew Nancy was tired from the experience, and per her request, I took the driver's position. I tried to lighten the moment and complimented her on how she'd handled it. She smiled, but I could tell she needed to calm down. She had a right to back off for a while. Once again,

I was impressed at her cool under fire. She never panicked and showed emotion only after the danger was gone.

We drove through the rest of northern New Mexico, eventually south through Arizona, and on to San Diego. Exhausted, we arrived after driving the last 300 miles in the early morning hours. It was just after five a.m. as I drove into the hotel parking lot and clocked in. For good reason, not too many people were around. Nancy was sleeping, and I felt bad that I had to wake her. I checked us in and when we got to the room, she just fell into bed. I must have been right behind her—I don't even recall hitting the pillow. We had come in seventeenth of fifty-six and clocked a time around forty-seven hours, or about 66 mph for the race. We had been able to complete the race without arrests, significant breakdowns, or other delays.

Finishing seventeenth was average but not exceptional. While only thirty-seven cars finished, I was still deflated—a little embarrassed. I had been humbled. I'd had such high hopes. Instead, we suffered one setback after another, mostly due to lack of experience. I started to ask myself how I could have built a better car or developed better skills to handle speed. More importantly, I regretted how I planned the route. I found myself listening to other drivers' stories to try to pick up some pointers. I was going to study my mistakes and consider running again.

But I wasn't sure I could take on that effort. The reality of underperforming in the type of race I had dreamed of running for the last eighteen years bruised my confidence. But I was amazed at Nancy's performance. She had no clue what she was getting into, and yet she recovered from the initial feeling of being overwhelmed and showed a toughness and coolness under fire that I did not expect.

I loved this woman; she was strong when she had to be, but vulnerable in a way that captured my heart. However, inevitable friction naturally develops in such a grueling race. Every experience for us up to then had been special and mutually supportive.

The race had pushed us emotionally and physically. I remember thinking I would do anything to smooth things over. As I snapped a picture of her standing on the Newport Beach Pier, I knew for certain that I deeply loved her, and I knew I wanted to make her my wife. At that moment, the setbacks of the race drifted from my mind, and I had become profoundly aware of how much she meant to me. I hoped the summer would allow us to reconnect. I thought perhaps later that year I'd ask her to marry me. But time, events, unsupportive friends, and destiny were not on our side, as I was to discover when we returned home.

One Mile at a Time

As we prepped the car for the race, Nancy was as happy as I'd ever seen her.

Edward M. Rahill

My mother insisted on taking pictures all afternoon, even with my shirttail hanging out. Nancy found this quite amusing.

One Mile at a Time

That night, we went out for dinner with my family. Nancy seemed on top of the world. In this shot, she was holding my hand. At that moment, I felt deep inside she was going to be my wife.

Final pictures before we were off to Boston.

The car I built. She had a solid suspension, good brakes, and was reasonably fast, but her lack of range on a tank of gas was a major disadvantage.

One Mile at a Time

In Boston, I saw early 1980s models of a Porsche 944 and an Italian Pantera powered by Ford.

Just before this photo was taken, Nancy confided that although she wanted to do the race, she was nervous about what we were getting ourselves into. I told her I would start and promised not to put her in a position she did not think she could handle. She could let me know when she wanted to give it a try. She ended up being a very good driver with good instincts and a real asset by the time we reached Ohio.

Before the start of our first race, we met the Blues Brothers for the first time. Tim Montgomery is on the right; Jeff is on the left. Nancy and I quickly became friends with them.

One Mile at a Time

Local and national media were well represented.

NBC Nightly News correspondent Douglas Kiker reported on the event. You can see why we were intimidated by this level of national attention. I did not want it because of the advance notice it gave law enforcement.

Edward M. Rahill

At the starting line waiting for our time ticket, and we were off!

After the race, Nancy and I drove up the Pacific coast and visited the Newport Beach Pier.

One Mile at a Time

Events and timing strained our relationship.

We spent the next couple days driving up the California coast, seeing the sights, such as the Santa Monica Pier. Then it was time to head home. On the way back, we decided to stop once for the evening, but the second day, we were eager to return home. So, between sleeping in the car and talking, we got back to Chicago in two and a half days. As I look back on our talks, I now realize that Nancy had been hinting at the status of my marriage to Carlene. When we first met, she was going through a divorce just like me. I was careful not to probe too much. But something was not right for her in that relationship. As I put the pieces together, I came to believe it had to do with promises broken—she was seeking stability and family. In that marriage, it just was not there for her. I can see that once her divorce was final, she wondered why I was delaying finalizing mine. When we returned to Chicago, there were a lot of stories to tell, and we could finally relax. We needed a bit of space from each other. We were practically living in a car together for almost ten days. We stopped focusing on our issues and spent time with friends and family who wanted to know about the race. Quite a few had seen the *NBC Nightly News* story and wanted to know more.

After a couple days to rest and catch up with friends and family, we went out to dinner. I revisited our conversation from the way home and told her I'd been thinking about her questions. I could tell she still didn't understand why I had to wait on the final divorce. I tried to explain it as clearly as I could: Carlene would be awarded an instructor position as soon as she completed her coursework at Northwestern. She and I had agreed to the terms and would be filed, uncontested, at that time. Until then, she needed my insurance coverage. Nancy seemed to accept that explanation, and she never brought it up again.

I was later distraught when I realized she had a need for stability and a deep desire to have a family—her family. My fear was that she did not believe that it was my goal too. Everything I strived for and accomplished in my life had at its core a goal to reach that moment when I would share my life with a woman I loved—to provide stability and have a family together.

I did not know what to do. I wanted to be the man she fell in love with, but I had to be the man who kept his word to protect Carlene. I wondered if I could have handled it if I was in her place. I had made up my mind that she was the person I wanted to spend my life with. Until I was free to marry, I did not see how I could ask her to be my wife.

But behind her concerns was a second issue I did not understand—a medical condition. Her doctor had told her she was showing signs of endometriosis.

Before the race one afternoon, she had just come home, and over coffee she mentioned her condition to me. I asked what we could do about it? She told me that her doctor suggested having a child could help. She then moved on to another topic, as if she didn't want to talk about it. I remember asking myself if it was serious. But with the change in topic, I did not follow up with another question.

At the time, I was unaware of the longer-term complications that could arise with endometriosis. I now know that in addition to her monthly discomfort, it would limit her fertility over time. She feared for her health and for the limited time she may have believed she had to start a family.

As much as Nancy and I were attuned to each other, I was not plugged into the depth of her emotions. I did not appreciate how the status of my marriage made her have doubts about our future. It turned out to be a significant issue that led to regrets for both of us. But at the time, I did not comprehend how much pressure she felt, how important it was to Nancy to move forward in her life, nor the emotional need she felt to finally find a stable relationship and marriage.

A third stress on our relationship was about to present itself. This was the time I needed to better understand her feelings and find ways to strengthen our relationship. I remember starting to explore if there were ways to build a bridge to resolve the timeline issues important to Carlene.

At the time, I did not know about Nancy's friends' concerns about our relationship. I was about to be stationed in Mexico for eight weeks.

Chapter 7
Everyone Gets a Break at Some Point

It was good to be back in Chicago. I relaxed for a week then headed back to work. Larry, my boss, gave me a heads up that I was about to be drafted for a special assignment in Mexico. I didn't really know what to think; I just waited to learn more.

The next day, I was called into the office of the president of ARCO Metals, Bill Chamberlain. Larry and two other executives were there. I was informed I was being assigned to a group to develop a financial plan to salvage the bank loan program and prevent Mexican industrial sectors from entering default by the end of the year. The catch? The plan needed to be in place by the end of the summer.

"We think you're someone who could add a lot of value, and corporate does, too," said Chamberlain. Then one of the guys told me that I had the right combination of finance, economic modeling, and actual plant manufacturing experience, which would complement the current team.

After the meeting, as we walked down the hall, Larry said, "Ed, this is a serious situation. Mexico and Latin America are on the brink of financial collapse." He then said, "I don't have to tell you this, but this is a high-profile assignment—it could make your career." He smiled the way he always did. He was the kind of boss I would strive to emulate in my future.

I had a week to get ready, including vaccinations, passports, and a plan. I needed a way to coordinate with people in the States who could support me and run economic scenarios. They were even giving me my own medical kit to treat myself if needed. I was going to be able to fly back to Chicago for two weekends a month. I thought about Nancy and hoped she would understand what this assignment could mean for us.

My grandmother taught me early on that everyone gets a big opportunity at some point in our lives. The challenge is recognizing it when you see it. I always wanted to make a difference, to make the world a better place. I aimed to accomplish what I had promised myself when I was a boy: to be the kind of provider my uncles had been for their families. My gut told me that this was that opportunity.

That evening, I tried to explain the situation to Nancy—that this was what I was meant to do, and if I did it well, it could open doors, not just for me, but for us. I wanted her to know I was thinking of our shared future.

Nancy was trying to wrap her head around what I had told her. It came as a surprise—eight to ten weeks, she was not prepared for that. As for what it meant for us, I could tell she did not understand. I sensed she was thinking about the here and now, just making her life work. I was a little frustrated. I kept feeling we needed more time to reconnect. But that was not going to happen. Even phone calls between us would be difficult. At the time, calls pretty much had to be planned, and spontaneous phone calls were seldom possible.

Nonetheless, we had a good final week. It was as if everything was okay. She was back to herself, showing me affection. She expressed her concerns about being apart for most of the summer. I promised her we would spend the time we needed when I was back. I finally went off to Mexico City to join the task force and support the consortium of banks and their due diligence, or so I thought.

The Problem Facing Mexico and Latin America

In August 1982, Mexico was unable to meet interest payments on its $80 billion debt. A collapse in oil prices in the early 1980s led to a recession. Their cash dried up. There were two groups of creditors: foreign debt managed by the International Monetary Fund (IMF) and large commercial banks, mostly U.S.-based. Both the government and its private sector needed additional loans to stay afloat. The national energy and materials industries debt payments were in arrears, and those industries risked having their loans called by the banks.

Their only recourse was to enter bankruptcy. In response, the creditors rescheduled Mexico's loans and devised a plan to reduce the crushing debt. In 1982, Mexico reached an agreement with the banks and the IMF to enter a fourteen-year repayment plan. American private banks would monitor progress and had provisions to terminate the agreement if progress was not made.

By the spring of 1983, Mexico was again in bad shape, attempting to repay the nation's debt and on the verge of financial collapse. Because a default one year after it was believed the problem was solved could have worldwide monetary ramifications, there was an attempt to downplay the problem. But the problem was there. Mexico and its industries could not meet near-term debt payments, and the banks had cut off new loans.

In response, the banks formed a consortium to address this common issue and approached the U.S. State Department for assistance.

In near-crisis mode, the State Department asked ARCO for resources to aid the consortium of banks to determine if there was evidence that the Mexican private sector and their sister Latin American countries could meet future obligations and repay loans in arrears.

ARCO was approached as many of the industries in trouble were in the same business—namely oil, gas, manufacturing, and minerals. While technically the banks had until December 1983 to revise their agreement, they needed to make a decision to restructure or pull their loans by the end of August.

The State Department knew that if the commercial banks pulled their loans, it was possible that the Mexican and Latin American industrial sectors would be crippled. If that happened, the already fragile Latin American economy could slide into regional economic collapse.

On the first day, I was introduced to Stewart Day, a Citibank managing director, who oversaw the assignments. He was a tall, well-spoken man, very congenial and refined. He had a difficult job pulling this team together. After a couple days, I got a feeling there were two camps evolving within the task force. Each had a very different view of the problem, the mission, and the solution. This could be a difficult summer. The two camps were comprised of professionals from different walks of life, the commercial banking staff primarily out of New York City, and a few of us from ARCO metals operations.

It did not take long for the two perspectives to surface. The analyst staff from the banking and ARCO treasury department were of classic East Coast banking lineage and educated at top universities—Harvard, Wharton, London School of Economics. My team—myself and two others from ARCO—were from company operations and came up through oil and gas and manufacturing operations. My academic background was in corporate finance and planning, but also macro and econometric modeling, which we used heavily in the ARCO planning process.

We had major differences in our approach to projections. The commercial banking and treasury crew relied heavily on forecasting, while I relied on scenario planning. Forecasting, with some degree of probability, implied you could tell the future, while scenarios reconstructed what would happen if events unfolded in a certain way. Then you studied the likelihood of those events occurring. This allowed us to view the big picture, comparing all possibilities.

The work that summer was intense. We had to come up to speed on the problems and find a solution in a limited time. That is why we lived in Mexico City that summer. Within weeks, my insecurities evaporated. It became clear to the team that I had a handle on the problems, and we were about to debate about how to deal with them.

> From the beginning,
> my instincts led me to
> think differently.

Despite our difference, the group got along. We were there as a team, and most of the guys were genuine in their approach. I quickly became aware that I thought differently than the rest of the team, and this led me to take a unique path to the solution. They started by gathering all the information they could to build financial models of the industrial sector. Their focus was to determine to what degree the Mexican industrial sector could cut back, reduce inventories, and reorganize and downsize underutilized sectors, such as mining. Raw materials were in surplus. From their perspective, it was a logical place to start. They hoped to increase free cash flow to be able to pay the debt service in arrears. I understood what they were thinking. From my experience, though, this was the worst thing we could do.

The next day, I found the other employee from ARCO Metals, Matt, and I asked if he would accompany me on a series of visits with the executives of Industrias Nacobre, an integrated producer of manufactured products like ARCO. Matt had fifteen years' experience in the manufacturing plants; he was a real asset. Our first visit was to the SVP of business operations, Eduardo Rodriguez. Initially, he was reserved in his interactions with us. After some pleasantries, I asked if he would set up a visit for us at one of the plants, and I was hoping to meet the people who managed the supply chain. That instantly caught his attention. I could tell by how he answered that he was impressed. We later learned that this was the first time anyone had asked to meet the people and see how the company worked.

The next week, we visited several operations, some quite large. I had seen operations like that in Buffalo—foundry, casting, machining, stamping, finishing, packing. They were making everything from tubing, wire, piping, and complex parts to decorative and brass plates. Matt even found an attractive copper plate table set in the plant store—the plant manager gave it to him as a gift to take home to his wife. He then asked if I'd like one for my wife. I remember smiling and saying yes, thank you, and asked if we could ship it back to Chicago, to Nancy. It was a nice set, a six-plate copper dining room setup that one would use for a Thanksgiving dinner.

That night, Luis, the company controller, invited us to dinner at his home outside Mexico City. It was a quiet neighborhood and a modest home with security gates. Inside, the home was well appointed and was a warm and family-friendly environment. The dinner conversation was very friendly and genuine. Luis's English was excellent, and his wife's was good. I was a little embarrassed because I did not have a command of the Spanish language to reciprocate. I enjoyed the evening and was glad to get to know the people behind the numbers.

Most from the neighborhood worked for Industrias Nacobre and the company's suppliers. I learned about their lives, listened to stories of their children. They were hoping to build a strong future. At dinner, Luis started to explain to the guests why we were there—to protect them, to make sure Mexico did not slide into bankruptcy. It was almost if he was saying that we were the good guys, we were going to find a way to save the day. I winced—I knew we had not yet found a way that would protect them from the liquidation option being proposed.

That night, I awoke from a deep sleep with a jolt. In a dream, I saw the people who I had just shared a warm human experience with being evicted from their homes. I felt helpless. That was when I heard a voice from my past speaking to me in a soft fading voice: *This is why you are here.*

The next day, Matt and I sat down to discuss what we saw. It was clear that we were looking at a behemoth of an integrated industrial enterprise. From raw metal ore to machined fittings, cooling tubes for air conditioners to on-the-shelf products at Pier One

Imports on Wells Street in downtown Chicago. We believed the banks were underestimating the complexity of the industrial sectors. The only thing I could do was bring up this issue to the team. If we followed their plan, this industry would not get back up for years. Sucking out the cash now would kill its ability to generate cash in the future. These businesses would likely go under in twelve to eighteen months—factories closed, employees terminated, assets sold off. Our task force was doing what it had been asked to do—answer one question: were there enough liquid assets available to pay off the debt? We were utilizing the typical methods of the lending sector in default situations: focus on what we know now, protect the current debt holders. But the payment on the debt was due in less than a year. As a planning and operations analyst, I was trained to focus on a different question: how to optimize a business enterprise, to fix troubled industries so it can profitably function—both now and into the future. This is where these two views of our mission were about to collide.

We had to do something. I knew what I was about to do would be viewed by the team as above my pay grade, but the dream from prior night compelled me to go on. I asked for a meeting with Stewart and the team leaders the next day. It had to be at eleven a.m., due to scheduling. Most of the key guys came in by 11:08 a bit restless and did not know what the meeting was about. I was nervous; they were a heavyweight group, and I was a thirty-year-old senior planning analyst from Rolling Meadows. I just said to myself, *Here we go*.

Stewart called the meeting to order. I knew all these guys, but this was the first time our meeting had a formal tone. I could see one or two of them were wondering why they were there. Then I jumped in, expressing my worries about the restructuring plan we were considering. I was concerned, I told them, that the path we were taking might not work, that it could lead to a more serious problem in 1984 and beyond. I could see a couple people in the room begin to dismiss what I was saying. I was trying to collect myself, appear cool and in control in the stoic way when under stress. Then Stewart, seeing my dilemma and the disruption in the room, asked me to elaborate.

I was frustrated. Not everyone agreed with me. Perhaps I did not have the credibility to be making this kind of point. Then I told myself, *Discuss your thoughts to the group as if you're speaking to just one person.* That calmed me down. I needed to make quick, concise points—an elevator pitch. I had just a few minutes, or I would lose them. If I could get just one question, that would allow me to elaborate.

I started as if I was just talking to Stewart. I said I understood the strategy behind balance sheet harvesting. But this was a one-shot deal, and it did not account for the time and cost to restart the industries the next year. If we executed this plan for what was basically the region's industrial sectors and harvested these companies' balance sheets to pay off the debt, where would the cash come from the following year?

I waited. There was some mumbling in the group, then one of the guys jumped in and asked, "Why are you thinking it would do more harm than good? Why don't you think they'll generate the cash when the economy recovers?"

I got a good look into his eyes; it's always important to make eye contact. "Supply chain lag time," I said. There were a few sounds of surprise in the room. I went on. "I'm concerned that the lag time for working capital to fill up the production, distribution, and marketing pipeline would suck more cash into the business than we'd get by harvesting the balance sheet this year." I paused. "And it could be worse than that—there is a reason the mines have not been shut down: it can take up to six months to shut down a mine and even longer to bring them online again. If we do shut them down, we can harvest the remaining ore inventory for the next six to nine months, get free cash, but what then? Up to six months just to get the mining up to minimum operating capacity and start providing a reliable supply of ore to the manufacturing operations. And what happens to the manufacturing sector without inventory to make products to pass along to the next stage of the manufacturing chain? Where does the cash come from to meet debt payments next year? We could be looking at well over a year of negative cash flow." He momentarily looked away, not out of rejection, but he was processing what I'd just said.

You could feel the energy in the room. We went back and forth with the team for a few minutes. Stewart was watching and listening. Finally, he stopped the discussion. "Ed, what's your point? What are you suggesting?"

I did not show it, but I was apprehensive because what I was about to suggest was the opposite of what we'd been planning. "I think we need to avoid shutting down any operations this year. We need to be prepared to inject cash into these companies early next year. We need to 'prime the pump' and get them ready for the recovery that's going to come in 1984 and beyond."

There was a second eruption of discussion in the room, but Stewart saw what was going on and responded in a thoughtful way. The room listened. "As you all know, we are well along with the plan we have in place. There's not a lot of time left. But we're here to help solve a regional financial crisis that has global implications. Let's stay focused on our task at hand." He started to walk away, then turned back. "One more thing. I called this meeting because I want us all to check our work, check our assumptions—measure twice, cut once. Ed, Matt, please continue your work on this. See what else you can come up with in the next ten days and get back to me."

After we left the meeting, Matt looked at me and said, "What are we gonna do now?"

I looked back at him and said, "I don't have a clue." Stewart really impressed me, he was doing the right thing, he did not dismiss me outright, but he was still going with his senior guys. I would have done the same in his shoes.

The next day, Mark, an analyst from ARCO's treasury group, stopped by. "You sure have a lot of balls, buddy," he said to me. I was a little embarrassed, and I started to respond when he stopped me. "I want to help. You're an ND guy, right?" I said yes. "Well, I'm USC, but I'll put that aside. I was thinking about what you said yesterday. At first it sounded crazy, but the more I thought about it, you might be onto something."

Mark was a godsend; he had already spoken to Stewart and gotten approval to work on our project. I'd been on the phone with our planning team in Rolling Meadows and gave them a heads up that we may need to be ready to run full scenarios on the manufacturing sectors of the Mexican economy. The response was not pretty. Finally, after a day of waiting, I had an idea. With Mark on the phone, I suggested a quick fix. "We don't have to model or run scenarios on the entire Mexican economy, only its manufacturing sector." To save time, we could use ARCO treasuries macro scenarios as a model. I was trying to prove a point—we needed to invest, not cut back.

We were able to show that a change in assumptions could impact both time and cash flow in different stages of the supply and manufacturing chain. At ARCO Metals, we had the value-added manufacturing models, and I'd already had my team develop economic models that would tie into macroeconomic scenarios to the manufacturing performance models. What we didn't have was independent respected economic probability models for the world and regional economies for the next twenty-four months. That was where Mark came in.

Mark's skill set was currency valuation, and he helped us protect against the possibility of Peso devaluation. We agreed that he'd stay on top of it with the commercial banking team and make sure it was addressed in the proposal for additional investment. I realized that it's simple to get things done if I had a great and supportive team. I kept them at the front of my mind.

One final hurdle was how to reengineer our value-added manufacturing models to reflect how the Mexican sectors worked. We were going to use Industrias Nacobre as a proxy. What were the asset relationships between that company and ARCO Metals, and how would we adjust the inputs to scale to Mexico's industrial sector? Mark, Matt, and I got together to figure out the problem. Matt knew the asset size relationships of our integrated manufacturing chain; he would work with Luis and Eduardo to get the corresponding information from Industrias Nacobre. Mark was already on it, getting the latest projections from his team in L.A. and coordinating the data and scenarios with the Mexican government on reining in imports, especially over the subsequent couple of years.

The copper and raw material mines in Mexico were still running, mostly to keep almost 300,000 people employed. But there was a surplus of raw material increasing monthly. This made mining the number-one target of the consortium. We needed Eduardo's help. We needed to model the impact of various shutdown scenarios and figure out how long it would take to restart the mine.

Our objective was to determine if there was evidence to support the proposal that Mexico could do it in under eighteen months. We researched various statistical models of the timing and duration of economic recovery. It was a simple approach. The commercial banking system wanted reassurance that their loans would be repaid according to terms, which Mexico currently was not doing.

One Mile at a Time

Using economic data, I laid out the possible outcomes and their impact on the Mexican economy. My team back home produced models that analyzed each scenario for Mexican industries over the subsequent eighteen months. This approach had an interesting result. Under most scenarios, it established that Mexico and its industrial sector could meet their debt service obligations when running at a reasonable percent of capacity. The results showed that under most reasonable scenarios, the capacity necessary to reach a cash solvency level was significantly lower than the banks had expected, and therefore, the probability of solvency in the next eighteen months was remarkably high.

I was tired. It had been a long three weeks in Mexico. I was looking forward to a long weekend back home. I had decided to stay in the States through Monday morning to meet with the analysts in Rolling Meadows who were developing and running the scenario models for us. They were a tremendous help, and none of what I was doing could go anywhere without them.

I got into O'Hare Friday night around midnight, exhausted. I could not wait to see Nancy the next day. It was the first week in August.

Edward M. Rahill

Love hurts?

When I came to her cottage, I could sense something wasn't right. I started to tell her about our progress in Mexico when she said she needed to tell me something. As I sat there quietly, she told me it was over for her. I was shocked. Her words were toxic to my soul. I was in a daze. Reality did not exist for me. Why? What was wrong? I asked all the questions you'd expect from someone who is blindsided with that kind of news. I can only remember a few fragmented comments. Something about needing stability in her life, her counselor's advice, something about my behavior, needing the right fit for the life she wanted.

I didn't understand. I didn't feel it was real. It was especially difficult because she was not the Nancy I had known. She was reciting points in a deliberate fashion, as if she'd been coached on what to say. I tried to pull myself together. I put on that stoic face I'd practiced for years. I don't even remember leaving, and I have only a few numb impressions of the rest of the weekend.

I do remember a sudden feeling of panic as I let the reality of my loss sink in. I hardly slept. I tried to talk to her on the phone, but she didn't want to. Monday morning, I awoke from a deep sleep, not having slept the two nights before. I went into the office to meet with the team on the models and scenarios. Then I asked Angie to get me a car to the airport for a plane back to Mexico.

That week, I could manage the days, the work. The interaction with my peers was good for me. It was the nights that were difficult. The sense of loss was overwhelming. I was in Mexico City, desperate to find a way to reach her to try to turn it around. But the distance between us made that impossible. It took almost a week before I could calm down. To this day, my memories of that time bring up the same emotions—grief that never went away, although its intensity has long since subsided.

Later that fall, after I returned from Mexico, I found out she had started seeing someone else. This reopened the wound. From time to time, she would reach out. Angie once called, asking where I'd been the previous night. I asked why, and she blurted out, "Nancy called me last night. She was upset, and she said she couldn't reach you and asked me if I knew where you were."

One evening, she contacted me and asked to meet. She needed to talk. What choice did I have? I was emotionally compromised, drowning in confusion, but I still agreed to meet. The conversation drifted into restarting our relationship. I asked if she wanted to give it a second chance, and she said yes. I remember almost going into shock, but that didn't last. She soon pulled back, and I never understood why. At that point, I was losing any backbone I had. There were a few other times when she reached out only to pull back or not follow through.

One night she called and we talked for the better part of an hour, and she asked me to come over. We were intimate that night, but nothing came of it. Those encounters just made it harder for me because they were unpredictable. I wanted to hate her, but I couldn't. I understood my defense mechanisms stemmed from emotional pain. Hate was just that—a way to strike back, a shield to protect the deep wound in my heart that wouldn't heal, wouldn't stop bleeding. I loved her, and losing love caused the pain. There was a popular song that said love hurts. That's not true. It is the loss of love, the loneliness that comes from the absence of love. Loneliness hurts, rejection hurts.

I can only imagine what was going through her mind. Years later, I came to believe that those sad episodes about something in her past were connected to our breakup.

While at the time I did not know it, her support group and her best friend may have urged her to move on. Maybe my not being divorced was the trigger for them. They knew about her painful past and her concern that time was running out to have a family due to her endometriosis. What I did not know at the time was that her doctors gave her a timeline of a couple years before she would require surgery. I don't know what transpired between Nancy and her friends, but I can guess.

To be fair to them, their friend . . . had gone through a divorce, had a medical condition that was closing in on her ability to have a child, needed a stable, supporting relationship to start a family, but was seeing a married man, who, as far as they could tell, showed no meaningful signs of committing to her, and had just taken her on a ten-day vacation, not a trip to Europe, but a brutal 3,100-mile cross-country road race.

He sounds like the kind of stable guy you'd want your best friend to spend the rest her life with, right?

At the time, I did not understand her reasons for the breakup. I remember the lyrics to the Dire Straits' song "Romeo and Juliet."

"It's just that the time was wrong." The first time I heard that song, I was driving, and I had to pull over. I was devastated. It seemed as if the lyrics were written about what happened to Nancy and me.

One verse continued to play in my mind:

> And all I do is miss you and the way we used to be
> All I do is keep the beat, the bad company
> All I do is kiss you, through the bars of a rhyme,
> Julie, I'd do the stars with you any time.

I guess because I was young and idealistic, I was unprepared for the impact of such a breakup. I didn't know how to handle it. It ripped into my soul at night and saddened me for years. I had viewed Nancy as already my wife—the woman with whom I had emotionally become one with, with who I had intended to have a family, who in my heart, I had already made a lifelong commitment to.

The irony still haunts me. After reliving the good times with Nancy while writing this history of my life, I felt I would trade all my successes to have those moments back again, to have the opportunity to show her how close we were to her dreams of commitment and a future family. Later, when I came to fully understand the issues she was facing, it compounded my feelings. To some degree, I still carry this loss. There is almost never a day when a memory of Nancy does not cross my mind. Mostly, though, I remember the good times.

Edward M. Rahill

My Return to Rolling Meadows

The rest of that summer in Mexico City is a blur, perhaps because it was overshadowed by my heartbreak. As I look back, I'm impressed by how well I held it together at work. Perhaps it was the resilience I had learned from my grandmother that helped carry me through.

Our econometric and probability models came back with strong correlation results. Mark, Matt, and I had individual meetings with members of the task force to fill them in, to make them feel they weren't being excluded from what we were doing. We had several one-on-ones with Stewart to make sure there were no surprises for him. Also, I wanted him to know that I understood his role and I was not going to undermine him. This was his task force; I was on his team.

Behaving as a team player was how I was raised and how I was going to play this situation. I remember another thing my grandmother repeated from the Bible: "You reap what you sow."

Toward the end of the project, there was a flurry of activity, and everybody on the team got on board with our approach: to invest rather than harvest. The idea I had once argued alone in the conference room was now theirs too. It made me feel good. I backed away from the process, let them argue the case. The more they did, the more they believed. As I looked at the task force plan coming off the printer, I took a deep breath. I was proud of the role I played in making that happen.

We presented our report to the executive team at Atlantic Richfield. They seemed impressed and, to my surprise, relieved. With other banks, an ARCO executive team presented our work to the Treasury and State departments that week, and I was told they were equally impressed. Our task force's work was done. We said our goodbyes and went back to the lives we were living before we had been tapped for this mission.

A couple weeks later, Bill Chamberlain's secretary asked me to come to his office. The executive committee and my boss were there. I sat down, and Bill thanked me and the task force. He then announced that the Consortium of Banks agreed to extend the terms of the loans at a lower interest rate, and the International Monetary Fund agreed to supply the Mexican government with additional temporary loans. The banks also agreed to waive near-term repayment covenants, and new "working capital loans" to the industrial sectors would be in place by 1984. They would continue over the next few years, according to the original 1982 restructuring plan.

"Ed, two days ago I received a call from my friend, the CEO of Industrias Nacobre, to thank me and ARCO for sending the people we did," Chamberlain said. "His message was that if Mexico defaulted, he was facing a difficult restructuring." In the end, he said, the necessary shutdowns would have meant letting go of thousands of jobs across his company alone. For the mining sector, he estimated 90,000 jobs on the line. It could have been much worse. There were almost 150,000 people in some way employed in our integrated operations across Mexico. The ripple effect was incalculable. Industries across the nation would have faced the same shutdowns and layoffs. The Mexican executives, he said, believed that my actions were instrumental in bringing about this solution.

Bill also said that the company was awarding me a special bonus for my leadership role. I was stunned. There was clapping, and I thanked him and left. Larry walked out of the meeting with me. "Ed, the number of jobs impacted that day may have been 240,000. But what is not taken into account is that those employees have families. In Mexico, there are no safety nets, no unemployment insurance. If you're unemployed, you're falling into poverty. Well, just do the math. I believe the number of lives you impacted is closer to a million." That night, I shuttered at what had happed in Mexico and all this meant.

As it turned out, by early 1985, Mexico and other Latin American partners successfully paid back $108 billion to the U.S. banks within eighteen months as we had predicted. They were able to generate the cash flow. I take comfort in the idea that thousands of people, perhaps even hundreds of thousands, had their livelihoods and had homes to go to in 1984, because I chose to make my case in that conference room on that July day. I had a part, even a small one, in saving a nation from economic collapse. If not me, who else was there to do it?

At the time, I didn't know it, but what I'd accomplished in Mexico changed the trajectory of my life. Twenty months later, I was to start a new position as Vice President of Planning and Development with a public company unit of Bell & Howell. I was the second youngest VP and officer in the history of the corporation.

Mom was right about recognizing my one opportunity and seizing the moment. My regret was that this new venture would unfold without Nancy.

I had pulled it together for the Mexico mission. But the emptiness without the one person I had genuinely loved became obvious once I was back home. I had lost my passion. I was spiritually broken. I remember looking at myself in the mirror and seeing a shell of a man. I was about to descend into the darkest period of my life.

For the next ten months, I went through all the emotions. At times I felt normal, having fun, joking, and enjoying other people's company. But then something would remind me of her. I could put on a smile or talk enthusiastically about something, but it was just a front, an act to cover up the wound that would not heal. However, I would not allow myself to collapse to the point of letting my job suffer. I continued to perform, and at times, excelled at my work. By that time, stepping up to professional challenges was not a choice, but part of my DNA. I was in emotional shock, but with the help of friends, I held it together one day at a time.

There was no better friend, no one who gave me more support, than Angie. She would listen to me as I recounted the same regrets. From time to time, she invited me to her house where I met her husband John, who I liked very much. Her kindness helped me through many days. But the worst was yet to come.

When I was alone at home at night, I would try to bury the pain by taking the Firebird out on the backroads of Barrington Hills and Algonquin, and just drive—drive fast. When I got in the car and listened to the engine fire up, I felt a passion in my soul that

I just couldn't wait to experience: the sound and the G-force of her winding out.

Driving fast while listening to tunes on the radio kept me from what I had seen in other broken men—drinking to dull the heartache. Occasionally, I'd go to the Red Door Tavern across the street to seek an escape from my anguish. I may have had one drink too many to numb the pain. But it was my drives at night when things got bad, rather than the bar, that kept me from falling into the abyss.

I remember my wide range of emotions as I played Springsteen's "Backstreets," which ripped through my soul as it recanted a man who had lost his love, or "Darkness on the Edge of Town." I loved Hank Williams Jr.'s "Queen of my Heart" and the haunting guitar of Fleetwood Mac's "Silver Spring." But it was a song from the distant past, one I hadn't heard for years, that touched me to a point of tears. Gordon Lightfoot's "If You Could Read My Mind" made me shutter as the lyrics came over the speaker and I relived what happened with Nancy. The song narrated his sudden breakup with his wife. The wound that wouldn't heal haunted him through the rest of his life. Here I was, driving through the night, listening to Lightfoot's lament. I choked as I realized I would carry this wound in my heart for the rest of my life. That was when I understood pain. True pain comes after experiencing a complete emotional connection with someone special, and then comprehending that I was now a man without love. You now exist alone; pain is the absence of love. It was terrifying and there was nothing I could do about it.

With my car and my radio, I found sections of road I could drive all out and push my limits. I also looked forward to taking on life's challenges and someday finding someone to share my life with. Back then, I had a lot to look forward to.

One late night while out on one of my drives, something different happened. During my scan of radio stations, the radio briefly stopped on a distant rural station. It was playing Judy Collins's "Amazing Grace." I quickly reached to press the scan button to skip ahead, but then thought twice. As I listened to her unique voice and the lyrics, I slowed down and pulled over. I turned off the engine but kept the radio on. I stepped out of the car and listened to the silence and that song. It was a cool, clear night; I could feel how expansive the universe was. I looked up at the stars, and thought about the meaning of life, the world, and God. Then I decided to talk to him.

"God, it must really piss you off that we only think of you when our lives suck." I felt like he heard me, and he was laughing at the comment and my sarcastic tone. I wanted to be free from this sense of loss and abandonment. "Amazing Grace" was trying to bring me home. I shed a tear and tried to uplift my soul, but it was not to be. My mood turned somber; I was struggling to pull myself out of depression. But it was not enough. I found myself back in the trap of self-pity.

I drifted through this state for the better part of a year, until one June night, when everything had fallen apart, and I had little hope of pulling it back together. I was a broken man. I was going to be faced with a choice: accept the setbacks and give up, or look deep into who I was, to my past, and regain my strength in the face of seemingly impossible odds.

But that choice was in the future. For the moment, I needed help making it through my day-to-day life.

Chapter 8
If at First You Don't Succeed

Tim Montgomery and I had stayed in touch after the first race, and we became friends.

We had similar backgrounds when it came to cars and driving. His father owned and ran Montgomery Car Care in Fremont, Ohio. He grew up making his driving mistakes on the back country roads of northwestern Ohio. We were both Midwestern small-town boys who lived and breathed cars. We were a natural fit.

It was not long before we started to talk about the race, what we'd learned, and what it would take to compete against those sponsored cars. We talked about the fact that we'd both run that race with friends. The race was supposed to be for the fun of it. As we found out, driving over 3,000 miles at 100+ mph was not fun. It was stressful, it was work, and it was a strain on racers both physically and emotionally. I don't think Tim and his co-driver spoke to each other for a couple weeks after they returned home, and he told me it took a while for the friendship to get back to normal. And as I found out, the stress of the race set the stage for the perfect storm in my relationship with Nancy.

One weekend, Tim and a few friends were getting together for pizza and beer to watch a game in Fremont, Ohio. Tim asked if I could come down, and I agreed. The next day, I drove the five-hour route alone, and I was in a reflective mood. I couldn't help thinking about last year's race and what I could have done differently. I had a few regrets, and I worried that I didn't have what it took to compete in such a demanding race. I was more sensitive than usual due to my recent breakup.

Once in Fremont, Tim, Jeff, and I were sitting around telling stories about the race, and I contemplated the possibility of doing it again. Jeff had made it clear that this type of racing was not for him, but I could tell Tim might just be considering it. I started feeling a little nervous. Then came a memory of advice from my past. *"Life's odds are that everyone gets at least one opportunity to pursue their dreams sometime in their lives; the challenge is recognizing it when you see it."* I had a premonition that this might be the last time I'd have this opportunity.

Tim was a good mechanic, and he was a very good and aggressive driver, and at times I would need to rein him in. But he was the type of guy war veterans would talk about. He was a guy I'd want to share a foxhole with. But I was not yet emotionally stable enough to throw myself into that race again, a race that had gotten the best of me the year before. I needed more time to get my backbone, to collect my thoughts and search my soul to find the nerve to do what I'd have to.

Tim and I continued our conversations about the race into the fall. By then, we were over our bad experiences from the previous year. I remember thinking that this might be my last chance to run a race I had dreamed of as a boy. At long last, on one phone call, I finally said, "Life is short. I want to run this race again. I want to go for a win. Do you want to become a team?"

"I was waiting for you to say that!" he exclaimed. Once raised, it was done. We were going to run the Four Ball Rally again, and this time, we were going to take a shot at placing.

Tim and I knew the odds were against us. We shared the feeling that we were possibly getting in over our heads. But we had learned a lot about the race from our experience. We discussed how we prepped our cars, what modifications we made, and why. We spent more time on what we had learned to be competitive—the type of car, strategies for different conditions, the stress we'd feel during the race, the friction that would inevitably arise between drivers, and the teamwork it would take to run 3,100 miles.

Clandestine Help from GM

We planned everything from the routes we would take to the equipment we needed. But one thing was missing—the car. My '78 Firebird was out. I had an attachment to the car. She did run well, but she didn't have what it was going to take to run the race the way we wanted to. We were going for a win. We needed a car that could run at the next level, with the big boys of the racing world. That was when we got the break of a lifetime. Some engineers at GM's proving grounds in Milford, Michigan, had been following the race over the previous few years and noticed the same thing: American cars were not competitive. Porsche, BMW, and Mercedes won and placed most of the time.

Our lucky day came when a friend of Tim's father's, a guy named Bill, happened to be visiting family in Milford, Michigan. At a local bar, he'd met a couple of GM engineers and mentioned our plan to race the next year. The proving grounds tech guys were on him to learn more. Word got back to Tim and his dad that some of them were interested in the race and wanted to learn more about our plans and what cars we were considering.

We knew we needed help to take on the best Europe had to offer. I suggested we ask GM to sponsor us or at least help where they could. Later that week, Tim received a call from one of the engineers. They discussed it in their group and were willing to help, but only if it never got out that they were involved. It took Tim and me two seconds to say yes.

Later, the team at the proving grounds set up a call with us. We understood it had to be a GM car, and we knew what we wanted in a car to be competitive. The question was what car we'd choose. We came up with the following criteria: (1) a make and color that would not draw too much attention from other drivers or the state police; (2) a car with a bulletproof engine, drive train, cooling system, and suspension; (3) the sustainable power to hold 125–140+ mph for an extended period (basically the entire race) with short peaks above 170 mph if needed; (4) brakes that could stand up to a 3,100-mile road race; (5) upgraded seatbelts to racing safety harness level (one strap across the chest was fine to not draw attention, but the harness had to hold you in place during high-speed driving); (6) room for support provisions and supplies to keep life bearable during the grueling two-day race; (7) increased fuel capacity, from my experience last year, lack of range was a race breaker; (8) finally, a reclinable passenger seat for the other driver to get some rest after his four-hour shift. Brakes became critical, especially since Tim finally agreed to my brake-and-go racing strategy that would be hell on the drivers, pads, and rotors.

It became clear that none of the GM sedans had the performance capability we were looking for. Corvettes provided the best drag coefficient and top-end performance, but they were out because they did not provide enough driver comfort nor room for support provisions, additional fuel, or equipment. Basically, the Corvette was a quick around-the-town sportscar, not a cross-country road racer.

That left only two cars in the GM fleet that might work: the Chevrolet Camaro and the Pontiac Firebird Trans Am. Both were of the GT class, a car size popular in racing circles worldwide. A grand tour (GT) is a type of sports car designed for high speeds and long-distance driving, due to a combination of performance and luxury attributes.

The interior was already laid out the way we wanted it. The cockpit was perfectly designed for an endurance race, and the instrument panels, gauges, and ambient night lighting were ideal. No changes were needed, except for an auxiliary power harness and an mph to km/h conversion, which was done at the transmission. It was everything we wanted for the race. Finally, the back end of the interior was open to the cockpit, allowing easy access for the interior and a perfect bed for a future high-capacity racing fuel cell.

While both the Camaro and Firebird had a sporty but "redneck" reputation, they were surprisingly good. They came with a small-block V-8, which was important in road racing contests like the one we were going to run. Big-block engines are constructed using iron and weigh around 685 pounds fully assembled and had higher cubic-inch displacement combustion chambers. Big-block engines were capable of 500–575 horsepower running under naturally aspirated fuel systems. Small-block engines weigh approximately 525 pounds and could handle about 400–475 horsepower with a slight variance depending on camshaft and the engine heads. The reduced weight was worth the decreased power because it allowed for more of a fifty-fifty weight distribution, a critical factor in controlling the car under road-racing conditions.

The small-block Chevy engine was based on a proven durable design with good cooling and oil flow, and it was built to accommodate performance modifications. These engines could be bored out and stroked, resulting in more cubic inches to produce exceptional horsepower, while keeping the weight down. Because both cars' front and rear weight distribution was balanced, their skid pad/lateral acceleration numbers were surprisingly good, within range of the top sports cars on the road. And that was before adjustments. The body design, especially the Trans Am, had some serious wind tunnel design testing. The drag coefficient on the Trans Am was superior to that of the Camaro. That meant several things. The Trans Am had a higher top speed and could hold it longer before overheating. The Trans Am would also give more efficient miles-per-gallon at a high speed. So, it was the Trans Am.

But there were major problems that needed to be addressed. Its overall performance capabilities and durability were not up to the demands of a race that it was being designed not just to run, but to win. The 5.0-liter, 305-cubic-inch engine lacked sufficient horsepower and torque to meet the demands of a 3,100-mile endurance road race. Basically, the car had insufficient performance and power for a racing environment. Tim and I believed we needed to double the horsepower rating to get the performance we wanted. It lacked the mechanical durability (power train, brakes, suspension) and fuel capacity, which was something Tim and I had already planned to fix. But the other mechanical issues were subpar for the grueling road race we were planning.

The lure of the Firebird Trans Am came from the wind tunnel design. It had an incredible .299 drag coefficient, racecar numbers. Racecars with that drag coefficient and with the proper downforce enhancements had a theoretical top speed approaching 200 mph. The interior was functionally laid out, so you could get all the information you needed about how the car was running with just a glance. The final attraction to this style of car was its driver and passenger comfort and its modification-friendly engineering. Comfort was very important; we both had to live in the car for almost two days. As for engineering design, the car was easy to modify for performance—something you could not do with European cars. Tim and I believed every one of the good-but-not-good-enough issues could become excellent in the hands of the right mechanics.

Edward M. Rahill

When this was explained to our proving grounds contacts, they got back to us: "Get the car, and we'll take care of the rest."

I would order a car with special equipment as instructed by the proving grounds team. After receiving it, I was to bring it to Fremont, Ohio, to spec it out for future modifications Tim and I wanted, and we added some options that we knew GM would not provide. Once we received the car back from GM, Tim would do the additional work at his family's auto repair garage. When I say special equipment, well, let's just say that the local Fremont Police were enthusiastic about the race and helped us obtain equipment to defend against those nasty radar guns. Once specked, it was off to Milford, Michigan, and we would not see it again for four or five weeks.

When Someone Upstairs Is Looking Out for You

One day, I was so touched, I felt like the hand of God was reaching out to help me through one of the most difficult days of my life. It was a cold, gray March day, a Saturday. The night before, Friday night, was filled with gut-wrenching despair. Nancy was to be married the next day.

I don't remember if I even slept. I was sobbing on the floor, with almost convulsion-like contractions of my diaphragm, crying with no sound, gasping for air, begging God why. I thought it was a nightmare. I imagined that Nancy would come back to me. Then, I'd open my eyes, and the darkness of the night was still there. The sobbing would begin again.

I sat in the kitchen making my second cup of coffee. It was around ten a.m. I was tired, numb. The phone rang. I picked it up with indifference. The emotions of the prior night had drained me. It was the Pontiac dealership.

"Mr. Rahill?"

"Yes? What can I do for you?"

"Your car was delivered, and it's prepped and ready to go."

"The Trans Am?" I asked.

"Yes, it's ready. Just bring your trade and title, and we can get you out of here within an hour." I hung up. She was being delivered a month early. I suspected our proving grounds contacts had pulled a few strings to move the manufacture date to the front of the line.

But that's not the point. The point is that on the darkest day of my life, a little gift was given to me—a gift of hope, a gift that lifted me out of the hell I was in and replaced it with thoughts of what the future might hold. It also helped when I called Tim to give him the news, and he exploded with excitement.

Awkward moments still happened that day. At the dealership, while I was taking possession of the car, I ran into a woman from the office. The way she looked at me and spoke, I could tell she didn't know what to say. She was not upbeat with small talk, the way you are when you suddenly meet someone from work. She spoke gently, like she knew I was in pain.

But as I gazed upon the car I was going to race across the continent, I recalled the moment as a seventeen-year-old boy, when I fell in love with the '67 Shelby Mustang. At this moment, an ember in my soul that should have died the night before had reignited. There were many months of emotional sorrow ahead of me. But the seed of my soul was not dead. Unbeknownst to me at the time, the fire of my passion for life just might have survived into the future.

I've come to believe that what unfolded that day was not random. The delivery of this car was a gift that allowed me to focus on my future instead of falling further into despair. There had to be somebody looking out for me to help me get through Nancy's wedding day.

I took the delivery and was instantly impressed. I drove the car all day, putting her through her paces, and finally slept well that night. The next day, it was off to Fremont to have Tim do an inspection and run an upgrade checklist before the car was to be shipped off to the Michigan proving grounds for racing modifications.

Chapter 9
God Works through People

In those long months, my breakup with Nancy was never far from my mind, not to mention the preparation for the race. But there were other things that tested my convictions. In the end, staying true to my personal moral code helped me through those times.

ARCO corporate merged the Louisville subsidiary with my company. Corporate had concluded that a more efficient business could be created with less overhead. Unfortunately, overhead reduction invariably meant laying off employees, and older employees tend to be more expensive.

Departments where there were duplicate functions were the primary targets. Employees in administrative positions, marketing, and research and development were at the greatest risk. By law, no one could not be told they were on a target list. People were going to lose their jobs. As part of the planning team, I knew who they were, and I was told under the threat of termination not to disclose anything. The legal team included a prominent section about confidentiality in their presentation of the plan, describing the consequences if we ever disclosed what was about to happen.

We were required to sign a non-disclosure agreement acknowledging that any violation would result in disciplinary action, including the possibility of immediate termination and possible litigation. To drive the point home, the legal team presented cases of actual violations, which they'd won against individuals who had violated past agreements.

The process became more difficult when I discovered that termination and layoffs would occur in two stages. First, they offered an early retirement for employees over age fifty-five, with full health insurance, and then they would terminate employees who did not take early retirement during a second phase. In phase two, all employees, regardless of age, would receive a severance based on years of service and temporary health insurance. We were told that the process had to be followed confidentially and to the letter of the law. The process was designed to protect all workers, old and young, from discrimination. But, in fact, by not being able to take age and years of service into account for key benefits such as healthcare, older workers, with fewer remaining productive years and without retirement health insurance, would be significantly disadvantaged if they did not volunteer for early retirement.

I knew Tony, an engineer in his mid-fifties who'd been with ARCO for the better part of twenty years. He had relocated from Waterbury, Connecticut, with his family to take a job in the metals research and development group. This worked well for his wife, who was originally from Michigan and had family there. He was one of my favorite people to work with. He went out of his way to help; he was the kind of guy who always saw the good in people.

Tony would rib me about Notre Dame. His wife's family were Michigan and Michigan State fans. I could tell he was going to tease me about something because he would approach me in a good-natured way, saying, "Hey, Irish!" His wife of thirty years became disabled eight years earlier. He never told me much more, but the ongoing medical expenses were significant.

They had a daughter in Arizona, but other than that, they had each other. He'd often talk about his family on our coffee breaks. Over time, he shared how much he owed to ARCO. The medical benefits alone covered many aspects of his wife's treatments that other companies did not. I knew that ARCO was exceptional in this way—it was the reason Carlene and I had stayed legally married. ARCO had one of the best insurance policies in the country.

Tony would tell me he didn't know if his wife would have been able to make it if it wasn't for the company. He would say, "You know whenever we're faced with a crisis, somehow it always works out. I believe it's my guardian angel watching out for me." And then he would smile.

In that staff reduction and budget meeting, I reviewed the names of the personnel being promoted or reassigned and the people who were going to be let go with just a severance and five months of insurance. I flipped to accounting, and Nancy was not on the list. Then I turned to the product engineering group, and I saw that Tony was number three on the list for future termination.

The night before the staffing reduction was to start, I was thinking about Tony's situation. I was deeply conflicted. What made it so difficult was that I had been brought up with a moral code—an outdated, old-school moral code that my grandmother had instilled in me.

That night, my pulse was racing. I struggled to overcome my fear of the consequences for what I was considering. I took seriously the potential loss of my position, and even worse, I would carry the stigma of having violated an agreement with ARCO that would stay with me into the future. The company was serious about prosecution. If that happened to me, I'd face the termination of my career, ending any hope of executive management with any company in the future.

I sat at the kitchen table, and I poured myself a stiff drink. I ran through the whole thing in my mind. I had a routine I had come to rely on when it was time to make important decisions. I would contemplate the choice I was making and its consequences. I would think about feelings and ideas and take into account my beliefs, my truths, and the kind of person I hoped to be.

I thought through the consequences of behaving as expected, of doing nothing. As I drifted back and forth between the decision and my reaction, I found my mind and heart in opposing camps.

When I considered finding a way to help Tony, the logic told me it was impossible—it made no sense. Risking it all, for what? Then I shifted to how I felt: cowardice and shame for turning my back on someone in what could be the most difficult time of his life. And I was the only one who could make a difference.

I was paralyzed. Fear was winning the day. But I did some more soul searching, thinking about who I was and the life I had lived. Then, the memories of what had happened in the past came flooding back—most notably, my decision to help Carlene. I recalled what I'd learned as a young man: *"When faced with another's plight, and you have the ability and the opportunity to do something about it, God will leave the decision up to you, because he wants you, not him, to make the choice ... to make a difference."*

I sat there and stared across the kitchen table. There was an internal battle going on. I just let it slowly rise from my soul to my head. Despite my fear, I knew what I had to do.

There were two others who worked with Tony: Jack and Steve. Then an idea flashed into my mind. I looked at the clock; it was almost eight p.m. I knew they were working late that night. Jack could still be at the office. I started to dial Jack's number, then stopped. Twice. I put the phone down. Making this call was ringing a bell that could not be unrung. I did one more gut check, and I picked up the phone. As luck would have it, both Jack and Steve were still at the office. I asked Jack to get Steve and call me from the conference room and to make sure the door was closed.

"Guys, listen," I said. "Tony's going to lose his job. And tomorrow, if he doesn't present early retirement papers by the end of the day, he will be let go the next morning."

There was silence, and Steve said, "I thought they'd keep Tony."

I went through the series of events that led up to this moment and explained my dilemma. I asked them to trust me. I asked them not to tell Tony about our chat. If he was questioned, it was best that he didn't know it was me. "And as far as you guys are concerned, this call never happened. If anything happens to you with the company, I'll protect you. I'll take care of it."

Steve jumped in. "What if he doesn't listen to us? What do we do?"

I paused and ran my hand through my hair. I understood their fears. Tony had openly said he would not take the package. Finally, I said, "If Tony doesn't want to buy it, just tell him it's his guardian angel watching out for him. If that doesn't work, give me a call." I hung up.

I just sat there on the couch. For all the anxiety I had faced on this issue, it was resolved. I'd made my decision. I felt the stress evaporate; I was a little numb and was calming down. I didn't even need to finish the drink to fall asleep. About forty minutes later, the phone rang. I jumped from my sleep. It was Jack and Steve.

"Ed, we don't know how to thank you for what you've done. You know we love the guy." I tried a follow-up question, but they kept going. I could tell they were very emotional.

I listened to them recount the call they'd had with Tony, how he'd said no, that he and his wife had talked about it, that he loved his work and wanted to take his chances to stay with the company. Jack and Steve walked through the pitch about the benefits of the package and the consequences if he did not take it.

"Tony started to become despondent, confused, and at a loss for what to do," Steve explained. "Then, out of frustration, he belted out, 'How do you know you can trust this guy who's telling you this? Why should I trust him? I don't even know who he is!'"

Steve was getting a little choked up on the phone, so Jack continued. "It was then we told him what you asked us to say. 'It's your guardian angel watching out for you.'"

Tony was quiet, and Jack said the silence must have gone on for twenty seconds. "Guardian angel," Tony repeated. He paused, then in a softer voice: "Guardian angel." Jack said there was another pause, and they were worried. Finally, Tony said, "I'll have to let my wife know I'm gonna take the package. I'll see you tomorrow." Then he just said, "Thanks," and hung up.

A few days later, the mood in the office was not great. Several people had been given their termination packages; it was hard. I sat at my desk trying to prioritize the day's work. Angie was at my door. "Ed, Tony's here to see you."

He had a smile on his face. He sat down, and I was at a loss for words. I started to tell him I understood he took the package, and that was when he jumped in.

"You know, Ed, I told my wife a few days ago that all my life when things were bad, I had faith that somehow things would work out. The early retirement package was a gift. My wife and I are taking it." He told me all the things he had to do, and as he rose to leave, I could tell he wanted to say more. "You knew I was on the list, didn't you?" I didn't answer. Then he looked me in the eye and said, "I do believe in guardian angels." He then took my hand in both of his and with a firm handshake, he said, "My wife and I will always remember this."

And then he left. I was a little choked up, but I tried to distract myself by turning to my IBM XT and skimming the list of documents. There was one I hadn't opened in a while. It was titled quotes.doc. It was a list I'd put together over the years of some memorable quotes or sayings. I clicked on it and glanced through it for a few seconds. It's funny how some things pop up at the right time. I stopped when I saw a quote from Mom: "God does not make miracles happen; he works through people who do."

A few minutes later, Angie reappeared to drop off a file. "So, I hear Tony took the package."

"Yes, yes he did," I said.

"That's interesting, because a few days ago, he seemed pretty set on not retiring."

"I know, quite a change of heart," I said.

Angie went on. "The amazing thing is he didn't know he was on the list; he was going to lose his job." Her technique was familiar. She was trying to set me up. She paused. "Well, I asked Tony why he changed his mind. You know what he told me?"

"What?"

"It was his guardian angel who showed him the way."

She used one of her extended pauses this time, the way she did when she was trying to get a response. "It was you, Ed, wasn't it?" She just smiled and said, "How you handled this is why I still work for you!"

When I look back on the choice I made and think about Tony, I feel good about myself. I had survived a test of character. Perhaps the risk to my career was not as big as I believed; maybe it was. But at that time, when I was emotionally compromised, I thought it was. When I was most vulnerable to the feelings of personal survival, I listened to my conscience. One thing was for sure: Tony and his wife's lives would have been devastated if I had not taken action that night. His visit to my office that day revealed that he knew that. For that one day, I actually liked myself. There was still enough of a man left inside to listen to what my moral code was telling me to.

Later, in a period of reflection, I recalled my mom's encouragement to pursue a life that would make the world a better place because I was here. A smile came to my face, for in this instance, in making a difference in one family's life, I had not let her down.

Chapter 10
It's Time to Get Ready

She's back... and she is fast!

I can still hear Tim's excitement over the phone when the Firebird Trans Am arrived from the Milford proving grounds. That weekend, I drove to Fremont. There she was, a good-looking car for its day, and when we put her up on the lift, we could see the changes. Upgraded suspension, linkages, and an added oil cooler. I was impressed with the four-wheel disc brakes, definitely racing grade, and the high-speed Goodyear tires, rated to 160+ mph.

She had subtle changes to the body, mostly ground effect additions under the front end and lower side panels. These additions were set back just a little under the car so they wouldn't draw undue attention. That was good to see, because the key to stability and top-end speed is not just horsepower, but the car's drag coefficient. Under-car drag, which depends on how much air gets under your car, is a hidden limiter to top speed. But more importantly, the stability of the car at high speeds is also impacted by the amount of air that passes under the car. The more air, the less stable the car.

Under the hood, the engine appeared to be a "standard stock" small block, but on closer inspection, we suspected it was not. Once we fired her up, we knew she definitely was not. The engine had more of a loping idle, a sign that it had a more aggressive cam shaft. Later that day, we went through the upgrades with an engineer at GM. We inspected the fuel and air intake and fuel-injection systems, electronic timing, added oil cooler, heavy-duty belts, battery, upgraded aluminum radiator, and headers on the exhaust system. The heads, the more we studied them, didn't appear to be stock heads, and we concluded that they had replaced the cast-iron intake manifold and heads with aluminum racing heads. He also told us the five-speed transmission, clutch, and rear-axle gears were modified for high-speed driving. The gear box was also tuned to the new power curve of the engine.

Even the pollution control system had been modified to reduce the draw on the engine vacuum. When it started up, you could tell there was no catalytic converter. This was to reduce back pressure on the engine. We knew the C-3 onboard computer was most likely reprogrammed for performance, but we came to believe it had been replaced. We never learned with what, but the car tended to want to pounce when fired up. We quickly learned to go light on the throttle; she responded instantly to any tap of the pedal! Our contact dropped one more upgrade on us: the original 5.0-liter, 305-cubic-inch engine was replaced with a 5.7-liter, 350-cubic-inch engine, a much more capable one. Both the 305 and 350 were based on a small engine block to start, but the 350 was bored out to increase the size of the combustion chamber. So that was how they met our need for more horsepower and an expanded power curve without adding the weight of a big-block engine. Our contact explained that they wanted to err on the side of engine toughness and durability, so the rating was limited to 475-to-505 horsepower at 5,800 rpm depending on temperature, with a torque rating at 4,700 rpm in the 520 foot-pound range. At the proving grounds on cool days, he said she was reaching speeds of 175 to 180+ mph on the straights.

One minor change inside the car could be seen on the instrument panel tachometer. Tim jumped with excitement when he saw it. The tach had been replaced with a new version, and the engine's redline had been increased to just under 7,000 rpm. This was a legitimate racing engine! This was a racecar. I felt good. I was born an American car guy. If Ford had made competitive Mustangs at the time, I would've gone that way out of respect for my grandmother. She asked me to always be loyal to Ford because Ford took a chance on her when she needed it most. But in 1984, Pontiac made what Tim and I believed was the best domestic car to take on the world's best. Little did we know just how good it was. We'd find out when we went up against the best that Porsche had to offer, but that was in the future. For now, we just wanted to get a car into the race.

We added our modifications: a radio scanner, CB, and a radar detector. An important addition was the reengineered police radar gun borrowed from the Fremont Police. It had been modified to jam police radar by sending out a signal at twice the power rating of the gun. We set its frequency at 56 mph. We added aircraft lights to the front of the car and taillight kill switches for night driving, and most importantly, a second fuel cell bladder with an extra fifty-five gallons of fuel. We were able to carry almost eighty gallons, giving us a significant range advantage over the 911s and other two-door coups. We had a car that had up to a 1,200-mile range at racing speeds.

As we finished our work on the Firebird, Tim and I agreed that it had just the right performance, mechanical robustness, range, room for equipment and provisions, driver comfort, and durability to win the race. But one last question remained: did she have the drivers who could get the most out of her and get her to the finish first?

Preparation, training, and planning

Part of preparing for the race was preparing ourselves. That was good for me. We modified our diets and exercise routines. But the most important single thing we did was focus on actual high-speed driving training. We selected the Skip Barber program at Indianapolis for this. It was a weeklong course for advanced Formula 1 driving.

Over the course of that week, we'd drive every day and then meet in the afternoon to discuss what we learned and how we could do better the next day. Although we were both experienced, Tim and I were humbled the first two days. Spinouts and missed gear shifts were more common than I want to admit. By the third day, it got better—much better. I was driving the line at high speed and refining my trail-braking and acceleration timing going into and out of the curves. My reflexes were getting better.

Finally, I was able to accomplish what we were told we wouldn't be able to—powershift on the straights. Powershifting is basically shifting gears without a clutch while the engine is accelerating—hard to do with gears squared in their cuts. As my reflexes improved, I found that if I just reduced the rate of acceleration and executed the shift at the right rpm, I could do it. But the engine was always under power. This took several seconds off my lap times.

When we left, I felt I had the training to run the race the following month, but that didn't change the fact that this race was going to be physically and mentally demanding. I knew that from the last year's race. Racing a car for a day and a half over 3,100 miles without a break will take a toll on anyone.

Edward M. Rahill

This is a 1984 Pontiac Firebird Trans Am identical to the one I purchased and equipped. It was silver sand metallic and designed for stealth. It pretty much stayed that way after the GM proving grounds upgrades. The only noticeable change from this car was the substitution of turbine wheels for added brake cooling.

One Mile at a Time

My first day at the Indianapolis Motor Speedway. It wasn't until the end of the course on day five that we convinced the instructors to allow us a brief run with the Trans Am on the track. Each of us was allowed three laps with instructions not to exceed 90 mph on the first lap. We were also instructed to end the run at any time if they raised the warning flag. Tim and I both exceeded 160 mph on the final lap. It was unfortuante that we did not have the opportunity to run again; we felt the car had not yet reached its true potentiel.

Edward M. Rahill

On the Indianapolis Motor Speedway road course, Tim and I took the Skip Barber training seriously. Although those cars were only Formula Fours, they had a 140 mph top end and were very unforgiving if you weren't paying attention.

For me it was not until day three when I felt experienced enough about how she drove and her idiosyncrasies to be in command of the car.

Lessons Gleaned from Experience

One thing Tim and I learned from the previous year's race was how important it was to do our homework. For example, there had been numerous delays and setbacks due to construction, which could have been avoided if I'd had a better understanding of local traffic patterns. Even small cities can have significant delays depending on the time of day and day of the week. It was also extremely helpful to study the policing patterns along possible routes.

We laid out a plan that represented our preferred and alternate routes. The next step was to schedule a trip-planning meeting with the American Automobile Association, Triple A. It was the best source for maps and planned construction projects across the nation. In addition, they had good information on fuel stops. With this in hand, we started a deep dive into possible routes and what obstacles we might face along each one.

We contacted each state's Department of Transportation to confirm the information we had on scheduled road work and identified any law enforcement issues we may not have been aware of from our meeting with Triple A.

With the 100+ mph performance demands and constant attention to driving details, you've got to prepare for the brutal demands on your body, your car, and your mind. We reminded ourselves that this was not just a drive across the country, it was cross-continental endurance racing. First, rest periods: there was no real opportunity to sleep, unless you reached complete exhaustion, but you could rest. We'd impose four-hour shifts to help each driver stay fresh. Four hours had become the norm on the pro circuit, so it was good enough for us.

Diet and hydration are key for maintaining optimal mental performance during a race. This is something we'd both learned the hard way. We researched the best strategies to maximize time on the road, including reducing solids, consuming laxatives, and sticking to a liquid diet of shakes just before the race. During the race, we would consume carb-heavy foods, such as Snickers, graham crackers, and Reese's Peanut Butter Cups. Fluids were mandatory. Both Tim and I had suffered from some degree of dehydration the previous year, which we said would not happen again. Hi-C was a favorite. We made sure there were plenty of pee bottles to go around.

One thing we wanted to get better at was identifying highway patrol methods. When in action, the combined air, highway, and radio communications could make speed enforcement a formidable barrier to victory. Tim and I interviewed experienced truck drivers and retired police officers. In previous cross-continental races, several states seemed to rise above the others in arrests. An interesting pattern presented itself: states east of the Mississippi, the Oklahoma City area, and California seemed most aggressive. We understood the Ohio methods of air patrol and radar enforcement, as well as patrol cars that were not easily identified from a distance. So, we focused on the eastern states in our trip plan.

One state, Indiana, stood out. There was a disproportionate number of arrests without a clear pattern of methods used. We decided to do a series of test runs—Tim in Ohio and me in Indiana—to gain insight into police enforcement methods.

My method was to purposely get arrested. I drove from Chicago to the eastern part of the Indiana toll road and turned back toward Chicago. I then set the cruise control to 71 mph when the limit was 55 mph. That was a difference of 16 mph and 4 mph below the reckless driving classification. I just waited to get pulled over.

About an hour into the run, I was approached from behind by an Indiana patrol officer who hit his lights. I immediately slowed down and pulled onto the shoulder. After a couple minutes, the officer approached me and asked me to return to his car. I sat in the passenger seat, and we went through his citation procedure. I was quiet and cooperative. I apologized and when I got the chance, I let him know I was surprised. Then, I asked how he caught me. That was when I learned the technique used by Indiana and other states with obstacles and bridges. Police tended not to use radar, as most drivers thought. They used time-to-distance measurements to determine the speed of a vehicle. So, Indiana was not relying on radar to arrest speeders. This was a major insight that we incorporated into our brake-and-go racing technique.

I was lucky to have found a teammate like Tim. Taking a serious run at this race was not a one-man show. This type of race requires dedication from both drivers. It's not enough to be talented behind the wheel; winners have to commit to doing everything right, and if it's not right, they do it over again

Edward M. Rahill

until it is. In *The Art of War*, Sun Tzu penned a favorite quote of mine: *"Every battle is won or lost before it is ever fought."* That was how I felt about the upcoming race. Unlike in the previous year's race, I wasn't going to be caught unprepared.

Tim and I spent countless hours, days, and months preparing. The time was spent preparing the car, researching what we needed in a car to win, and coordinating with the engineers at GM, making countless modifications if something did not work right. We both understood what teamwork meant. As one final symbolic gesture to the team, I agreed to grow a beard until the race was over.

Tim and I laid out a race plan and researched the challenges we might face along the way.

Chapter 11
Strategies for Racing 3,100 Miles

Our drive across the country required two different driving styles, which was why we needed the right car. Boston to St. Louis was a congested roadway, and I had insisted on a brake-and-go strategy. West of the Mississippi, the driving techniques were wide open. The lighter traffic, less frequent speed enforcement, and wide-open highways allowed for higher sustained speeds. In the West, brake-and-go would be used less frequently and only as we encountered traffic.

The brake-and-go technique was simple, but it punished the drivers and their cars. In the presence of other vehicles, the driver always takes a defensive approach, not an aggressive style. The technique was to apply the brakes, then downshift one or two gears utilizing the engine's braking power to help reduce speed.

Brake-and-go tactics include:

(1) to decelerate when approaching a grouping of vehicles,

(2) to apply the brakes to get down to about 15 to 20 mph faster than the group of vehicles we were passing,

(3) then to accelerate as fast as possible once we passed the slower cars.

The downshifting was critical because even the upgraded brakes would not last 2,000 miles, let alone 3,100, without engine braking assist. The mechanical downside to this technique was that it relied on the engine and gear box to absorb some of the force of slowing down, rather than the brakes, and still hold together for 3,100 miles. For safety reasons, I felt that extending the life of the brakes was critical. Another note on safety: while driving at speed, we knew to make any lane changes or pass other vehicles slowly and predictably.

The key reasons for the brake-and-go technique were as follows:

(1) It was safer when passing a group of vehicles as one could easily adjust for sudden lane changes than at higher speeds. The objective was to allow the driver of the vehicle you are passing to anticipate your moves. I remember telling Tim that the key was to make directional changes without the other vehicle having to use its brakes.

(2) State patrol officers and aircraft focus on the movement of individual vehicles relative to other cars in a pack. (I learned this through my own research.)

(3) In the previous year's race, we both noticed that some drivers of eighteen-wheelers enjoyed suddenly changing lanes as we approached in the passing lane or would go tandem to try to block our lane and just play games with us. By the time we left the Massachusetts Turnpike, the truckers were becoming aware of the race, and many of them wanted to play with us. Brake-and-go gave us a safety margin when a truck driver decided to play this game. It allowed us to choose the next move before he could react. Our two most common moves were to suddenly use the breakdown lane or

quickly shift into the lane he was moving out of under full acceleration.

Brake-and-go was the correct strategy east of the Mississippi. It was also why the driver needed to know what the car could do and choose the right gear to engage the trucks at their game.

This was why we needed a car with a lot of mid-range rpm torque to accelerate quickly. Once the truck driver had committed, he had a limited chance to react to the speed of the Trans Am. However, some aggressive truckers anticipated this move and tried to quickly move back and cut us off. This basically turned into a game of chicken and a dangerous situation. Therefore, racing-quality brakes were important to deal with this type of aggressive move.

Another technique was driving the racing line to minimize the distance traveled while maintaining optimum speed on a road or track. Often referred to as apex driving, the technique uses all available road surfaces to travel as fast and straight as possible during the race. This meant the distinction of driving lanes, including breakdown lanes, was irrelevant. Our objective was to find the optimum speed and distance to travel through a curve.

By utilizing the entire available road, a driver will enter a righthand turn, not from the inside lane, but from the outside lane. Then the driver will gradually adjust his turn by drifting to the inside of the turn until he reaches a point in the turn called the apex. The driver will drift back toward the outside lane until he reaches the end of the turn, then prepare for the next one. The advantage of this is that a driver can effectively reduce the degree of twisting and turning, thereby running higher average cruising speeds. Over the course of a 3,100-mile race, this technique could save a significant amount of time.

Trail-braking is a blend of braking and turning at the same time. It enables a driver to brake slightly later while entering the turn, but more importantly, to enter the turn at a higher speed. This technique is not the racing school method of braking that teaches the driver to always brake in a straight line before entering the turn, release the brakes, and then turn into the corner.

The trail-braking method has the driver recognize the best drive-the-line path through the turn, stay under power while entering the turn, and then apply full braking power when in the turn. But trail-braking is not necessarily braking all the way to the apex, although that is possible. Once the car passes the apex, the driver reverses the technique, this time accelerating. Trail-braking generally results in a faster time completing the path through the corner, however, because it's a more aggressive method, it is riskier.

The degree of trail-braking I would employ depended on three conditions: the speed at which I was approaching the turn, the steepness of change in direction of the curve, and the duration of the curve. If the curve had a steep angle of turn or generated a relatively high G-force during the turn, I would revert to the "racing school" method of braking. Under those conditions, I found applying acceleration to the rear wheels early in such a turn increased my traction, stability, and control going through the turn.

An added complication of trail-braking to get through a turn is downshifting the gear box to choose the rpm level you want exiting the turn. It takes experience and knowledge of the car to find the optimal time and gear to make this move. But generally, it is advised to make the first downshift before entering the turn and the first upshift while exiting the turn.

A crucial element that can be overlooked is the role of the navigator. The navigator position is more demanding than it looks. In addition to studying routes for potential adjustments and planning fuel stops, the navigator ran communications between truckers and our car and monitored the scanner for patrol communications. This information was valuable in adjusting routes based on real-time information. This person also operated the radar-jamming gear and was responsible for scanning the sky for patrol aircraft and helicopters. While at race speeds and in near emergency situations, the navigator was responsible for observing the entire field of play, to be aware of everything on the highway. The driver concentrated on controlling the car and the immediate road ahead. The navigator gave a heads-up on everything else.

Off to Boston

Monday evening, May 28, I drove into Rolling Meadows for a small, good luck gathering with my work friends from ARCO. It was good to see Angie, Larry, and the whole groups wishing me the best. I had no expectations. After a while, I had to get something off my chest I'd heard the previous week. I asked Angie about the rumor I'd heard that Nancy had made a few comments about me.

When I brought it up, Angie didn't want to talk about it. She was trying to be a class act, not speak badly about anyone. Finally, I just asked her as a friend to give it to me straight. Apparently, when Nancy learned that Tim and I were running the race again, she became uncomfortable and said some disparaging things about me, my planning, and how things hadn't gone well the previous year. She said she'd carried me through the race. Basically, she was saying she didn't think I had what it took to do better. It hit me hard. I thanked Angie for telling me the truth.

I agreed with Nancy that I'd made mistakes in the previous race, but her comments still hurt. Later, I came to believe she was dealing with unresolved feelings about how our relationship had ended. But at the time, it was just more weight piling onto my already fragile spirit. Her comments stayed with me and haunted me well into race day.

The next morning, I drove to Fremont, Ohio, where Tim's family and friends were waiting. It was a bit festive, and Tim had his team stocking the car with last-minute racing provisions, including the final attachments for the fifty-five-gallon racing cell.

The next day, it was off to Buffalo. This was a real party with my mother, brother, sister, and high school friends, two of whom ran a bar named the Heritage Inn Two. I was amazed by the way Tim could walk into a room of strangers and within twenty minutes, it was if they'd known him all their lives. My mother was usually to the point, and I felt she sensed the turmoil deep inside me. Of course, Nancy and I had stopped over for a couple days the previous year to stay with her. But now that Nancy wasn't part of my life, she knew something was wrong.

She asked me with her classic direct tone, "What happened?"

We went to a corner of the room, and she listened. I gave her the short version, but an honest one. She said, "From the moment I met her, I knew why you two were together. But at times, I felt like she didn't fully understand the quality of the man she had." I hugged my mother. There might have been a little truth to it; Nancy didn't understand why I was waiting for my divorce from Carlene.

Reflecting on these simple events, I am profoundly grateful. The people at the sendoff liked being with us not because we'd done something special—at that stage, we had accomplished nothing. They wanted to throw a party for us just to be good friends. The next morning, there were a few hangovers, but Tim and I had been careful not to imbibe too much. We said our goodbyes, and we were off to Boston. We drove east on the New York State Tollway, the same road we'd be racing on in the other direction just two days later. The reality that we were going to run the race again was beginning to set in. It was time to start thinking about Saturday morning. The future was not predetermined. We were becoming serious about what we were going to face. I felt nervous, but I needed to keep that to myself.

Edward M. Rahill

One Mile at a Time

We posed with the Trans Am on our stopover in Buffalo to say hello to my friends and family, and we smiled at the surprise party thrown for us by my family and friends the night before.

The day arrived.

It was a gray, rainy day when Tim and I arrived at the hotel in Boston. At least two dozen racecars were already there. The sponsors tried to keep the field under thirty because the previous year's fifty-six entries were unmanageable. Because Tim and I had both finished the race a year earlier, and given the fact that Nancy and I were seventeenth and Tim and his partner were twenty-first, we easily qualified.

We parked in the designated area. As we looked over the other cars, we saw a mix of domestic and foreign models. It was interesting to see some of the personalities associated with their cars, including the driver of the 934 Carrera who'd made a splash the previous year. There was a Ferrari 308, two Mercedes-Benz sedans, several BMW sedans (including a 1984 5-Series Alpina and 533i), several Porsches (including a 928S, 944, and the 934 Carrera mentioned earlier), and two Ford Panteras. Domestics included another '84 Trans Am in addition to ours, two Corvettes, a late-model Mustang that we later found out had added a turbo charger to its 5.0 high-output engine, a couple Camaros, and a 1984 Dodge Royal Tradesman van. One of the Camaros was a '72 and over the top. It was all black and looked like it was set up for a county fair rally. The driver was from California and had driven his car to Massachusetts for the start of the race. He was known to shout, "God bless America!" several times a day. A team we believed was from Japan had arrived the night before with a premium performance rental car. They had planned on dropping it off in San Diego before flying home to Japan.

But the cars we were looking for were the ones with an understated appearance like ours. The prior year, the police had a field day chasing down racers that stood out. We noticed a Ford LTD Crown Vic sedan. The car presented itself as a government vehicle and was gray. But the tires were rated for 140 mph. There was no way to know what was under the hood or how much fuel it carried. The rear bumper held a slightly enlarged license plate frame. We later learned it held realistic-looking federal government and local plates for several states. They simply electronically changed plates as needed.

Tim located what he thought was a radar jammer. Looking inside the window, it almost resembled a cockpit. This car was well thought out. With its stealth gray shade and official unmarked government appearance, as well as the extra fuel capacity and police interceptor motor, it was a serious threat.

As we looked at our Firebird in the middle of the fleet, we felt good about our car. She was Ohio state trooper gray, and except for those high-powered running lights, she did not stand out. Later that day, one of the more experienced team members stopped and commented on our Trans Am. In a friendly way, he said, "You guys are serious, aren't you?" He looked at our tires and what he could see of our brakes. "Your entry has a lot more capability than it shows." We thanked him, talked previous race experience, and gave him our rationale for our choice of car. We found all kinds of personalities at the event. They were all high achievers in some sense, and a few tended to exhibit a bit of narcissism.

Suddenly, one of two men who'd been standing about ten feet away jumped in. "You guys can't be serious if you think you know what you're doing with that toy car."

I gave him a stern look, but Tim, being Tim, responded, "So what piece of crap are you driving?"

"You really think that Pontiac is going to be competitive in a race like this?" the guy retorted.

This was not going well. I grabbed Tim's arm and said, "Just get lost. We don't need this right now." A couple other drivers noticed the exchange and started coming toward us. The two men walked away. We later found out they were driving a black Porsche 928S, and they were from New Jersey.

That evening, we went to dinner, more to see who was there than to eat, since Tim and I had switched to a liquid diet for the race (restroom stops cost time, and a bottle could be used in the car, but that was it). It was a lively crowd, but you could tell everyone was just a little careful. It had a competitive undertone. Our friends from New Jersey were on the other end of the room, which was okay with us.

Ed Preston addressed the group and reminded everyone that one bad actor could tarnish the reputation of all the racers. He explained that they had reduced the number of participants for safety and had decided to limit press access at the start of the race to keep it quiet. However, he was inviting the press to the finish in San Diego. We also got an update on weather conditions across the country and on what he was hearing about traffic enforcement. He said he had contacts across the country that would give him an update by seven a.m. the morning of the race. He wished us good luck, and we went through the process of randomly selecting the start positions for each car.

The Night before the Race

I couldn't sleep. I got up and went outside to the parking lot for one last look at the cars. Approaching the Firebird, I saw Tim checking the wiring on the high-output lamps.

"Everything okay?"

"Yeah, I just wanted to make sure the connections were good with these running lights. They draw a lot of amps, and the gauge of the wires needs to be right. They're okay." He seemed a little agitated.

I looked around at the other cars. "I think there are more experienced drivers here this time—international, too."

"I know," Tim said. "Did you get a load of that Austrian team at the banquet?"

"Yes," I said, "they were a lot more comfortable speaking German than English." And we laughed.

"Did you know one of the guys with that Crown Vic from Texas is rumored to be ex-law enforcement or ex-CIA?"

"Really?" I said.

"A couple other racers got a look in their trunk, and in addition to a large fuel cell, it seems their car is loaded with electronics, detectors, jammers, and even night vision. In addition to standard CB and scanners, they might even have a shortwave radio and the new Motorola phone to stay up on situations and call ahead, to set up stops. Not to mention the dozen federal and state plates they have hiding in their bumper."

Tim had been the socializer of our team, which helped me understand what we were up against, who the other racers were. "There are several teams here who make their living by racing," he said. "Not by winning the races, but by placing. They make $60,000 to even $75,000 a year. They travel to state fairs and regional races, and they supposedly do well. You and I have day jobs. Where does that put us?"

"Bottom line, Tim, what are you trying to tell me?"

"Hell, I'm just going back to Fremont after this race to my day job." He had one more thing to get off his chest. He paused and finally said, "Tonight, for the first time, I wondered why I'm doing this. Don't get me wrong, I'm excited, but I'm not gonna kid myself. As far as experience, we're outclassed. On top of that, there seem to be more assholes this year."

"Are your referring to those Porsche guys from Jersey?"

"Yeah, those guys."

"Hey Tim, what's up? What's eating you? Are you thinking we don't stand much of a chance?" I asked.

"I'm just remembering how brutal it was last year. This year's likely to be worse. There's a rumor going around that the cops are already waiting for us. That they plan on giving us a lesson because of the way we caught some of them napping last year." I could tell he was feeling the weight of the challenge.

"As far as our run-in with those Jersey guys, I believe in karma. Somehow, some way, those guys'll get put down. What goes around comes around." I paused for a second. Then I said, "Once I heard Brock Yates talk about his first Cannonball Run. He pointed out that Dan Gurney, a winner of the 24 Hours of Le Mans, said that the raw nature of this kind of race made it the most challenging one he'd ever run. In my view, this is the most challenging race in the world."

In a frustrated voice, Tim quickly responded, "Yeah, I know. You don't have to tell me! I drove this race last year, too." He then paused as if he was realizing his mood and smiled.

I decided to challenge him. "Tim, do you still think we have a car that stands a chance in this race?"

I could see him bristle at the thought. "Hell, yes! We got her right where we want her. I just wish I had a chance to run those two from Jersey one on one. I know this Firebird can run with them. You know, just like Springsteen said, 'We shut 'em up and then shut them down.'" I smiled.

"I know you're frustrated. I'm a little apprehensive too," I went on. "When you're out there, you're on your own. Every state trooper across the country is after you. Traffic can be dense. Trucks are playing chicken with you; there's no pit crew, no real time to rest. And there are thirty other cars trying to do the same thing: make it to San Diego first! No rules—just first."

I wanted him to know he was running a special race tomorrow, so I added, "At Daytona or Le Mans, you get to leave your car every four hours for a rest. Here, we live in ours for a day and a half. On a track, you know the road ahead. At Le Mans, hell, you drive the same eight-mile course at least 350 times. Not here! You're driving 3,100 miles on roads you've never seen, and you don't even know what you might be facing 200 yards ahead. Challenging? You bet!

In my mind, no other endurance race can stand up to it." I looked right at him. "I've seen you drive, Tim. You're good, a little crazy for my taste, but you're good, and I chose you as my partner because of that." I was trying to encourage him. "You're more than good—you're one of the best." It showed on his face that he appreciated the compliment.

He looked down and then into my eyes. "Same here, Ed. I can't think of anybody I'd rather be racing with tomorrow."

I thanked him and said I was going to turn in. As I walked back to the hotel, I focused on the next day's event. I needed Tim. I needed his head in the game, and the role I just played with him was team captain, except I was the one who needed a pep talk. I hoped that somehow this race could rebuild my spirit, which had been beaten down over the last year. Tim and I had been determined to put together a team that could win this race. But I was having my doubts; I was nervous about the grueling experience we were about to have. I knew I was not 100 percent. I was emotionally compromised. My passion had dulled, and my confidence was diminished. I no longer had faith in myself. I wasn't even the man I'd been as a teenager. To stand up and not break under pressure—I wasn't sure I was there. I just tried to hide it.

One Mile at a Time

Tim worked feverishly to reinstall our night running lights and get the Firebird Trans Am ready to go. Beautiful in a stealthy way, the car's aerodynamics tell you she will be fast with her high horsepower output engine.

Edward M. Rahill

Warning: They know we're coming!

About an hour and a half before the start of the race, we ran into Ed Preston, the race organizer. It was raining and overcast. He said that he'd learned about a coordinated national police and highway patrol enforcement plan. It had been organized three months earlier in anticipation of this event. Each state was in active communication with adjacent states about race activity. They prepared to run double-shift patrols at the times when they anticipated race teams would be passing through. A notice was sent out nationwide that the race would be underway by eight a.m. Eastern. Local and state law enforcement were told they should prepare to take any action necessary.

"Basically, the entire country knows we're coming, and they plan on doing something about it," Ed said. "It was last year's NBC news coverage that brought this kind of press and law enforcement. So, good luck, guys. Keep your eyes open."

We thanked him. I just looked at Tim and said, "Okay, guess it's gonna get busy out there."

Over the previous fourteen years, various versions of the Cannonball had taken place; all had attempted to keep the events quiet. But it was increasingly difficult to avoid publicity. This all came to a head in 1983 when the Four Ball Rally, the largest and longest race ever run, got positive national coverage on the *NBC Nightly News*. The NBC correspondents had interviewed and recorded racers speeding across the country.

The race became even more reputable when it was rumored that the German team—who had set a record the previous year—were not shipping brokers, but Porsche factory team drivers under cover. Tim and I later learned that was a factor in GM's decision to covertly sponsor us, ending their noninvolvement policy. They just did not want corporate to know about it. The proving grounds team had had it with European cars dominating an American race.

Local and state law enforcement could no longer ignore it. Some believed the race had become a source of humiliation for them, which motivated them to organize nationwide to stop it. This, of course, created a huge challenge for us racers, making it perhaps the most challenging race ever. Every department knew we were coming, and they would be communicating with each other about our progress and locations.

A few minutes later, Ed Preston raised a bullhorn and asked for attention. He told the teams about the news and asked us to be careful. "I fully expect a coordinated nationwide enforcement effort unlike anything we've seen. It won't be like last year when they were caught with their pants down. They will be ready with tougher police actions than we have ever experienced in the past."

We didn't realize how right he was. Of the twenty-seven cars scheduled to start that morning, fewer than half were to finish.

A 1983 Mercedes 6.9-liter SEL-AMG four-door sedan. The car was equipped with blue police lights to aid in getting cars out of the way.

Ford Crown Vic with a stealth persona. We later learned it was powered by a 5.8-liter police interceptor engine and had recessed police lights.

One Mile at a Time

1983 or 1984 BMW 5 Series Alpina

1983 Porsche 934 Carrera

Edward M. Rahill

934 Carrera warming up his engine and oil a half-hour before his start

Highly modified turbo-charged 1983 280-Z

Chapter 12
Gentlemen, Start your Engines

The race started at eight a.m. Just like the previous year, the cars were staggered in three-minute intervals. We were eighteenth in line, toward the end of the starting order, or about twenty minutes ahead of the last car. Finally, after an hour wait, we took off.

It was raining as we drove through the streets to the Massachusetts toll road. Tim took the first shift, while I managed the electronics and made final adjustments to our route. As the day progressed, we focused on keeping the furious pace we'd set for ourselves. We found ourselves arguing about everything: how hard we were pushing the car, whether we should stay with the brake-and-go strategy, how many stops we could afford and still be competitive.

It got nasty at times, and Tim said some not-so-nice things about my driving. I always approached a string of cars and trucks at 15-to-20 mph over their speed, then accelerated. Tim preferred pedal-to-the-metal, to drive as fast as he could. His argument was the ten-to-twelve seconds lost by slowing down and then speeding up could cost us over an hour and a half in race time.

"Sometimes slow is fast," I argued. "Slow allows you to assess how the situation is evolving, and when to make your move."

Edward M. Rahill

I believed we needed to control our speed for safety reasons because other vehicles often make unanticipated lane changes that we wouldn't be able to adapt to if we were overtaking them at 50+ mph, especially when passing a group of vehicles. We were stressed out and argued vigorously about it the first day. Eventually, we remembered the pressure of the race and realized we'd each experienced this behavior before. So, we made a conscious effort to calm down.

When it was my turn to take the wheel near Albany, Tim sensed something wasn't right with me. Behind the wheel, everything I was saying was right—the strategy, the approach—but he could tell my will and passion weren't there. I was struggling, becoming more anxious as my speed increased. I was losing my nerve, and he knew it.

The First Time I Was Arrested

I was driving through upstate New York running just north of 100 mph when, as we cleared a rise in the highway, our radar detector started screaming. I immediately jammed the brakes. Tim shouted, "Stay on the brakes! Their radar guns can't lock onto us while we're rapidly changing speed." Our radar jammer was mounted to the front of the car and couldn't jam radar coming from behind. Two patrol cars appeared behind us. I slowed again and pulled to the side of the tollway waiting for them to catch up. After a minute, an officer approached and asked for license, registration, and tollway ticket. I complied but said we couldn't find our tollway ticket. The trooper became irritated, and he walked back to his car. Tim and I concluded that they'd been unable to get a lock on us and the officers couldn't prove we were speeding. They had neither visual nor radar evidence. They had hoped to secure our toll ticket with a timestamp, which we had anticipated. So, we threw the ticket away as soon as we entered the tollway. The trooper returned and instructed us to try to find the ticket, and we behaved as if we were. Tim opened his door, and a trooper barged into the car searching for anything. We knew this was illegal, but they weren't in a good mood, so it was best not to escalate. We could tell they were a bit pumped and frustrated until they discovered our Bearcat radio scanner in the glovebox. Out came the handcuffs, and, as the owner of the car, off I went to jail/court. Tim was left with the car and one state trooper to keep him company.

After a ten-minute drive, the trooper pulled into the parking lot of a small municipal building, and I was escorted out of the back of his car to a room where there was a woman behind a desk. The plaque on her desk said she was a judge, but she was dressed in summer clothes. She motioned the trooper to bring me over. She started the hearing with an announcement that she had a wedding to go to, so "let's get to the point."

I stood before her in handcuffs as the trooper cited the charges. It had something to do with being in possession of an unauthorized radio receiver that scanned for official police communications. The judge asked if I had anything to say. I answered that in 1934, Congress passed the Radio Communications Act that guaranteed every American the right to receive radio communications, and that a license was only necessary if someone wanted to broadcast on those frequencies. Then I reminded her of what the officer had just said—that the scanner was a "receiver," and it did not broadcast.

The judge looked at me, then at the officer, then back at me. After a short pause, she cracked a smile and turned to the officer. "He's right. Get the cuffs off, drive him back to his car, and release him. Case dismissed." As I left, I saw another member of the rally team standing in the hall waiting for his turn.

We later discovered that the New York State Police had obtained descriptions of our cars from the Massachusetts State Police and had set a trap to intercept racers.

On the drive back to my car, the officer didn't talk to me. I had to ask him for my Bearcat scanner back. I could tell he was unhappy. I said thank you and got back into the car. Tim was agitated, and I understood why. While he was pulled over waiting for me, he saw several cars from the race pass us. We'd lost almost two hours, and we were barely three hundred miles in. I got back into the driver's seat and took off. I was also aggravated.

"How come you got off so easy?"

I told him how I made the case that the use of a scanner is protected under federal law. Tim said that when they put the cuffs on, he assumed we were done. "I was just planning to pick you up from the jail tomorrow and head home."

We eventually settled down to talk strategy and monitoring. We agreed we'd be more active in our CB communications to help us stay aware of state police "wolf pack" operations. The reality was that the race would be more challenging—nothing like the previous year's. I drove for another hour, then Tim took over. I think he just wanted to settle down. I was able to shake it off, which felt good.

Over the next several hundred miles, we saw three other racers who'd been pulled over. Most appeared to be getting traffic citations, but one team had handcuffs on. This level of enforcement was starting to impact our driving. It is human nature to avoid a threat. It required determination to maintain an aggressive driving profile under such pressure. An added issue was that Tim and I had got off to a bad start. The New York arrest and going to court might have been enough to take us out of the competition. Little did we know, more bad breaks lay ahead.

Road Emergencies and Cool Heads

As we approached Dayton, Ohio, I was driving and the outer belt expanded to three lanes, and the traffic got denser. Tim and I had talked extensively about the types of emergencies we could face. High-speed accidents from unanticipated lane changes by other vehicles could send a stream of cars into uncontrolled spins. Then there was equipment failure, especially on eighteen-wheelers who tended to rely on low-cost tire retreads. Blowing a tire was not uncommon.

From the moment we encountered heavier traffic, I adjusted my speed accordingly, but maintained a good 20 mph advantage. Suddenly, up ahead, our worst fear unfolded. There was a cloud of smoke, debris, and a sudden uncontrolled movement from an eighteen-wheeler. He had blown not one but two tires while changing lanes, causing him to dog-track down the highway over two lanes. It couldn't have happened at a worse time, given the traffic. This sent a group of cars into a tizzy. A couple cars were out of control, and their direction was completely unpredictable. I had to maneuver around a car ahead of me who'd slammed on his brakes. One car ahead of us in another lane was rear-ended because he had applied his brakes with multiple cars behind him. It was a pile-up.

Tim immediately called out the situation and yelled to downshift one gear and warned me to prepare for evasive maneuvers. "Be careful! There are still several cars behind us."

I was fixated on the road, and I downshifted into fourth gear to get the car into its power-curve sweet spot while Tim quickly sized up the situation. Suddenly, one of the cars ahead of us lost control while reacting to the pile-up. It was careening sideways on the highway. He yelled, "The eighteen-wheeler is off the road! Your problem now is that car."

As the car about a hundred yards ahead started spinning, I focused on its wheels. They were spinning, not locking up as they would have been under heavy braking. Tim saw the same thing and yelled, "Aim for the front wheels!" I set my path directly toward the front wheels of that car and brought our car up to full throttle. Sure enough, the out-of-control vehicle did what I expected and spun over to the side of the road, slid along the side of a guardrail, and stopped. One remaining car was having problems, it looked like a flat tire, and he was trying to pull over. I threw the Trans Am into the far-left lane to give him a wide berth and continued to accelerate straight through the remaining debris. The danger was now over, and we just settled down and drove on. We were lucky not to have suffered any damage to the tires or undercarriage.

All of this occurred within seconds of the eighteen-wheeler's tire blowout. It happened so fast that all we could do was react in the way we had been trained. From our driving and racing experience, we knew the key to predicting a vehicle's path in an uncontrolled situation was the wheels. If they were locked, the car would continue in the direction it was headed until the wheels came free. If the wheels were spinning, the car was going to end up anywhere but the direction he was heading. That's why we learned to target the car's current position. The specific reason for targeting a car's wheels instead of its center is to minimize the risk of injury to the driver of that car. The safest place to hit a car during an accident is the wheels. The energy of the impact is concentrated on the car's axles on the front or back side of the car and not the driver's seat. I was reminded of my first real road emergency when I was a teenager driving the parts truck for the dealership.

Engage the mind, bury the emotions.

There are two ways to get yourself out of trouble in an emergency. You have your brakes, and you have your accelerator. Most drivers on the road instinctively use their brakes when they see trouble ahead. But as we'd just seen, this can be a dangerous choice at expressway and higher speeds. Experienced racers will try to drive around the problem first. Anyone who's seen an accident at Daytona or NASCAR will know that whenever possible, change direction and use both the brakes and accelerator to get out of trouble.

My Second Arrest of the Race

While I was driving through Ohio, west of Dayton, Tim was trying to estimate how fast we needed to go to recover from that two-hour delay from my arrest on the New York State Thruway. Suddenly, our radar detector sounded, and Tim immediately dropped what he was doing and hit the jammer. I'd been running somewhere north of 120 mph trying to make up time. But it looked like we were unprepared for the dragnet put out by the Ohio State Police.

Another rule that we made for ourselves was to never run from the police. I hit the brakes, then hit the taillight kill switch so as not to broadcast that we were slowing down. It was to no avail. We watched the Ohio state trooper cut across the median with his lights on. I carefully pulled over to the side of the road and waited for him to catch up.

"Do you believe this?" I asked Tim while we waited. "The whole country seems to know we're coming, where we are, and what we're driving."

The trooper approached the car. I held my license and registration out the window with both hands where he could see them. He took the documents. "Mr. Rahill, do you know how fast you were going?"

I acknowledged I was going too fast. He said, "Please step back to my car." Normally, it would be a mistake to admit any wrongdoing at a traffic stop, but my instinct was to cooperate and not give the officer any reason to get irritated with me.

As I got into his car, I was nervous. It was my second arrest in the same day. I was fully aware that law enforcement was out to make a point—that they were in charge. But once in the car, I sensed he wasn't upset at all. As a matter of fact, he was in a good mood, almost pleased with himself. He proceeded to tell me that there was a nationwide All-Points Bulletin (APB) out for me and the other racers. This was his day off, but he volunteered to come in and bolster the patrols in Ohio when he got the news that the race had started. Ed Preston was right.

The trooper read a section of the APB to me and said he'd been looking forward to this day all year. He explained that this was a chance for him and the other troopers to have fun testing their abilities against some pretty good drivers. This was one of the few times he didn't have in the back of his mind that the driver might "have a gun waiting." He finally revealed that there was a national command center that had been set up to follow the racers. I was amazed. Just for us? It started to make sense. How else could they have followed us the way they did?

"Now for the charges." I acknowledged I was over the limit.

He just smiled. "Son, for some reason, my radar gun was telling me you were traveling at fifty-six miles per hour, but I have been doing this for fifteen years, and if you were moving at all, you were doing north of 120." He grinned. "I was trying to decide what charge I could get you on, but I noticed that as you pulled over, you didn't use your turn signal. So, this is going to be a little like Monopoly—you are going to lose one turn. You are being fined for a turn signal violation and will lose one hour. We have twenty minutes left, then you can go."

We started talking about how much he liked his job, what I did for a living—stuff like that. Finally, he said, "Time's up. Don't drive too fast in my zone. I won't hesitate to pull you over again." I thanked him and got back into the car. Tim was anxious; we'd fallen further behind. I was just relieved we got off so easy. His name was Sergeant Rodger Teague, and as fate was to have it, this was not the last time we would see him.

One Mile at a Time

```
/OHALLTERM
OHOHP0030 080 16:46:20 06/02/84
AM.NY1010100
12:17 06/02/84 01526
THQT QHQT
02207          FILE 13  SP TROOP T HDQTRS ALBANY NY1010100   JUNE 2-84
TO             SP ALBANY NY - REQUEST NATIONWIDE BROADCAST

------------------------- POLICE INFORMATION -------------------------
A HIGH PERFORMANCE HIGH SPEED RACE FROM BOSTON MASS TO SAN DIEGO CALIFORNIA
IS IN PROGRESS AT THIS TIME. VEHICLES INVOLVED ARE HIGH PERFORMANCE SUCH AS
PORSCHES,CORVETTES,BMWS,CAMAROS AND FARRARIS. THE NUMBER OF VEHICLES INVOLVED
FROM INFORMATION RECEIVED IS APPROX 40. THE FIRST GROUP WAS OBSERVED WESTBOUND
ON THE NEW YORK STATE THRUWAY - INTERSTATE 90 - AT APPROX 12:25 PM DATE. AFTER
A HIGH SPEED CHASE IN EXCESS OF 100 MPH SUBJECT WAS STOPPED AT MILEPOST 239 WB
ONEIDA COUNTY, NEW YORK. ARREST WAS MADE FOR SPEED AND ALSO A NUMBER OF VEHICLE
WERE STOPPED AND OPERATORS ARRESTED FOR HAVING RADIO RECEIVING DEVICES WITH
FREQUENCIES ALLOCATED FOR POLICE USE. UNKNOWN ROUTES OF TRAVEL, PRIMARY
ROUTES BEING INTERSTATES. VEHICLES CONTAINED SOPHISTICATED RADAR DETECTING
EQUIPMENT AS WELL AS HIGH TECH NIGHT VISION GOGGLES. THE CARS STARTED THREE
MINUTES APART AT 10:00 AM DATE WITH TWO DRIVERS PER CAR  ANY ROUTE MAY BE USED
ALTHOUGH THE FASTEST IS ABOUT 2,900 MILES THROUGH MASS, NY, PA, OH, IND, ILL,
MO, OKLA, TX, NM, ARIZ AND INTO CALIFORNIA TO SAN DIEGO. TO FURTHER IDENTIFY
VEHICLES SEVERAL ANTENNAS ARE ATTACHED TO EACH VEHICLE. MOST VEH ARE EQUIPPED
WITH RADAR DETECTOR EXTENDERS AND RADIO SCANNER EXTENDERS. AT THE PRESENT TIME
THERE HAVE BEEN 7 ARRESTS MADE IN THE SYRACUSE AREA ON THE NEW YORK STATE
THRUWAY - INTERSTATE 90.

AUTH CAPTAIN B M ARNOLD             GAUNAY  2-29 PM
  ACTING TROOP COMMANDER
```

The All-Points Bulletin from the New York State Police put out a nationwide alert that the race had started. Ed Preston had a contact there, who sent him a copy. Ed especially liked the reference to the two of us: "Operators arrested for having radio-receiving devices with frequencies allocated for police use."

Chapter 13
Leaving the Past Behind

Now some guys they just give up living, and start dying little by little, piece by piece.
Some guys come home from work and wash up and go racin' in the street.
—Bruce Springsteen

Tim took over. I couldn't drive; I needed some time to recover. I was overwhelmed. Two arrests and the shock of avoiding the pile-up in Dayton really put the pressure on. These surprise events on top of my compromised emotional state affected my desire to continue. I just didn't want to drive anymore. Tim was also showing signs of stress. The mood in the car was subdued. We weren't even talking to each other. Neither of us had imagined there would be so many setbacks, and we weren't even 1,000 miles into the race. The highway patrols were out in full force, and they all knew who we were, where we were, and what we were driving.

Another thing I didn't appreciate until we were running the race was all the lane changing and braking/accelerating we had to deal with. I didn't anticipate how stressful and exhausting it would be. We underestimated the traffic density on highways east of the Mississippi. Looking back, those first 1,200 miles were the most difficult. We became exhausted quickly and punished the car.

Edward M. Rahill

In Indiana, we saw another rally racer getting arrested; the handcuffs were out again. It was the Porsche 934 Carrera. It looked like both drivers were under arrest. Tim just mumbled, "Well, he's done. The race is over for them." That team had started later than us in the rotation. Catching up to a car that started after you is not an indication that you are doing well.

But our pre-race research had paid off. We'd avoided a line-of-sight speed trap because of what we'd learned about Indiana's passive speed-tracking techniques. Two troopers were on the side of a bridge, partially camouflaged by brush. I gave Tim a heads-up, and we reduced our speed to under 60 mph. We would have been arrested if we hadn't been aware of that technique, based on what we'd just seen twenty miles before. Forty-five minutes later, we were in Illinois on our way to St. Louis.

Suddenly, out of nowhere, the engine died. There were a lot of four-letter words being thrown around, but we were lucky. We had sufficient momentum from the speed we had been traveling to glide to the next exit. Added luck: a service station was at the corner. Tim did a great job of bringing her in without power brakes or steering. We coasted into the station.

Within fifteen minutes, he found the problem: a blown circuit in the ignition system. He was able to work with the mechanic, and it took another fifteen minutes, but we located a replacement from an auto parts store a few miles down the road. Tim was back with the part twenty minutes later, and he had the car up and running in less than thirty. We took a few minutes to fill the auxiliary tank and top off our main fuel tank.

Tim and I looked at each other. I could see the stress and disappointment in his eyes.

"Ed," he said, "this has been a hard run. I wanted more than this." He slammed his fist against the car and turned away. I'd never seen him like that; he was usually positive and joking around, but now I understood he was hurting. It was painful to hear him say that. I felt powerless, and my demons from the past were eating away at me. I could tell he sensed my distress. At that moment, I became aware of how self-centered I'd been for the previous ten months. That's not who I am. We finished topping off our tanks and were on our way. We'd just lost another hour and change. Tim asked to drive. He needed to get the frustration out of his system.

The sun was setting. We were both beginning to feel that the race was a bridge too far. I'd reached a point of mental numbness after our third setback. We didn't talk for a while. An hour later, a few miles east of Highland, Illinois, Tim asked me to take over. I hesitated; I didn't want to drive. He was very tired. I just sucked it up and agreed. I drove toward the afterglow of the sunset on the western horizon.

He was working on a few time-to-distance calculations. I knew that what he was finding out about our progress was not good. He seemed dejected. After reviewing the time to cover distance from interviews with previous years' rally drivers, it became clear that we had little or no chance to make up for lost time. True, the route from the Mississippi River to San Diego historically had a higher average speed, but our arrests and breakdown had cost us too much.

"I think we're in last place," he said. "Of all the teams still in the race, I know we are. We're not even doing as well as we did last year. We haven't made it to the Mississippi, and we're already done." He paused, showing his exhaustion. "We'd have to make it to Texas by dawn to stand any chance of being in one of the top five spots."

"Illinois to Texas by dawn. It's already damn near midnight," he said in a dejected tone. "In all our research, we never found anyone who recovered from this many lost hours. It's never been done," he said in a low and tired voice. He then turned to adjust his pillow. "I'm gonna try to get some sleep. Maybe we should just chuck it and go home." He'd reached a state of complete exhaustion, having gotten less than two hours of sleep the night before. This final setback broke our will.

It was somewhere before midnight, and as I drove, I could see the city lights on the horizon—it was St. Louis. Seventeen hours on the road, and we were beaten down. I believed that the race was over for us. I'd lost not only my desire to go on, but my will to face adversity.

I looked down at the speedometer, barely doing 80, and my thoughts drifted back to my youth when I first discovered endurance racing. As a kid, I dreamed of someday running such a race. I'd spent years envisioning this road contest, thinking about what it would take to win. But now I was deflated. I came to realize it was all a dream, a fantasy . . . and I was facing a lost cause.

Then I thought about the prior year when Nancy and I were driving this same road. I was hurt as I recalled what Angie had confided the week before, that when Nancy had heard that Tim and I were running the race again, she had been disparaging about how I had performed last year, saying she didn't think I had what it took. Nancy was right to move on, I thought. I'm a loser, just another Don Quixote tilting at windmills.

When your spirit breaks, everything else falls with it: your love of life, for others, and for yourself; your emotional stability, self-confidence, and self-worth. But I was most ashamed that I'd lost my nerve—the courage to continue the race.

At that point, I said to myself, *We're four hours south of Chicago; it would be easy to turn north and go home.* I wasn't there for Tim who needed encouragement. I didn't know if I could go on myself. I just wanted to give up. I was in despair. I felt the crushing blow of discovering I wasn't the man I thought I was. The mental exhaustion of the last ten months was taking hold.

Remember Where You Came From

Approaching the point of emotional collapse, my mind became quiet and almost numb. I was still conscious, but the sensation of reality was changing. Even the sound of the road was fading. It was as if my consciousness was fading. The world I was in was still there but becoming distant—very distant. The road was there, but I was watching it from afar.

Then, memories started appearing—slowly at first, but then they became thick to the point of confusion. My conscious mind had a jolt of fear from the lack of control of my thoughts. But just as quickly as the fear came, it started to leave as these memories from my past crystallized. Suddenly, I was back in the days of my youth with Mom during one of our after-school talks.

I remembered myself as a young boy and those moments when she was talking to me. I could tell that she was preparing me for something.

"Remember where you came from. Draw on the foundation of your character. That is where you will find the courage to reengage. It will help you recover from the emotions that are crippling you; it will set you on the path back to who you are."

It felt good to remember those messages from the past; they were nurturing. I hadn't relived the early part of my life for decades.

Then, in a flash, I returned to the present. There was only the sound of the engine and the road. I had a shock of fear at the thought that I might have been unconscious for a moment, but everything was all right. I only saw the amber glow of the instrument panel: the speedometer, tac, voltage, temperature, fuel, and oil pressure gauges. And there was the flow of the road markings as we passed each one at 68 mph. The car had slowed down, but everything was okay. When I was deep in thought, I brought her up to just under 90 mph. I was trying to reengage, trying to go on. I just didn't have the heart to take her to the next level. I was intimidated. I was ashamed of the thought of continuing the race. I just didn't have it in me to go on.

I was somewhere outside Rolla, Missouri, near a rise on the highway. I saw an off-ramp to a side country road and took it. I pulled off and got out of the car. I needed to collect my thoughts.

From the top of the rise, and I could see for miles—maybe ten miles. It was quiet, and there wasn't another car in sight. I heard crickets as I looked at the night sky filled with stars. The sky was as beautiful as I'd ever seen. A crescent moon in its last phase was in the lower western sky, shedding just enough light to reveal the pale outline of the terrain.

I was alone with my thoughts. I'd held out hope that somehow this race could rebuild my spirit, which had been beaten down over the last year. I felt that all hope of success had been crushed by the events we'd just been through. I reflected on my feelings of lost love, of being alone. I felt abandoned. Self-pity was overtaking me. I'd never recovered from Nancy's rejection. My will to love life was gone. I was overcome by the reality of how far behind we were in the race, a race I had imagined since I was a boy. I became misty-eyed. I felt defeated.

Perhaps it was time to do what Tim had suggested—to give up, to go home. This brought more pain as I reflected on having to face friends and family back home as a failure, just as Nancy had predicted.

I dropped to a knee, lowered my head, and shed a tear, overcome with grief. Finally, with the last gasp of my will I said, "God, what am I to do? I can't go on. Please help me." I was breathing hard; I felt my heart pounding. I felt helpless. I prayed for the strength to go on.

Edward M. Rahill

I looked down at the keys in my hand, then back to the stars. That was when a memory came to mind. I recalled a fall night back in Barrington Hills when I pulled over to listen to Judy Collins and look at the night sky. With tears in my eyes, I looked down at the road.

Just like moments earlier on the road, I felt my consciousness was fading. The emotions that had overwhelmed me moments ago were also quieting.

As I started to calm down, I gained a sense of clarity. A new presence was arising within my soul, and it was bringing new emotions, an energy I didn't understand. As these feelings became more present, they began to displace the anguish. I looked back up at the sky, down the dark empty road, and then back to the car. Shedding a few tears felt good—a release of the emotional pressure. Then I noticed my breathing had slowed down, and I was calm in a way I hadn't been in a long time. I looked back at the sky and thought, *Maybe this is what it's all about. Life isn't so bad when you're living for the moment.* In this state of mind, it seemed that the demons of the past and my fears of the future were fading away.

That was when I heard Mom's voice: "*Mick, the most devastating emotion you will ever experience is fear. It will break your will and turn you against everything you believe in. When that feeling comes, force yourself to recall your past and who you are. From your past, you can find the courage to reengage in the struggle, it will show you the way.*" I became alert to this message, searching my past for anything that could guide me.

It was then I recalled another time when I was also in a desperate, hopeless situation. I remembered standing on the starting line of a quarter-mile track at the regional All-Catholic Championship meet. In my mind's eye, I saw each of the opposing team's anchors pass me in sequence. They were all on their way to the first turn and ultimately the finish line. We were hopelessly out of contention. The improbable was quickly turning into the impossible, but I didn't care. I again dropped to my knee and prayed. "You made me fast. I don't know if it's enough. Please help me do what I have to do."

I got to my feet, and I felt like my soul was summoning all that my heart found true. There was an increasingly powerful feeling arising within my consciousness. I was in the process of reawakening to the man I once was.

My defeat in the face of what life had thrown at me was replaced with a new attitude. I felt adrenaline taking effect. My breathing was no longer shallow; I could completely fill my lungs. As I looked at the car and stared down that dark and empty road, I felt a passion building inside of me—a passion to reengage. The fear that had paralyzed me moments before was gone. After the most devastating year of my life, I was finally coming home.

As I walked back to the car, I was tuned in to the sound of gravel crunching beneath my feet. I got back into the car and fired her up, and when the engine came alive, my senses did too. I responded viscerally to the sound of the engine, its power. I left the side of the road and turned back toward I-44. I slammed the accelerator against the floor, and this quick motion briefly awakened

Tim. He mumbled something and was back to sleep in seconds. The wheels spun against the dirt road but gained traction once we hit the blacktop. I knew it was time to focus on the road ahead. As I accelerated up the empty road under full throttle, I rediscovered a sense of purpose. I was shifting the gears under power and brought her up to 85 mph, then 95, and then I broke 105. I allowed myself to bounce around 106 to 115; I had the will, but I still needed time to get back into it. I had to condition myself to faster speeds. I knew from experience that my mind would adjust, and that speeds that were intimidating in the beginning would become natural as I drove on.

Then, like an angry parent disciplining a wayward child, I started to rip into myself. I was embarrassed when I saw myself as less than the man I had wanted to be. Over the previous ten months, I hadn't been myself. I winced with shame when I realized how self-centered I'd been. I hadn't been there for my friends. I told myself that the devastation of losing the woman I loved was no excuse for self-pity. Feeling disdain for my past actions was a relief. I was breaking free from the self-imposed shackles of that last year. My mind started feeling fresh. It felt clean—not devoid of feelings, just in control of them. I thought about Tim. I'd let him down. He was frustrated to not have an encouraging teammate as he faced the bad breaks. That was about to change.

I made up my mind. To hell with the devastating setbacks. It was now about pride, self-respect, and willingness to embrace those who stood with me. I was going to reengage the rest of this race with all I had. *Life isn't so bad when you're living for the moment.* I needed to hold onto that thought and not drift back to thinking about how far behind we were, how far we still had to go.

Music had always been an inspiration. It was my connection to my soul, and to my car. I inserted a cassette into the player, kept the volume low, and shifted the speaker balance to the driver's side while Tim slept. I knew that the music would help me through the rest of the night. But that setup didn't work, so I grabbed the headphones and plugged them in. I now could turn up the volume and connect with the spirit within me and still be able to pull down the right side of the headphones whenever the CB signal meter alerted.

Springsteen and Seger dominated my playlist that night. Several songs had a serious or emotional theme, about a man fighting to recover from a crushing loss—just what I needed. I was listening to what my heart was telling me I had to do.

Two tunes just brought me over the top. They changed my mood from a struggle to a spirited run for the love of life. Springsteen's music made my pulse jump and helped me focus. The live versions of "Born to Run" and "Cadillac Ranch" reminded me to love the drive. I started to smile as I shifted gears to bring the Firebird up to her potential. I recall feeling my adrenaline-charged body pushing the car and looking down at the rpm gauge, then over to a cheat sheet Tim had put together to tell us our actual speed beyond the pegged 140 mph. I was running faster than that. I immediately slowed down to make sure I was in control. I was planning to run the car as fast as she could handle across the flatlands of the southern Great Plains; I just needed to make sure I used the speed when it was the right time to open her up.

That was when everything started to come together. All my life lessons were coming into play. I viscerally ran through everything I learned from my past, every time I'd made a difficult choice to press on when backing down would have been easier. I was going to run fast, flat out. I got nervous, but settled down when I embraced how good it felt to live for the moment. I then returned to my memory of the last quarter-mile race in high school. I started to repeat my racing mantra from that fateful day: *"One moment at a time, one stride at a time, one runner at a time."*

At that point, Seger's "Little Victories" started to play. It hit home. It was time to forget how impossible my quest was, how far I still had to go. Now I knew how to do it, how to run the race: one mile at a time. Each step would become a little victory.

I felt a surge of adrenaline, and my breathing sped up and deepened. I repositioned the car to deal with the traffic ahead. Speed would come once my rhythm was established. I ran through the gears in sequence. It felt good to be alive. I listened to the engine change from a low buzz to a high-pitched hum, then to a roar as the needle passed 5,400 rpm. The speedometer had already jumped past 130 mph was on its way up. I gave myself over to the experience, both mentally and physically. I felt the car's vibrations as she ripped through the air. Then I shifted into fifth gear, and the pattern of the engine sound started again with a roar, then an increase in pitch and an increase in rpm. I was now cruising at around 135 mph.

As I approached Springfield, Missouri, I continued to focus on the here and now. The late-night Springfield traffic, although light, started to feel like an obstacle course. As I sat behind the wheel of the most powerful car I'd ever raced, I recalled the years I'd dreamed of the chance to run a race like this. And at that moment, while I believed we were out of the race, I remembered a saying from my youth: *Sometimes lost causes are the only ones worth fighting for.*

We were well into southwest Missouri, and as I approached the Oklahoma line, I could see that the road had opened up. I put the odds out of my mind, and I started to talk to the car.

"Come on, babe, we can do this! One moment at a time, one vehicle at a time, one mile at a time." This newfound confidence settled me down. As I focused on the moment at hand, nothing could faze me. With the tunes in my ears, I smiled to myself and thought, *I was born to do this, I was born to run.*

Every time I opened the throttle, the car talked back as if to say, "I can give you more!" The brake-and-go was out; we didn't need it on the open highway. I was going to drive the line as much as possible. This increased some of the risk, but vehicles were few and far between that night, allowing me to maintain a maximum cruising speed. I became fixated on the road, watching for every detail, every sign of a change in conditions. It was here I was overcome with the feeling that I can do this. I dropped in another tape—Mitch Rider and the Detroit Wheels' "Medley: Devil with the Blue Dress On." This was another level of energy that gripped me as I pushed the car. But now it was time to settle down, just focus on each moment.

I saw the open highway, and then the traffic was gone. It was early Sunday morning. Rural sections between cities were empty, except for occasional eighteen-wheelers. All I could see was an uncluttered road. As the night progressed, the outside temperature dropped. Once in Oklahoma, I was able to open her up to her full potential for the first time. Outside Oklahoma City, I took advantage of a slowdown in traffic to take a quick bladder break in a bottle and grab some water and a candy bar, and I was off. I brought some caffeine pills, but they didn't seem necessary. With the hours behind the wheel and this level of intense driving, I should have been exhausted, but I was gassed up on adrenaline.

I could feel the car eagerly respond to my gas pedal's request for more as the cool night air fed the engine. The outside temp read sixty-eight degrees. The fuel-injection system was being fed all the O_2 she could breathe, and as a racing engine, she added all the fuel she could burn. I listened each time the car's sound changed from a guttural growl to a heart-stopping roar, then to a high-pitched whine, and my car's speed with it: 110, 120, 130, and at times faster, much faster. As the speed shot up, so did my awareness and control. The faster I went, the more it seemed like time was slowing down. My mind was operating on a new plane. Each lane change, each drift into the curve of the road was as natural as each breath. Speed did not seem scary anymore.

Despite driving that fast, it felt like the car was on rails. This was a result of its superior drag coefficient and the added ground effects enhancing the under-car vacuum, optimizing atmospheric downforce on the Firebird. I was fixated on the road and the markers ahead. I was covering over 200 feet per second. Therefore, I needed to focus past the next hundred yards. I focused on the next quarter mile and beyond, to allow enough reaction time to make adjustments.

I picked up I-40 outside Oklahoma City and was heading due west toward the Texas Panhandle. Deep in the rural, flat, sightly rolling areas of the southern Great Plains, I was amazed at how empty and wide open the road was. I was cruising at speeds in the 125-to-140 mph range. For up to five minutes at a time, I had the speedometer needle resting on the 140 mph stop peg, and she wanted to do more. I opened her up, asking her to accelerate—and she responded. I drove as fast as the car could go and still hold it together for the rest of the race. From their test runs, the GM team had said she should be able to sustain up to 140 mph for extended periods and over 160 mph for shorter periods. And if the conditions were right, and the engine did not overheat, above 175 mph was possible. They were right. I was approaching redlining the engine, 7,000 rpms in fifth gear. She had to be running north of 145 mph. We had 1,500 miles to go. I slowed to 130 to protect the engine. But I now knew she was a special car that could give me what I needed when I needed it.

I was living every second of the drive; I had almost forgotten how good it felt to experience driving this way, but now I was grateful it was back. Along the way, I would briefly experience a physical slump. Energy dissipated from my body and appendages. But as quickly as that happened, I reengaged with something like an adrenaline surge. There was a will to go on that would not let go. It was almost as if my body was tapping directly into my body's energy reserves, to go on.

When you are truly in tune with a car, it is not just your eyes and hands that tell you what's going on—the car talks to you through the vibrations in your seat, your legs, and your back. It communicates the changes in relative G-force when you are under a controlled rapid acceleration and when you are drifting. These signals made me aware of when I needed to back off and when she could do more. The sounds and vibrations of the car is its own language. When this all comes together at high speed, you're no longer driving the car; it's as if you are flying your car.

As I drove on, in the distance, I saw the flashing lights of a police cruiser. He had pulled over a BMW—it was one of ours. I slowed so as not to attract attention. For a moment, I wondered why we hadn't encountered more highway patrol cars. I overtook at least three other rally cars that I was aware of that night and had a run-in with a car I didn't recognize with Oklahoma plates. I was coming up on him and slowed to 90 mph as I passed him in the passing lane. It looked like a high-end BMW. I pulled back into the driving lane. He must have been surprised and pissed because he brought his car up to speed and passed me, then abruptly pulled in front of me. Here we were, approaching 110 mph, and I just wanted to move on. I pulled within ten yards of his bumper to draft his wake; I downshifted to fourth gear and began a slingshot around him. I could tell he'd hit his accelerator, but it was to no avail. The Trans Am just let out a roar and blew past him as I shifted into fifth gear. I hit 140 mph, and he backed off; his top end couldn't match mine.

For a couple minutes, somewhere between Oklahoma City and Amarillo, Texas, the speedometer was pinned at 140 mph. I then looked at the rpm gauge, it was at redline—in fifth gear. That could only happen if the car was running over 150 mph, just as the GM proving grounds techs said she could. I smiled as I realized that the back end of the Firebird's exhaust pipes had to be glowing red hot. In the dark of the night, it had to be spectacular.

I could see dry lightning in the distance. It brightened the entire nigh sky with every flash. It was breathtaking. I could feel its energy running through my veins. I suddenly felt, at least for this part of the race, that we were about to be part of something amazing. As the car ripped through that Oklahoma night, I could feel every beat of my heart. I noticed my shirt was damp with sweat from the intense muscle work I was putting my body through driving and shifting at those speeds. I sped through every curve, past every car and truck, and opened her up on every straightaway. I treated each vehicle as a new contest. I would continue to say to myself, *Another little victory.*

Every time I passed a vehicle at speed, I could hear the increase in pitch as we overtook it. There was a slight thud as I felt the Trans Am's encounter with the air wake from the vehicle, then a whoosh and a decrease in pitch as we passed it. Each time, I was reminded of how fast I was traveling. It was as if the other vehicles were just standing still. I was impressed by the car's willingness to hug the road, brake when asked, not drift, and accelerate on demand. I felt my mission, my purpose. I enjoyed the times when I had to slow down and navigate around cars traveling at the speed limit. Because

Edward M. Rahill

I knew that when I broke into the open, I'd hear that sound I'd first discovered as a boy, the most beautiful sound I had ever heard—the sound of an American V8 winding out toward redline.

I became emotional when I realized that I'd never again have the opportunity to experience such a drive. Memories came rushing back behind the wheel of a car. The bad breaks and believing we were out of the race no longer mattered. Now I was driving my car, I could open her up, I could be at peace, and my car was giving all it had for the rest of this race—that was all I asked.

I drove for six and a half hours that night. I focused on the highway and went as fast as I could. The car was set for night driving. The taillight kill switch was activated, and the high beams on the front were on. The CB radio volume/squelch was set to a level so I could follow trucker warnings about what was ahead, but it was low enough so Tim could sleep. The radar jammer was on with the activation switch moved over to my side of the car. The auxiliary fuel cell was half full, and the main tank was full. We had more than enough fuel to get us through the night.

In retrospect, I'm amazed at my sheer determination to maintain my attention to the task at hand for more than six straight hours. Four hours is considered to be the limit for continuous driving. But at the four-hour mark, I felt alive and responsive. I just let Tim sleep. I was running on adrenaline and willpower, my mind on the task at hand. But there was one more thing: it is the reason I believe in divine intervention—not in events themselves but in changing people's hearts and souls. I was reborn that night, and it was by the grace of God and the loved ones who came before me.

One Mile at a Time

Alone with my thoughts on the road, I had made peace with what had happened over the last year. As I drove, I recalled those special moments with Nancy and then how it ended. I couldn't deny that I had deeply loved her. Acknowledging this was part of my healing. But she was not to be for me. I could deal with that. Until that moment, I could not let her go, but it was time. Now I was driving into what Bruce had written in "The Promised Land."

At just after five a.m., I was running across the Texas Panhandle at speeds consistently north of 130 mph. The predawn haze helped me define the road ahead. I had switched from the auxiliary fuel tank to the main tank an hour before.

Tim woke up. "When do we get to Oklahoma City?" he asked, still groggy.

"We passed through Oklahoma City about two and a half hours ago. The traffic was not too bad. We passed through Amarillo a little less than a half hour ago. Right now, we're in the Texas Panhandle, just coming up on Adrian. We are about twenty miles from the Texas–New Mexico line."

I recall the expression on his face as he processed what I'd just said. Still half awake, he grabbed the map and began to study it. Then in a loud, thunderous voice he shouted, "No fucking way!"

Anyone who knew Tim knew how excitable he was. He immediately jumped to wide awake, and map in hand, redid the calculations. I could hear enthusiasm return to his voice.

"Let's see," he said, "Illinois . . . Adrian, Texas . . . Can't be! That's more than eight hundred miles! Holy shit, in a little over six hours! We averaged over 120, no, almost 125. Hell, I don't know, maybe more!" He blinked a couple times, and I could tell he was processing what had happened. He'd passed out from exhaustion six hours before, believing all hope was lost.

I just told him I was tired, and it was his turn. We were coming to a gas station where we could make the second fuel stop of the race.

I stopped the car, and then my mind and body started to shut down. I could feel my muscles in my arms and legs tremble and go numb as the adrenaline dissipated from my body. I had trouble getting up from my seat, balancing to get out of the car. I stumbled and couldn't walk. I fell to the ground, and Tim stopped refueling to help me to my feet. He almost carried me to the passenger seat.

I was drained in a way I hadn't been in a long time. It was a feeling that only comes from having gone all out. There was something satisfying about that feeling. I had a flash of the time I collapsed at the finish line on that track after the quarter mile in high school. I fell back into the passenger seat, exhausted, muscles quivering. I had gone beyond what I thought I could do that night. There was peace with that feeling.

I drifted into semi-consciousness, and memories of my race with Nancy came to mind. Even with the demands of this race, I couldn't stop thinking about her. But the thoughts were different now. The sense of hurt and worthlessness had been replaced with sadness. I knew I could live with that. That was the stoic way. What had happened the year before was now a memory; I was finally living for the moment. Four minutes later, the fueling was complete, and we were on our way.

The first hint of sunrise was behind us in the eastern sky. I recall the dawn light painting the flat terrain in reddish and yellow hues. It felt like I could see forever. As a rejuvenated Tim took the wheel, I remember saying, "We can do this."

The last thing I remember before my mind went dark was Tim saying, "You got us back into this race, now we have a chance. It's time for me to show what I can do." Then, in my last seconds of awareness, I heard the engine rev to high rpms and rubber squealing and felt the car lurch ahead with every shift Tim made. He proceeded to run through all five gears under full throttle. You could hear the tires screech as he powershifted through the next three gears. We still had a thousand miles between us and San Diego, but Tim was back. I was back. We were back!

Chapter 14
A Thousand Miles to Go

After about three hours of deep sleep, I awoke as we were cruising across rural New Mexico. I felt as if I was in a new world. We reflected on what we'd accomplished the night before. It didn't seem real, but it was. We were moving at speeds we'd never experienced the year before. This was when I felt something had changed between Tim and me. We shared the type of camaraderie that develops when two people go through a stressful challenge together.

"Tim," I said.

He could tell something was on my mind. "What's up?"

"I think we got a break last night. I think our bad luck may have opened a door." How could I have driven that fast for so long and not been detected?

"What do you mean? Yesterday was hell—how can that be a break?"

"I'm saying I drove like hell last night. The Missouri, Oklahoma, and Texas highway patrols should have detected me, but they didn't. I only saw one patrol car last night."

"Yeah, so? I don't get your point."

"What if we were so far behind that they didn't expect any more teams to come through? They were running double shifts for the race—there might not have been any cops left to run the night shift. We averaged 130 mph during my six hours and twenty minutes of driving. If that isn't a miracle, I don't know what is."

When we planned the trip, we discussed the problems we'd each had heading into California from New Mexico the prior year. To learn how to cope, we consulted as many people as we could to hear about their experiences driving through New Mexico and Arizona. Rather than follow the standard route on I-40 through Albuquerque and into Flagstaff, Arizona, as we both had last year, we decided to run I-54 south from Santa Rosa to I-70 to Las Cruces and I-10. That took us through the White Sands Missile Range. Although it added more distance to the race, the backroad route presented us with little traffic or state police enforcement.

We were starting to think that we might be able to have a respectable finish in the race. The previous year's winning team had set a record of thirty-six hours and ten minutes. We estimated we needed to average at least 95 mph for the rest of the race just to compete for a top-five position. That would be difficult since the previous year's winners had averaged 83 mph for the race. And that estimate had to include stops for fuel, unanticipated traffic, and no arrests.

We were a little nervous, thinking we'd miscalculated. As we began to question the risk, we were taking by traveling the backroads of New Mexico, I shared one of my favorite quotes with Tim. It was from the legendary Brock Yates, the founder of the very first Cannonball Run. When a debate would arise about what the team should do, he would ask one question: "Are you having fun yet?"

One Mile at a Time

Tim stopped. "Hell, yeah! Let's have some fun, let's just do it!" That ended the second-guessing. We would focus on the moment and enjoy being on top of our game and doing our best.

The whole race felt different. We started to relax, and it felt like we didn't have a care in the world. As the Smashing Pumpkins' song "1979" played over the speakers, we had fun driving. I realized how different this felt from where I'd been the day before. It was almost like I'd awakened from a bad dream, a very long one. This new world I awoke to was filled with promise. It was not long before we were just giddy with ourselves on a two-lane blacktop—great conditions, straight as an arrow, and you could see miles down the road. As a bonus, we'd only see another car once every twenty-five to thirty minutes. As it turned out, this was a gift of insight. Due to the national All-Points Bulletin, most law enforcement was focused on the northern route—not ours.

The sparse traffic allowed us to rest our minds, and I thought back to my days driving on the back roads and the Southern Tier Expressway of Western New York. I noticed that some of my intuitive reactions to potentially dangerous situations during the race found their roots back on those roads. I understood why I was so calm at these speeds: I'd seen something similar before. It's hard to explain unless you've raced, but over time, your mind adjusts. It is like the world around you opens up, everything seems to slow down, and speed is no longer unnatural. Going 120 mph almost feels like 70 or 80.

It wasn't long before we just lay back listening to the same cassettes and cruising north of 130 mph for a few hours before we were on I-54/70. Tim put on a tape his teenage cousin Christy had made especially for him to use on the race. The tape was of her favorite songs that she thought he'd like—mostly by girl bands. The first song was Blondie's "Union City Blue." It blew Tim and I away on the first chord.

"Holy shit, Tim! You're kidding me, this is a girl band?" In addition to Blondie, we heard tracks from Cyndi Lauper, Melissa Manchester, Bonnie Tyler, Katrina and the Waves, and Madonna. We could feel the energy of Blondie's "Dreaming," Cyndi's "She Bop," and Katrina's "Walking on Sunshine" reverberate through the car. But the one song we sang along to was Cyndi's "Money Changes Everything." We didn't have a care in the world. I remember laughing and just slapping the dashboard and steering wheel like they were drums. When Bonnie Tyler's "Holding Out for a Hero" started to play, I looked at Tim and said, "So, are you her hero? Your cousin must really like you!"

He smiled. "She's my favorite." This was one of the happiest moments of my life, spending time with a good friend, great music, and a fast car. We were just out on a Sunday drive through rural New Mexico . . . at 140 miles an hour.

It was during this section of the race that our speedometer needle snapped. We were playing with bringing the car up to its top speed on open, long straightaways and then bringing her down. During one of the high-speed runs, we had the speedometer needle against the 140 mph stop peg and were still accelerating. The speedometer needle just broke off the center cable. We had to calculate our speed from the rpm gauge for the rest of the race using

Tim's cheat sheet taped to the dashboard. It only worked when we were in fifth gear, and it was in pencil, but it was all we had.

Both of us had become physically and mentally one with the car. It was an extension of us, of our bodies and minds.

I am convinced that the reason our intuitive and reactive driving skills improved with time. It was because we were constantly learning from hour to hour as the car reacted to certain situations, and we adjusted accordingly. This was why speed and quick adjustments became second nature as the race went on. It is why making adjustments at 150 mph in the middle of the Oklahoma night didn't even faze me.

You need a car that can take advantage of this type of highway when it presents itself. We were able to cruise between 120 and 140 mph and dabbled at over 160 mph.

Edward M. Rahill

Car-ma for Those Jersey Boys

We entered a section of the route that was breathtaking. It was amazing how open it was and how far we could see. This experience was new to us because the previous year, we'd both taken the northern route with more hills and mountains.

We drove for miles with a clear view of the road ahead. Gradually, we began to overtake a car ahead of us. As we approached, it looked familiar. It was the black Porsche 928S with the New Jersey drivers who'd given us trouble the night before the race.

"It's those assholes from New Jersey," Tim pointed out.

I could tell he didn't want to be diplomatic. "Just be cool about this," I said. "Let's see their reaction before we play our hand." We must have caught them by surprise because we were already up on them before they reacted. They brought the Porsche up to speed and pulled away.

Tim downshifted and was about to open the throttle, but I said, "Just wait. Let's play with them."

"What do you mean?"

"Let's just match their speed and every move they make. Stay on them but always in the opposite lane. That should drive them nuts."

Tim laughed. "So, you think we should really mess with them?"

"Yeah, buddy. Have some fun, and when the time is right, let's run them and see who has the better car. Back in Boston, they mocked our Trans Am as a toy. Okay, if we're a toy, let's play with them." Tim got it; he was laughing so hard our car started to weave.

The next several miles were a little crazy. The road had too many winding curves to count. We were running against the Porsche heading toward the rise we knew was ahead, running tandem through the curves in a game of chicken. Because of our car's position in the oncoming traffic lane, we were the ones to back down when a car appeared heading our way. Then it was back to running in tandem pushing each other side by side. The 928S was fast, a match for our Trans Am, but we started to feel we had a little more.

I studied the New Mexico road and topographic map and said, "The next three miles we should be running uphill, curves all the way, till we reach the summit for a mile. Then the fun continues—a steep descent into the desert floor."

Tim responded, "Okay. I wanna just lay it out after that. Let's see how the Jersey team responds to a road this long and steep into the valley floor."

"Yeah, buddy, I'm tired of this game," I said. "We are here to run this race, not them! Let's for now pull in behind them. Then, at the top of the hill, pull left to give me a chance to check down the road for oncoming traffic. If it's good, pull back behind again, draft them, and then try a slingshot around them."

We stayed with the Porsche for the next three miles, running the hills. As we cleared the crest of the last one, I could see the valley below. The road descending into the valley went on for miles, and it was stunning. It must have been a straight shot for the next six or seven miles. I grabbed the binoculars to check for oncoming traffic. There was none.

"Are we clear?"

"You bet. Go for it!"

In a NASCAR racing maneuver, Tim dropped back and pulled in behind the Porsche, downshifted from fourth to third, then floored the accelerator, drafting in the slipstream of the 928S to increase speed. He then swung back out into the left lane, slammed the accelerator, and we were off. The heart-pounding roar of the exhaust and the sound of the screaming 350 motor was thrilling. The 928S responded, accelerating as fast as it could, and we could hear its engine coming alive. Tim upshifted to fourth gear, and both cars benefitted from a gravity assist as we plummeted into the valley. Tim was in his element. For a minute or two, the 928S stayed with us, running abreast. The driver of the Porsche gave us the finger, and Tim looked over and gave one back.

"Just drive. I'll handle this." I turned toward them, smiled, waved, and mouthed *fuck you*, then flipped them birds with both hands. I saw the driver's angry face scream some obscenity at me. "Tim, with a prayer to the mother of divine acceleration, get us out of here now!"

Tim was standing on the accelerator, then let up slightly to shift into fifth. We were running nose-to-nose with the Porsche until we reached the desert floor. That was when it got a little hairy. We were starting to level out. We could feel the G-forces coming into play. I was pinned to my seat. Tim started to squeal, and then, by the grace of God, we began to pull away. Our American car was outrunning the best Porsche had to offer. I laughed. Within minutes, they cut their losses and dropped back. Five minutes later, we could no longer see them behind us.

We were ecstatic with our car's performance. We knew that the 928S had a factory top-speed rating of 162 mph, and we'd just pulled away from it in a wide-open run. I knew we had something special based on my run the night before, but what we experienced against one of the best production sports cars in the world just confirmed it. But streaming down the mountain with the 928S, with a gravity assist, we had to be running faster than 170 mph—it had to be approaching 180 mph, as the Firebird's tachometer was over the rpm redline. That was airborne speed, especially for a car of that period. A little scary when we thought about it.

A recent picture of a New Mexico highway reminiscent of the section of road where the Trans Am made its epic run against the Porsche 928S. (Photo license through Pixabay)

After we were in the clear, Tim told one of his jokes. "Hey, what's the difference between a Porsche and a porcupine?"

"I don't know, what?" I played the straight man.

"With a porcupine, the prick is on the outside!"

Just south of Chandler, Arizona, we left I-10 and took I-8 toward California. It was getting hot outside, but the car didn't seem to mind. Tim had just driven for over five hours, and it was shift-change time. We took advantage of some slow construction traffic to top off the tanks before San Diego. We had only stopped twice for fuel in over 2,800 miles—this was the third stop. I got back into the driver's seat. We both needed some down time, a chance to decompress. The next hundred and ninety miles through southern Arizona would be easy.

That run-in with the 928S really made us feel good about the car and the team we had fielded. We were having fun. It was a bright, sunny, wide-open day with light traffic, and we were just drifting between cars and lanes like they were standing still. We had no expectations of winning; we were just trying to collect our thoughts.

We talked about what we were going to do that summer when we got back home. Tim started to tell me about a girl he'd met who he was looking forward to seeing on his return. It was good to see him unwind and talk about life beyond the race. Most of our interactions for the previous six months were about getting ready. Now that we were on the last 350 miles, it was time to think about life after.

Then he got serious. "Ed, I don't know what happened to you last night, but you're back. I was worried. I could tell from the moment we started the race that you were off."

"I know..."

"After the two arrests and the breakdown," he confided, "I was ready to throw in the towel. I really didn't want to go on. But after your six-hour run, I was amazed! I got my mojo back!" I could tell he had something else on his mind. "You don't have to answer, but what happened between you and Nancy?" he asked.

I was caught off-guard. To get a little time to think, I said, "What do you want to know?"

"You guys were a great couple; I really liked her."

I sucked it up and said, "It was just that the timing was wrong."

"I get a feeling it was more than that," he said. "And don't tell me that what was bothering you yesterday had nothing to do with her. One guy to another, I know it did. Like I said, I don't know what came over you last night, but you're back."

"Thanks, buddy. It's been a long road, and I appreciate your comments more than you know."

"If you ever want to talk about it, just let me know."

"Thanks, Tim. I appreciate it and I will."

It meant a lot to me that he understood what I'd been through without any explanation. It had been a rough ten months. Sometimes it seems like society expects men to take the emotional blow, to suck it up like we can't be hurt, to act like it doesn't matter—but it does. But now I was feeling great, we were on a roll, life was good, and I was looking forward to what was next. I didn't say anything else. As I drove, my mind was wandering. I was thinking about where I was headed.

Tim and I continued to talk. He wanted to start his own garage business when he got back to Fremont, and maybe even save up to buy a boat. I told him it was time for me to buy a place with some land, five or ten acres, build a pole barn, restore cars, something I knew I'd like to do. My first choice would be a '67 or '68 Shelby Mustang. I had first fallen in love with that car when I was a sixteen-year-old kid working summers as a lot boy. I asked Tim if he could help, and the businessman in him piped up. "If you pay for the beer, sure!" This was a feel-good moment. We had become good, good friends.

We drove for the better part of an hour at speed and just took the experience in. But we weren't giving the best level of attention to detail if we wanted to avoid being detected. We were cruising at 115 mph. Twice the national speed limit . . . plus five.

The hell I'm gonna to be arrested a third time!

It shouldn't have caught us off-guard, but it did. From our research before the race, it was clear there were two possible routes to San Diego once a team had reached New Mexico. There was the northern route, which took I-40 from Amarillo to Flagstaff, Arizona, then I-17 South to pick up I-8 into San Diego. The northern route was being used by most of the teams. It offered more resources along the way. But it was also the route that police enforcement expected the race teams to follow.

The route Tim and I chose was I-54/I-70 South through New Mexico, then exit to I-10 in Las Cruces, then pick up I-8 in Arizona. The key here: I-8 was really the only practical route into San Diego. Which meant that almost all the cars would funnel onto that section of the highway. The California Highway Patrol knew this and were waiting. We should have anticipated their actions.

As we passed through Yuma toward the Arizona/California border, Tim estimated we had 175 to 180 miles to go. About twenty minutes west of Yuma, I came up from behind on a California Highway Patrol car cruising westbound and blew past him before I even realized he was there. *Shit!* It was one of their new high-output Mustangs. They were rated at 120 to 130 mph. Then Tim noticed two more patrol cars behind an abutment sitting on the side of the road. The two of us had just been shooting the bull, cracking jokes, and we didn't even notice him until it was too late.

To add fuel to the fire, there was a helicopter flying eastbound patrolling the highway, and he was swinging wide as if to make a U-turn to head west. I vividly recall our scanner breaking with a heads-up to the patrols in the area. Tim and I listened as the patrol car reported over is radio, that our car had just passed him traveling at a high rate of speed and that we were ahead of schedule. They seemed to be preparing some type of response; it could have been a roadblock. I immediately dropped the car into fourth gear and accelerated.

We then heard that the patrol car was engaging in pursuit and the helicopter was too. As we surveyed the road ahead, it looked like we were about to be blocked. An eighteen-wheeler, who was on the side of the road almost two miles ahead, started reentering the highway. About ten to twelve cars were reacting to his move and slowing down. Then, we saw another California Highway Patrol car coming from the opposite direction, lights on, crossing the median and turning around toward us. This extra stress was the last thing we needed. I started to wonder how bad it could get. Were there other surprises awaiting us down the road?

"Tim, where are we?"

He was already on it. "According to this map, we're about to enter the Imperial Valley, and I'm estimating we're a little over eighty miles from the foothills of the Laguna Mountains." He thought we were just under 140 miles from San Diego. "If we can reach the mountains, we should be able to buy some time because the police only have line-of-sight radios." This meant they had no direct radio contact with patrol cars on the other side of the mountain range without radio relays, which was hard to do.

"We can reach the foothills of the mountains in about forty minutes if we get into the open and get some speed." The California troopers ran their patrols in teams of two, and both were behind us. Tim recognized the make of the copter as a Bell 206 series, the performance patrol helicopter of the day, which maxed out between 135 and 140 mph under standard operating conditions. From what we'd learned about the Trans Am during the race, we knew she was a match for the helicopter. But the impact on our performance in this extreme desert environment was the unknown variable. Our in-car outdoor temperature reading was already 108 degrees, and it was rising.

It was beginning to look like we were driving into a trap. After making it this far, could this be it? Was I good enough to pull through? The physical and emotional exhaustion from that last thirty-three hours, combined with the sense of a trap closing in, made me anxious. I didn't know what to do. I started to become emotional as I realized this was my chance, and I was not going to let it go. That led to an emotional stiffening of my will, and I thought, *Fear kills more dreams than failure ever will.* I was going to give it all I had. I refocused and thought, *Engage the mind, bury the emotions. We will find a way out!*

Tim was feverishly trying to devise a path out of this morass. I needed his help because the traffic was all I could handle, and he came through. "I don't think the copter can run near their top-end in this heat," he noted. "That's if we don't overheat, too! I don't want to be arrested for a third time." Tim laughed.

"You know, I think this time, if we get caught, we're probably going to jail," I said. "Can you handle that?"

There was silence, and we both smiled and said at almost the same time, "Let's go for it!"

I was in my element, which was a gift. After a day and half of being targeted by the most coordinated national traffic enforcement event in history, we were up against the best they had, and about to find out how good we were. I broke left and accelerated the car up to 130 mph despite the intense desert heat.

At that point, winning was not on our minds. We had been through our version of driving hell the day before. Now we just wanted to drive our way out of the trap. That was when Tim shut off the air conditioner to reduce the drag on the engine and aid in engine cooling. He then broke out the water bottles. In a matter of minutes, we were sweating unlike anything we'd experienced in our lives.

As we drove toward the pack of cars and the eighteen-wheeler, the challenge seemed overwhelming. Once again, I felt there was a possibility of not making it out of this. I could tell Tim felt it too. There was no clear path around the situation. We dropped our speed to 100, then 80. Finally, we decelerated to just under 60 mph, blocked by cars ahead of us. I just started to repeat my approach, my mission: *one car at a time, one mile at a time.* That settled me down. I had been accelerating and seeking gaps in the line of vehicles before the highway patrol could execute whatever plan they had. It was turning into an obstacle course, in which I needed to constantly shift gears, braking, accelerating, and steering past one car at a time until I finally reached a pack of cars and the eighteen-wheeler. We were blocked. There were three cars in the left lane, just sitting one car length behind the eighteen-wheeler in the right lane. There were two cars between us and the truck and at least a dozen cars behind us in both lanes.

I pulled to the right to give Tim a look. "Breakdown open but not for long!" he barked.

I immediately downshifted and jumped on the throttle, pulled right, and was off. But I was quickly running out of road. The two cars in the right lane were momentarily startled and slowed long enough to open a gap between them and the eighteen-wheeler. It was enough room for me to swing the Trans Am in. Now we were really stuck. This was going to be difficult. For the next few minutes, I needed to wait for things to develop. After thirty hours of running all out, the best strategy was going to be patience. I upshifted to fifth gear to lower the rpm as I noticed the engine temperature beginning to rise. I remembered my comment to Tim the day before: *Sometimes slow is fast.*

By this time, Tim noticed the California Highway Patrol cars gaining on the pack of vehicles that included us, still at least 150 yards back. The helicopter had already reached us and was cruising about 200 yards high and about 100 yards off to our left. Tim was watching this all develop.

"It looks like the two patrol cars were planning on lining up on each side of the road," he said. "I bet they intend to overtake us once we get past the truck and force us to the side of the road."

"Is there any chance to drive off road to get clear of this truck?"

"No, there's no breakdown lane. It's gravel and brush, and the truck is behaving like he's looking for an opportunity to pull over."

"I want to take a chance and run these guys. Do you see an opportunity to break free of this jam?"

I could tell he was thinking the same thing. He sized up the situation. The patrol car in the right lane was backed up by a line of cars. With no breakdown lane, he was stuck. The patrol car on the left side had made progress and was attempting to clear the string of cars ahead of him with his lights.

"If you can cause that line of cars to back off, that could temporarily slow the patrol car, and you might be able to take advantage of it."

We were in the right lane behind the truck, momentarily blocked by a vehicle in the left lane. The driver was flustered and didn't know what to do; he seemed to be looking for a way to get into the right lane, but we were already there, followed by the two cars behind us, and there was nowhere for him to go. If he had his wits about him, he could have accelerated to get ahead of the truck and then flipped into the right lane. But most drivers just freeze when they see a highway patrol car coming up on them. Their instincts are to just find a way to pull over. At that moment, I made a plan. The truck and the pack of cars were traveling at between 55 and 60 mph.

"I'm going to try brake-and-go one more time," I told Tim. We were already in the right lane lined up behind the eighteen-wheeler. I needed to find a way to get into the left lane before the patrol car reached us. Once he was on us, I wasn't going to be a fool—it was over.

Slow braking would cause the traffic behind us to react and hit their brakes. This would have a ripple effect on the cars in the right lane behind us and effectively keep the last remaining cars in the left lane from clearing to the right out of the way of the patrol car.

I tapped the brakes to give the string of cars behind me a warning. I intended to slow down, I then downshifted into fourth gear and hit the brakes. We dropped behind the truck by four car lengths and were running at 3,200 rpm. While dropping back, as Tim had suggested, I swerved slightly into the left lane to give the cars in that lane something to think about as I prepared my next move. This maneuver temporarily stopped cars from changing lanes to let the patrol car through. I hoped it just might open a spot in front of me for the vehicle to my left, blocking me to move into the space I had vacated. My heart was in my throat; if he did not take that moment to change lanes, we were dead—there was no way out of this dilemma.

He did! The driver hit his turn signal and was moving to the space ahead of me. But it was not over yet. With his change of position, the car behind him hesitated due to my previous intentional drift into his lane, but then began slowly accelerating to take his spot. I had to move fast. I tapped the brakes one more time, and to get the car in its optimum torque curve, I downshifted into third gear and opened two-thirds throttle. I accelerated until almost hitting the bumper of the car ahead of me, and swung the Trans Am into the space he had just vacated.

We were finally in the left lane, and the road was wide open. Still in third gear, I immediately stood on the pedal, and we exploded past the truck, from an estimated 55 mph to just under 100 mph in just a couple seconds. We had finally broken free of the trap and the traffic. Now running at 6,200 rpm, I upshifted into fourth gear, dropping the rpm to 4,800. I opened up the Trans Am to just below 5,200 rpm and shifted into fifth gear to reduce engine heat. We had a top speed higher than the California Highway Patrol Mustangs, and we knew we could outrun them. But a new problem arose: the brakes. As I ran the last brake-and-go to get out of the traffic jam, I noticed brake fade from the front rotors.

"Tim, we're losing the brakes. Soon they will be as useless as a hand brake on a jet." Three thousand miles were finally taking a toll on them. This meant the brake-and-go was done. We could only drive one way—all out—and it wasn't over yet. We could no longer drive aggressively with these brakes.

The patrol copter had fallen behind as we broke free of the jam, but he was still there. He dropped his nose to pick up speed. He had to have been surprised by how quickly the Firebird accelerated out of the jam, but now he knew what he was up against. He was flying over the eastbound lane matching us in speed.

"Well," Tim said, "I guess we're gonna find out who's faster in this heat."

For us, high temperatures had two negative effects. Less dense air feeding the engine reduced its power. Second, the impact on the engine's components could cause overheating. Overheating exacerbates the impact of high rpm on engine components, increasing the rate at which each component expands relative to the others, creating more friction. It just gets worse; it's a compound problem—heat creates more friction, and more friction means more heat. This results in the engine components increasing their drag and a reduction in overall horsepower and power output. In the end, there's also a risk of component failure.

The helicopter had the same problem, but not to the same degree. His engines were turbine shafts and ran at a very high rpm and at much higher temperatures. A bigger issue for him was that

One Mile at a Time

as the air temperature rises, there's a decrease in air density. It's an aerodynamics problem. The helicopter's main rotor, basically what a helicopter's propeller blades are called, depends on the density of the air to create "lift" to pull it ahead through the air. The less lift, the less potential for speed. Hot air temperatures generally result in a decrease in air density. Therefore, a helicopter would have less force pulling it though the air, which would reduce as the air got thinner. That is exactly what happens when air temperature rises.

We were at a make-or-break moment, and I knew it. There could not be a more extreme environment for pushing a car than the midday desert conditions we were facing. But the patrol helicopter was facing the same conditions. We continued to accelerate, and we had already reached and surpassed 115 mph. I gave Tim progress updates; the helicopter was staying with us. We were running somewhere around 110 mph when I shifted into fifth gear, and that was when I started to sense a difference.

The car's engine temperature gauge was rising, but our speed was too. Tim was calling, "Speed, 115 mph," and "Temp, high." With the engine temperature rising, he made our final move to cool the engine. He turned the climate controls from fan air to full heat and cracked the windows. It was about to get brutal inside the car. The Trans Am and helicopter were both accelerating. We could hear and feel the car's engine vibrate with a high-pitched hum and the roar of the exhaust as we passed 120 mph. That was when things started to break in our favor; we began to pull away, slowly at first, then faster—125, 130, then to just under 135 mph with the temp holding. The sound of the engine told me she was under strain, the temperature gauge told me she was running hot. But I could sense she was going to give me more.

Within a minute, we'd pulled almost fifty yards ahead of the patrol copter, and the rpm gauge indicated an increase of another 200 rpm in the previous ten seconds. Within three minutes, we were at least 300 yards ahead of the helicopter. We were drenched in sweat, and our Trans Am continued to pull away from the patrol copter. Was it fast enough?

Down the road, we could see waves of atmospheric shimmer as the pavement heated the rising air. This wasn't good news for the Firebird's engine, which was already straining in the desert heat. But a more immediate problem was developing: traffic. The eighteen-wheeler bottleneck had temporarily cleared the road ahead, but now we were catching up to the regular traffic. It was a Sunday in rural Southern California—not too bad, but still pretty dense. We came up fast on an eighteen-wheeler in the right lane and could see a couple cars that were just passing him and moving back into the right lane. I no longer had sufficient braking power to deal with the situation, so it was time to rely on the engine for help. I dropped the car into fourth gear and slowed down. The rpm gauge jumped almost 1,800 rpm, and I noticed the temperature gauge moving up. I tried shifting back into fifth to drop the rpm, but that caused the car to lose an acceptable throttle response and the ability to respond quickly at the speed we were traveling. I shifted her back into fourth gear.

"She's getting hotter!" I said to Tim. "She can't operate at these rpm ranges for long. What's the call?" Tim needed a few more seconds to see what the second car was going to do.

Waiting, I positioned us as far left as possible to give us a wide berth. We waited for what seemed like twenty seconds to get closer to the truck and cars. We were approaching at a much lower speed due to the reduced effectiveness of our brakes. Slowing down had another consequence—less air flowing through the radiator to cool the engine. Tim was calling out the progress of the copter. He had caught up and was on us; it was time to make the call. Tim announced that the vehicles ahead were staying in their lanes. Then he shouted, "Go!"

I downshifted into third with the throttle wide open to give us a jump and then moved quickly back into fourth, and we were off. As we passed the vehicles at speed, we felt a sudden thud as the Firebird encountered the air wake from the vehicles, then the decreasing pitch of the *whoosh* sound as we passed. The combined sound of our car's engine and exhaust under full throttle and the buffeting we felt driving through the air wake was impressive. Then I shifted back into fifth gear and let up on the accelerator to take the pressure off the overheated engine and assess the situation.

The Trans Am's temperature gauge was just over the redline and in the warning zone. Although we didn't say it, we were worried about the outcome of this chase. We hoped the move into a higher gear and lower rpm range combined with the faster speed would start to cool the radiator. The move seemed to momentarily halt the rise in engine temperature, but it did not drop. As we approached 120 mph, Tim could see that the copter stopped gaining on us. We were in a stalemate. We needed to resolve this chase; I didn't feel the car would hold together much longer.

"Tim, we need to end this now," I said. "If he stays with us into the mountains, he'll eventually be able to radio ahead."

"I know," Tim said. "They'll know we're coming and waiting for us on the downside slope." He looked at me. "You know the risks!" I nodded. He then said in a firm voice, "I feel the same way. What the hell?"

"Okay," I said. "If we blow the engine, it's been good knowin' you. I'll see you in jail."

He just laughed. "What's gonna happen will happen. Do you think they'll put us in the same cell?" With a big grin, he said, "After two days in the same car, I'd prefer my own."

I smiled back and said, "Let's get outta here."

I slammed the accelerator to the floor and opened up the throttle one more time, and she instantly jumped. We were momentarily thrown back in our seats. Even with the heat of the desert, she was still a powerful engine. One more time, the engine screamed, and the exhaust roared. We were running wide open; there was nothing more I could do. I glanced down at the engine temp gauge. It was almost off the scale. The pitch of the engine rose as we picked up speed. A minute later, I glanced at the rpm gauge, then at the paper estimating the equivalent speed. She was running north of 140 mph. I was waiting for the engine to seize.

Tim was still tracking the copter's progress. "He's trying to stay with us."

Then, suddenly, at the four-minute mark, he erupted with a shout. "He's got smoke! He's done! He's heading back! We did it, he's backing off the chase." I could see the joy on his face as he watched the copter turn and head back. At that point, the pilot must have concluded he could not stay with us in the desert heat and his systems were overheated, just as Tim had predicted. He just gave up. Done! Life was good! Tim was beside himself. For me, it was a huge relief; I started to laugh. For the previous twenty minutes, I really didn't know if we were gonna make it. The last ten, I'd been waiting for something to go wrong with our car. Now the chase was over. After a couple more minutes, the copter was out of sight. I took my foot off the accelerator and slipped the car out of gear to slow down and cool off. We coasted down to about 80 mph, then shifted back into gear and started to slowly regain speed.

Tim started to crack a few jokes, but then he paused and said, "What do ya say? Let's turn around and do it again! Except this time I wanna drive!" I just gave him the nastiest look I could muster. He started to laugh all over again. I was just relieved to get out of the situation.

The traffic was minimal, and the road was wide open. We estimated we were seeing about three vehicles per mile. After about ten minutes, the engine temperature gauge dropped back into the high end of the safe zone and Tim turned off the heat and gradually cooled down the interior of the car. None too soon. I drank a bottle of water in thirty seconds.

Tim turned to me. "You know, if you think about it, we technically didn't run from those California troopers."

"Why do you think that?" I asked.

"Well, they never got close enough to pull us over!"

I thought about it for a minute, then I started to laugh. "Tim, if I ever get arrested again, you can be my lawyer."

That last run was a little out of character for me. Running stealth has always been my style. I'd just taken several calculated risks to break free of the jam, including risking blowing an engine and outrunning a police copter—something I wouldn't have had the nerve to do even a day before.

Once we were well into the Imperial Valley, then the foothills, the traffic started to increase, and the outside temperature was falling. With more traffic and winding roads through the hills, we had to slow down, and the tachometer indicated we were moving between 80 and 110 mph based on the conditions. Finally, we tried to settle down and cruise in the 90 mph range from that point on.

Most cars can briefly hold high speeds. I know several in the race had near super-car capabilities. Those figures were test-track numbers. Trying to hold those speeds for more than five minutes was not realistic. But for a car to hold that speed for that long in a desert with over 100° temperatures was beyond all expectations, not just for our car, but for any car of the period. For a car that had just run more than 2,800 miles and averaged faster than 104 mph for the previous 1,200 miles, it was beyond all imagination. I thought about the car and all the support we received to get where we were. We owed a lot of people for helping us build a car this bulletproof.

One Mile at a Time

Modern-day photo of I-8 westbound heading into the foothills of the Laguna Mountains. Imagine the buildup of heat as we approached the afternoon and the extreme desert environment we were experiencing. I estimate this photo was taken about ten or more miles west of when we first had our encounter with the California Highway Patrol. Most of the breakdown lanes were not in place in the 1980s.

Chapter 15
Setting Records and Wrecking a Car

From the patrol radios, we could tell law enforcement was surprised by our appearance . . . and that we were early. As we drove on, Tim and I wondered if that could mean we were the first car into California. It didn't seem plausible. I realized that within a couple hours, depending on traffic, the race would be over, and then what? It had been a long run.

As I drove through the Imperial Valley and then the southern end of the Laguna Mountain Chain, the sun was already in the afternoon sky. If Tim and I had had any wits about us, we might have understood what that meant. We were two to three hours from the finish, and we were a little more than thirty-three hours into the race. After every setback, simple math meant we were running at a pace equal to if not faster than the record for cross-continental car racing. But after what we had been through over the past day and a half, we didn't care where we would finish. We were just cruising on I-8 at racing speed. We felt at peace; life was good.

As we approached San Diego in the afternoon, traffic on I-8 slowed to about 40 mph. Finally, we exited the interstate onto the San Diego side streets. At a stop, Tim asked if he could drive the car in, and I said okay. At that point, I didn't care who was driving. We switched, and he immediately lost his patience with the traffic.

Edward M. Rahill

Before I knew it, he had the Firebird over the curb, driving on the sidewalk for at least fifty yards. We were cruising down the sidewalks of San Diego. After I regained my composure, I suggested that he stay on the sidewalk and drive up to the intersection that was blocking at least thirty cars. As we came to the intersection where a stalled car was causing the backup, we turned right with the traffic and did a U-turn as soon as we could and headed back to the intersection, bypassing the stalled car. I couldn't control Tim, but at least I could join him. He was the crazy one on our team. I couldn't have pulled off the race without him.

I got on the CB to notify Ed Preston and the team we were coming in. Ed said there were a couple patrolmen at the entrance to guide us in. The communication was somewhat garbled because a lot of people were making noise in the background.

Five minutes later, as we turned onto the road leading to the hotel, there were quite a few cars parked along the side of the road. They were honking their horns, and people were waving at us.

"What's this all about?" I asked.

Then, as we approached the hotel entrance, there were two patrolmen on motorcycles. To my amazement, they were waving at us and pointing to the Hyatt Islandia parking lot. I noticed another helicopter hovering above the hotel with a TV station logo on its side. Tim got excited and almost missed the entrance. He blasted up the ramp where a crowd was clapping and cheering. With all his excitement, Tim had accelerated up the ramp too fast, and the brakes, which had served us so well, were finally shot. He plowed into the cement base of a parking lot floodlight.

Not even thinking about the possible outcome of the race, I got out of the car, running to the table with the time-stamp ticket while cussing out Tim and demanding that he pay me for the repairs. I handed the card to the timer, looked back at the car, and then looked around. There was a local TV news van. A crowd was looking at me and clapping, but where were the other cars?

Ed Preston grabbed my hand and said, "Congratulations! You guys are the first ones in."

"What?" I asked. "What are you telling me?"

He smiled and repeated, "You're the first ones to make it to the finish line." I smiled. I was not making the connection; what he said was not yet sinking in. Then, he let me know we had to wait another twenty-five minutes to make it official, to be sure that any cars that left after us did not come in under the time limit and win. I was then approached by a group of reporters with all types of cameras and equipment.

I asked them to wait a minute, and I sprinted over to Tim, who was still looking at the damage to the car he'd just rammed into the lamp post.

He just smiled and said, "It's not too bad. At least it's drivable."

I looked at him. "Tim, it doesn't matter! We're the first ones in!"

He blinked and then his eyes widened. "What?!"

"Another twenty minutes, and it's official!" I grabbed him, and we headed back toward the reporters and the crowd.

We looked around, and to our amazement, it seemed like a party. There were around 150 people in the crowd being served beverages from an outdoor cash bar that had been set up by the hotel. It had become quite an attraction. Then, reporters lined up to interview us. One reminded me that it was my birthday. I had totally forgotten. The twenty-five minutes quickly passed, and cheers went up again. We'd just won the longest road race in the world, and we did it in record time.

It was a surreal, dream-like experience. Ever since things started to get bad during the race, we'd forgotten any chance of being in the running. All we wanted was not to give up on ourselves, not to fail. In Illinois, we were very close to ending the race, and now to be standing there in front of those cameras, it didn't seem real. All my life, I'd thought about what it would take to win a race like this, and there I was—I had done it! We had done it in the face of the most aggressive, nationwide highway patrol effort in U.S. history. Of the thirty cars that entered the race, twenty-seven showed up race day (three dropped out before the race due to news of planned police action). Of the remaining twenty-four, two broke down, and eleven were arrested and detained by the police. Only eleven were to make it to the finish.

A couple cars came in over the next hour and a half, but they had both started well before us and therefore were ranked behind us. Tim and I had just set a new cross-continental record of thirty-five hours and forty-six minutes, beating the prior year's Porsche record by twenty-six minutes.

Our odometer recorded that we had traveled 3,066 miles. Later, we discovered that the km/h-to-mph conversion gear had underestimated our distance by approximately 1%, making our total

One Mile at a Time

3,126 miles. Our average speed for the entire race, including stops, breakdowns, and arrests, was 87.42 mph. Removing the time lost from arrests and breakdown, we had averaged 98.43 mph from Boston to San Diego.

The Ford LTD Crown Vic "James Bond Special" sedan, the electronic-laden car, came in second place. They recorded a time of around thirty-seven hours and change. I realized how close our margin was—just a little more than an hour ahead of the second-place car.

We averaged over 104 mph from Amarillo, Texas, to the finish, including necessary stops and some heavy stop-and-go San Diego traffic. That's what we told the press, but when you looked at the numbers from St. Louis to San Diego, it was faster. That six-hour nighttime run through Missouri, Oklahoma, and Texas was exceptional. But you won't see that in the news. I felt uncomfortable letting the press know our real average speed. Our fuel capacity gave us superior range, and we only stopped to refill twice and top off once.

It took a night of sleep before the magnitude of what we had done sunk in. It struck me that Tim and I had done something truly special to have been that far behind in Illinois and still win. If we'd given up for even an hour or slowed our speed by 3 or 4 mph over the course of the race, we would have lost. That perseverance and the tenacity to focus on every mile—that was the margin of victory.

That night there was a celebration at the hotel. I came down and was being congratulated by just about everybody. I was looking for Tim, who was with a large group watching TV. As I approached, I could hear laughing.

Tim was saying, "I'm so embarrassed, but it was fun!" They were watching a replay of that evening's local news broadcast of our arrival at the finish line and Tim hitting the base of the light. The cameraman had followed me running to the timer and yelling at Tim about damaging the car. The two anchors were laughing as they described what happened. I had no idea the exchange was caught on tape.

That evening was lively and fun, and later that night, the eleventh team came in with harrowing stories of their encounters with the police. Tim and I never did see our Porsche 928S friends. I suspect they fell victim to police enforcement and just went home.

The Prestons put together a dinner party. The atmosphere was lighthearted and totally different from the night before the race in Boston. The stress and competitive mood of that night was replaced with a sense of camaraderie. One final tradition that was part of the Four Ball Rally was to have each of the teams give a brief account of their run and recount any amusing stories they'd experienced along the way. It became clear that at least four of us had been arrested by the same patrol officer, Sergeant Rodger Teague of the Ohio State Police, the same trooper who'd pulled me over. The rally participants voted to award Teague the 1984 Four Ball Rally "Super Trooper" award. As the rally winners, Tim and I were asked to see to it that Rodger received his plaque. Tim called some people back home to have a trophy made in his honor.

The next day, we got up early to drop off the car at a nearby service station to do a quick front brake pad job for the drive back. The major repairs could wait until we got back. Then press interviews started again at seven a.m., and we were on the phone with the news outlets until well into the afternoon. The party continued in our hotel room. Fellow racers were drinking beer in the morning—can you imagine that? We were able to get two phones in our room. It was a circus. Once I caught Tim telling a reporter that at times, we were running north of 150 mph.

"Tim, don't tell them that!" I whispered. "Do you wanna scare some desk jockey working for a Ralph Nader type, who doesn't even own a car, and wants to go on a crusade to pass a new law because of us? Let's see . . . The Tim Montgomery Unsafe at Any Speed Law!" Tim and the room erupted in laughter.

I was getting baptized to the realities of press interviews. The number of reporters who wrote their stories before interviewing me was frustrating. I've never since read a newspaper article at face value. I did try to take advantage of the interviews to object to an arbitrary national speed limit passed by a congress thousands of miles away from the people. One of my talking points was, "There's never been a law broken more often since Prohibition."

Edward M. Rahill

The winners' plaque of the 1984 Michael A. Preston Memorial Four Ball Rally

Most of the publicity was positive. I believe it was because at the time, there was an underlying nationwide resentment against Washington, D.C. and what was perceived as an unjustified 55 mph nationwide speed limit. Seventy-three papers, from the *New York Times* to the *Chicago Sun Times* to the *Fairbanks News-Miner* ran articles about the race and our record win. *The Sun Times* ran an entire half page. On June 5, our story was covered by UPI and AP, resulting in national and international coverage.

My hometown TV station—Buffalo's WKBW—sent a news truck to interview my mother. I can only imagine the look on her face when she opened the door, and she was staring at five people from the local TV station and a camera, lights, and microphone ready to interview her. Later, I saw the three-minute tape. As a former reporter herself, it wasn't long before she had taken charge of the interview. Other TV and radio media picked it up across the country. But one of my most cherished reports of our race came from my favorite commentator, Paul Harvey. "Now you know the rest of the story."

Auto racer
in a 36-ho

By Dick Mitchell

It was like a Burt Re nolds movie, a darede from Barrington and h partner from Ohio drivi from Boston to San Die at 86 m.p.h. to win $10,000 prize and not ev getting a speeding ticke

Edward Rahill, 32, Barrington metals tec nologist, said from room in San Diego's Hy Islandia Hotel that t road race had proved t supremacy of Americ interstate highway syste and had been quite an a venture.

He and Timothy Mo gomery, 32, a mecha from Fremont, Ohio, h been so dedicated to w ning the event that th had gone to the India polis Motor Speedway t spring for a refresl course, one of the pages in a detailed set plans for the 3,000-n auto race.

Their studies paid when they won the chael A. Preston Memo

Edward Rahill of Barrington, Ill., and partner Timothy Montgomery of Fremont, Ohio, stand in San Diego yesterday beside car they used to win the Four-Ball Rallye, a 3,000-mile, cross-country race in which they averaged 86 m.p.h. and won $10,000.

CHICAGO SUN-TIMES, Tuesday, June 5, 1984

cross U.S. sprint

Four-Ball Rallye, reminiscent of the Cannon Ball Baker Sea-to-Shining Sea Memorial Trophy Dash of the '70s that inspired the movies "The Gumball Rally" and "The Cannonball Run."

Both Rahill and Montgomery had gone through the Skip Barber racing school at the track previously. It prepares drivers of races such as the Indianapolis 500 and Grand Prix circuits.

"On the very first day they start drumming into you that the hardest thing to learn is when to go slow," Rahill said. "We went to the school for a refresher course, and we made a pact: 'When in doubt, back down and wait until the highway clears out.'"

Rahill's 1984 TransAm came prepared: High-speed windshield wipers, a 50 gallon fuel tank contained in a fire retardant fuel cell and driving lights that project a beam five times the distance of those on normal autos.

He and Montgomery spent about $1,000 to make their auto the first American model to outrun the higher-priced foreign competition. Averaging 86 m.p.h. for 35 hours 46 minutes means that sometimes during the race that ended Sunday evening, the Pontiac was traveling well over double the national speed limit.

Rahill and Montgomery avoided a speeding ticket but were charged with having an illegal police scanner in their car. And in Ohio, they received a ticket for making a lane change without signaling. At least six of the 25 drivers in the cross-country run were arrested on New York interstates.

Rahill and Montgomery had bond cards and extra money to pay traffic fines. "You have to be willing to pay the penalty if you knowingly do something wrong. We accept that," Rahill said. "We're citizens of this society and abide by those penalties."

But Rahill emphasized that avoiding speeding tickets was not the object. "We chose to drive in accordance to the conditions," he said. "At times we drove 45 or 50 and at other times, especially in the West, we drove at 130.

"We were able to drive at those speeds and do it safely," he said. "The American interstate highway system is the best in the world. They are designed for much higher speeds and speed limits should be set at what conditions allow and not arbitrarily by someone in Washington."

For their efforts Rahill and Montgomery won "a little less" than $10,000, and achieved personal aims. "We set a world's record and accomplished a goal," Rahill said. "It's not my life's ambition to keep running the race. I may do something else. Something more exotic, perhaps something in Europe."

Chicago Sun-Times of June 5, 1984

National

Ed Rahill (left) and Tim Montgomery, with the car they used to win the Four Ball Rally, a cross-country race. They are shown Monday in San Diego, Calif.

Illegal Race Called Game Between Police, Drivers

SAN DIEGO (AP) — The drivers zipped across the country at speeds of up to 140 mph, and police handed out tickets when they could, but an illegal cross-country auto race was really "a game on both sides," said one police dispatcher.

The third annual Michael A. Preston Four Ball Rally ended Sunday when Ed Rahill and Tim Montgomery wheeled into the parking lot of a San Diego hotel less than 36 hours and more than 3,000 miles after the race started in secrecy in Boston.

Almost as soon as the 24 race teams pushed the pedal to the metal on Saturday, state police across the country began scouring the highways for the racers.

"We knew they were coming and they knew that we knew it," Aimee Emerick, a dispatcher with the Ohio State Highway Patrol, said Monday. "I think it was a game on both sides."

Some states did better than others in upholding speed laws. Ohio Trooper Roger Teague singlehandedly stopped four racers.

"It made his day," Ms. Emerick said. "They were trying to trick him and he just turned it around on them. He hid behind several semi-trailers and could turn off his radar until he saw them. Then it was too late for them to cut their speed."

Teague stopped Rahill and Montgomery for failing to signal a lane change. Rahill, of Barrington, Ill., and Montgomery, of Fremont, Ohio, finished the race in 35 hours, 46 minutes, a record for the event.

"We averaged 87 mph and did not get one speeding ticket," said Rahill, who clocked the distance at 3,066 miles. "The only way you can cross the United States at those speeds is to do it safely."

Six drivers were arrested on the New York State Thruway near Syracuse on Saturday for driving about 100 mph, New York State Police said.

Sgt. James Fisher of the New Mexico State Police said there were no arrests linked to the rally in his state.

Colorado Springs Telegraph

Cross-country auto race 'a game on both sides'

SAN DIEGO (AP) — The drivers zipped across the country at speeds of up to 140 mph, and police handed out tickets when they could, but an illegal cross-country auto race was really "a game on both sides," one police dispatcher said.

The third annual Michael A. Preston Four Ball Rally ended Sunday when Ed Rahill and Tim Montgomery wheeled into the parking lot of a San Diego hotel less than 36 hours and more than 3,000 miles after the race started in secrecy in Boston.

Almost as soon as the 24 race teams pushed the pedal to the metal on Saturday, state police across the country began scouring the highways for the racers.

"We knew they were coming and they knew that we knew it," Aimee Emerick, a dispatcher with the Ohio State Highway Patrol, said Monday. "I think it was a game on both sides."

Some states did better than others in upholding speed laws. Ohio Trooper Roger Teague singlehandedly stopped four racers.

"It made his day," Ms. Emerick said. "They were trying to trick him and he just turned it around on them. He hid behind several semi-trailers and could turn off his radar until he saw them. Then it was too late for them to cut their speed."

Teague stopped Rahill and Montgomery for failing to signal a lane change. Rahill, of Barrington, Ill., and Montgomery, of Fremont, Ohio, finished the race in 35 hours, 46 minutes, a record for the event.

"We averaged 87 mph and did not get one speeding ticket," said Rahill, who clocked the distance at 3,066 miles. "The only way you can cross the United States at those speeds is to do it safely."

However, some authorities disagreed. "They're not proving anything, they're endangering lives," California Highway Patrol spokesman Jerry Bohrer said. "It's stupid, and if we ever find them doing that in California, they will be jailed."

Six drivers were arrested on the New York State Thruway near Syracuse on Saturday for driving about 100 mph, New York State Police said.

Winchester Star, Winchester, Virginia

Edward M. Rahill

Returning to Chicago

Tim and I enjoyed Monday night's banquet and had finished the press interviews by lunch. We just hung out and partied into the evening, but Tuesday morning, we got up early and left town. Ed Preston gave us a heads-up that the California Highway Patrol was none too happy with what we had done, outrunning their patrol team on I-8. His sources told him that Monday afternoon there was an arrest warrant out for both of us. He said he couldn't get a second source, but it was better safe than sorry. So, we hid the car in the garage, checked out, and got one of the other racers to secure a room at the hotel under their name for us. At 4:30 a.m. the next day, it was time to get out of town, and it was off to Las Vegas for a celebratory stopover.

When we returned to Chicago, my office held a surprise celebration at Rupert's Club 33, a nightclub associated with the Continental Towers where I worked. Rupert's had three bars, a copper ceiling, and a dance floor. But what made it special was the live music and an exceptionally talented ten-piece band. It was the most popular club in the area.

One Mile at a Time

Here I am, co-winner of the 1984 Micheal A. Preston Four Ball Rally at a rest stop in Utah posing with our Trans Am, the super-car that took on all challengers. After a tradition of almost 100 years of endurance racing, I never suspected that Tim and I had just won the last true cross-continental endurance race ever to be run.

It was about 6:30 p.m. when we got there and found out what was going on. There were several hundred people there, and about thirty were from my office. I was shocked and humbled by all the attention. Tim was surprised. Here he was in a strange place, and all these people he didn't know were congratulating him. But that didn't last long. He had a knack for socializing, especially when there was beer around. It didn't take long before he had people mesmerized by his account of the race.

An hour into the party, Tim and I were asked to give a speech to the crowd. I was a little intimidated. But I tried to say something simple and lighthearted. I paraphrased a joke I'd once heard. "A funny thing happened to Tim and me on the way to Rupert's tonight. We took the long road and stopped in San Diego to pick up a trophy!" And I raised it above my head. It went over well; they were kind. It was a fun event with live music. Angie had set it up, and my boss Larry, Tony, and even Bill Chamberlain stopped by for a few minutes. In addition, Angie had invited Terri, a beautiful and charming girl I'd just started seeing before the race.

People from my office and complete strangers wanted to hear about the adventure. What I didn't know at the time was that Tim and I had become minor celebrities in the Chicago area due to local media coverage and Paul Harvey's report of the race earlier that week. We didn't have a clue. We were once again hijacked by a reporter, but we didn't mind. It seemed like the entire company was there having a good time. All except Nancy.

At about nine p.m. that evening, Angie, her husband John, and I sat down for a drink. I thanked her for organizing the surprise event. I started to understand that a lot of people had become aware of what we'd accomplished, and it had become a bigger deal than I ever would have imagined. Tim and I, being effectively out of touch during our return drive home, had no idea what was going on.

I gave her an account of the race and how we came out on top. We talked about how we were overwhelmed with bad luck at the start and how we'd come close to giving up and heading home—

just as other entrants had done in the face of the nationwide coordinated police action. Everything came together as we passed the Mississippi. Overall, this race was beyond what I'd experienced last year. Angie's face lit up.

She repeated Nancy's comment that I wasn't up to what it took to run the race. But then she said she wasn't sure that her comment was genuine—it might have been hiding deeper feelings. Angie then said she believed Nancy was not over our relationship, even though she had been married.

"Let me give you an example of why I think I'm right about this," she insisted. On the morning of June 5, after Sunday evening's finish in San Diego, people in the office got the news of my win and my new record from Paul Harvey's radio broadcast and the *Chicago Sun-Times* half-page coverage of the win. When Nancy got to work and found out what had happened, Angie told me she seemed distressed. She started to shed a few tears, threw her keyboard against the wall, and left.

I felt for Nancy. There was no sense of revenge, just a twinge of empathy for how she must have felt. She, more than anyone, knew what I'd accomplished. We had run the same race together, and I appeared to have been outclassed the year before. The very race that seemed an impossible quest to her, I'd just won—and in record time.

I allowed myself to think about what had happened, to remember the sadness I'd felt when I thought she never had faith in me. Then I realized that what Angie was telling me might be true—that Nancy may have still loved me, or at least she still had deep feelings.

Otherwise, she wouldn't have reacted the way she did. I recognized I still had feelings for her, and that just led to sadness. There was no going back. I knew at that moment I would have feelings for her for the rest of my life.

Tim and I drove to my place in Barrington for the night. The next day, we headed to Fremont, Ohio, to drop Tim off. My plan was to drive back to Barrington, get the car repaired, and have a get-together when it was fixed. Well, the people of Fremont were also planning a surprise party. As we drove toward Tim's home, we could see banners along the street and a crowd gathered around the house.

One of the banners was almost twelve feet long. Tim's parents, his friend Jeff from the first race, work friends, his girlfriend, and a couple Fremont cops who'd helped us set up the radar jammer were all there. Tim was under the hood of the Trans Am, so with a long-neck Budweiser in hand, I went over to see what was going on. He was disconnecting an electrical harness.

"Hey, what's that?"

With his sheepish smile, he said, "It's the radar gun from the Fremont Police Department. They want it back." I just laughed; it could not get any better than this.

This was a casual Budweiser, hot dog, and cheeseburger party. It was a welcome event for us, and it was perfect. It was wonderful just to chill out with great people and celebrate. Tim and I spent most of our time telling our story. Talking to the kids was the most fun. Talking to an eight- or ten-year-old boy about our adventures was one of the most rewarding experiences I can remember.

One Mile at a Time

Rodger got his due.

The real surprise was the arrival the next day of Sergeant Rodger Teague of the Ohio State Police with his wife. He was greeted by everyone as if he was a long-lost friend, and Tim's mother adopted his wife. He asked to take my car out on the road and see what she could do. Of course I said okay. It was good to make a connection with him. I know when he pulled me over that he was doing his job. But to connect with him as one guy to another felt good. He returned and told me she was faster than what he had, and that I was a class act pulling over the way I did. We all went out that night trading stories, and Rodger let us know he'd nabbed three other racers that day. We already knew this from the celebration dinner in San Diego when we all submitted copies of our tickets.

We finally surprised him and let him know about the Four Ball Rally tradition of naming the best trooper in the race. We presented him with a trophy with his name on it and the title of Super Trooper of the Year. He was surprised and speechless. About three months later, we received a copy of that month's issue of *State Trooper* magazine. On the last page was a full spread with a picture of him holding his trophy and comments from his peers congratulating him.

Edward M. Rahill

Signs like this were all over Tim's hometown street.

One Mile at a Time

It was special for me when I was talking to a boy who was in awe of what we'd accomplished. Kids are always looking for heroes. As I told him our story, it touched me to realize I might have fit that role, even for a moment.

Edward M. Rahill

The next day, here I am with Tim Montgomery and Sergeant Rodger Teague of the Ohio State Police. The cake congratulates the champions of the 1984 Four Ball Rally, and Rodger received the Super Trooper Award for the most arrests of race participants.

One Mile at a Time

Tim's dad parked the car in Tim's garage for the Fremont fans to see.

My hometown wanted to make a point.

The first night I returned to Barrington from Fremont, there was a surprise awaiting me. I was pulling out of my driveway on my way to pick up a pizza, and before I knew it, I was being pulled over by a Barrington patrol car and was asked to leave the car on the side street. I was handcuffed. They had to have been waiting outside my place for me to leave in my car. I asked what I did and never got a clear answer. At the station, I was told that my driver's license was not valid.

I stayed pleasant and said, "I disagree, but you're in charge." I was booked and held in a cell for a few minutes when a sergeant and a couple officers walked in and asked me about the race. They were smiling and joking around. Finally, the sergeant apologized, saying he'd been ordered by the chief of police to arrest me at the first opportunity to make sure I understood who was in charge. He asked me if I could post a $200 bond to go home. I had my wallet, but I didn't have the cash. "Do you have a bank card?" the sergeant asked.

"Yes," I responded.

"The cash machine works at the bank down the street. Why don't you go there and get the cash you need, then come back here, and we'll get you home?"

They were letting me out of jail and trusted me to return with the cash, and fifteen minutes later, I did. I asked about my car, and they drove me back to it. They joked that they were taking a break for a few minutes, and it would be nice if I could get the car home right now. I had a particularly good relationship with those guys from then on.

About a month after the race, I received a letter from the Illinois Office of the Secretary of State informing me that my driver's license had been suspended for unspecified traffic violations. After speaking with a lawyer, complaining that my tickets were not in Illinois, he told me that "with fame comes consequences." He investigated the suspension and basically said that the appeals process would take at least a year and that was how long the suspension was for. His contacts told him they were ordered to "send me a message." The next week, I was on a plane to Tampa with my passport and social security card to visit my brother for a week. I liked it so much down there, I decided to become a resident of the state of Florida and got a Florida driver's license. It just so happened I had to fly back to Chicago the next week with my new Florida license.

I did have one embarrassing moment at the local pharmacy I frequented. Walking to the counter, the clerk looked at me and cracked a big smile and she asked me to wait. *What's going on?* Then the owner came out, smiled, shook my hand, and pointed to the wall. There was a framed picture of Tim and me from the *Sun-Times* along with pictures of other local "celebrities" who came into his store. I spent the next fifteen minutes telling stories to customers about the race. In Barrington, for the next couple weeks, be it at the local grocery store or on the street, I would have to chat with someone new about the race. It was fun while it lasted. Several years later, after I'd moved on, I came back to that drugstore. My picture was still on the wall. The woman behind the counter was a different clerk and did not recognize me. I asked about the picture. She said, "Oh, he was a local hero. He used to live here for a while."

Edward M. Rahill

Later that year and minus the beard, I was often asked to give my account of the race in brief talks to family, friends, and sometimes groups I didn't know. This one was at Thanksgiving in Buffalo.

GM

After the race, I had two more interactions with the GM proving grounds team. When I returned to Barrington, one of the first things I did was get the Trans Am into the dealership to fix the brakes and repair the damaged front end. Two hours after dropping the car off for service, I received an irate call from the service manager at the Pontiac dealership about the condition of the brakes. He finished by telling me that the rotors were cracked beyond repair and the only way that could have happened was if they were glowing white hot! Then, he said he wouldn't put this under a warranty repair.

I tried to calm him down, then politely asked him to call the number I had been provided by the engineers, at the proving grounds. Ninety minutes later, he called me back. He was calm, and in a steady voice, he said that GM had told him to fix the car and not ask any questions. He was to order new rotors because the rotors were not standard—they were racing components. They would be there the next morning, and the car would be ready by the end of the week.

Later that year, I received a call from my contact at GM asking for a favor—to trade the car in. I'm not sure why, but it could have been that the news of our success was percolating through the halls of GM headquarters, and some of our comments about help from the techs at the proving grounds were beginning to raise some questions.

By that time, I was joining Bell & Howell as a vice president, and they had a requirement that all executive cars be four doors. It took some sleight of hand, which raised eyebrows from some senior execs, including my new boss and CEO, when I negotiated a Grand Touring as my company car.

But as it turned out, I might have had a secret ally in the chairman of the board. His name was Don Frye, an ex-Ford executive during the famous Ford vs. Ferrari battles of the 1960s at the 24

Hours of Le Mans. I don't know how much he had to do with me getting hired, but I believe he knew about my victory the year before and my work in Mexico.

We owed the GM guys more than we could ever repay them. I never could have won nor set a record without them sticking their necks out for us. So, I gladly went through the added pain-in-the-neck paperwork and made it happen. Although I was a little pissed when I discovered the '85 was not as quick as the '84!

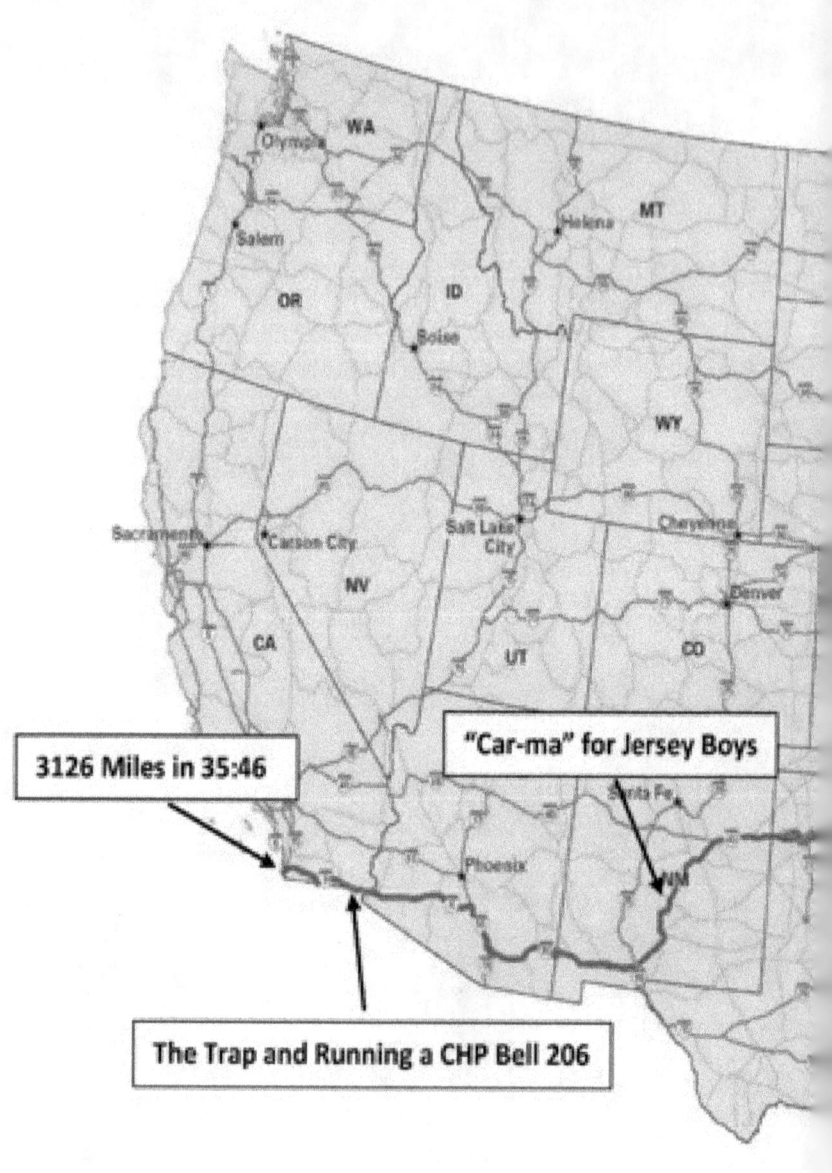

The 3,126 Miles of the 1984 Four Ball Rally

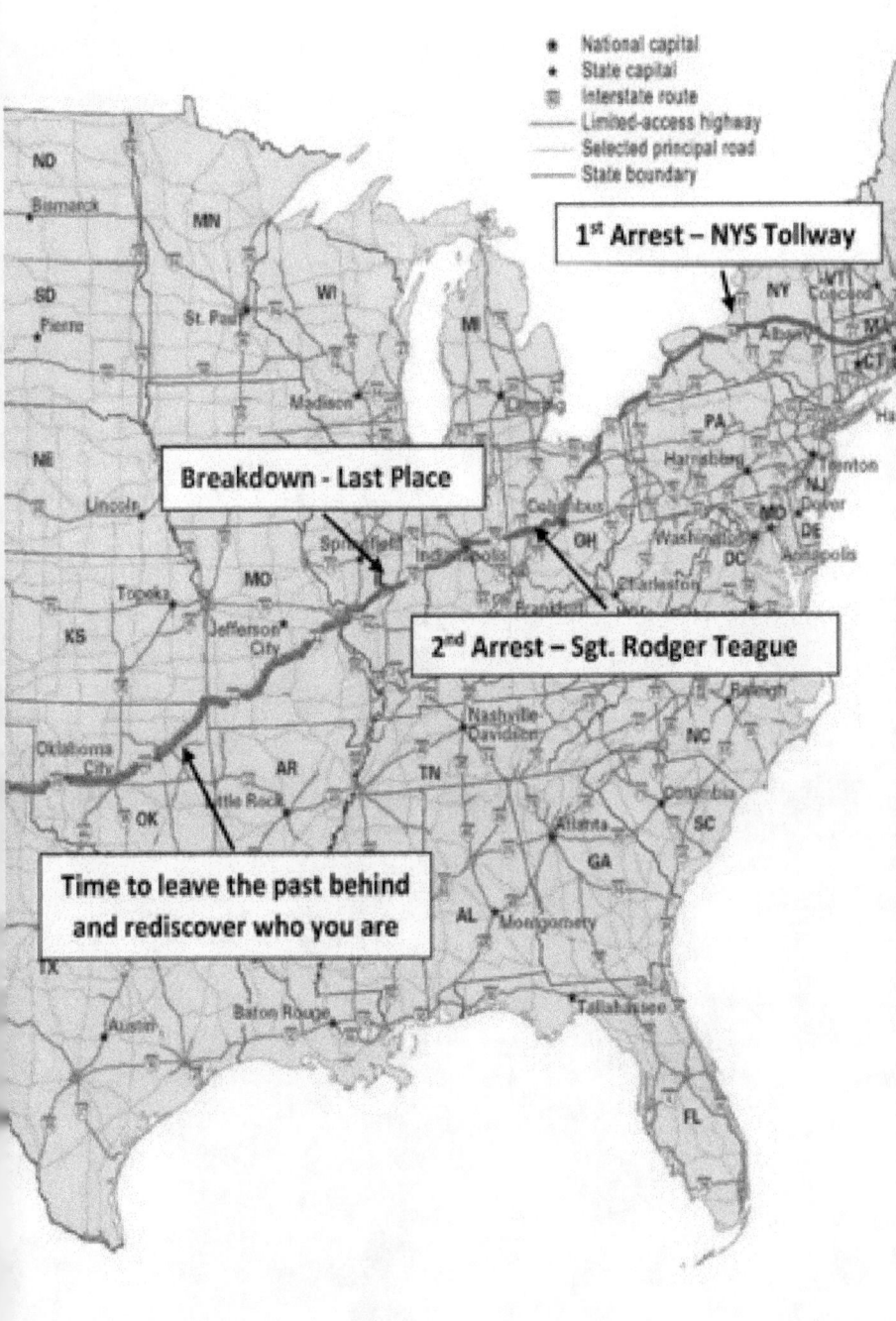

Chapter 16
And Now the Rest of the Story

Nancy

In December of that year, I received a late-evening call from Nancy. I was surprised. It had to be more than a year since I'd last spoken to her. While we talked, my hands trembled. I was on the phone with the woman I loved who I thought I'd never speak to again. Her voice was somber, and she asked if we could meet the next evening at a local restaurant.

I walked in. She had already found a booth and was waiting for me. Our eyes met, and I slightly smiled. We were both a little awkward, but then settled down. I could tell she was a little unsure what to say, how to start the conversation. She looked tired, and her voice was subdued, the same as I had sensed during her call the night before. She was a couple months pregnant with her baby. I was anxious, and the pain I'd tried so hard to forget was reawakened. My feelings were intense—I didn't know what to say. I was hurt, angry, and in love all at once.

We made small talk, and after a few minutes, she told me more. She and her husband had bought a home, and she caught me up on her sister, a new assignment at work, and a problem she was having with her horse. She even told me how sweet her husband was and how he took care of her the time she had to go to the emergency room because of an infection on her leg she had developed from riding. It was almost like nothing had happened, and she was trying to talk to me just like those evenings when we were together. She was open, and seemed to trust she could share her feelings and thoughts with me.

I remember thinking, *Why is she telling me this*? She had to know how I felt about her and how hard I'd taken the breakup. If she only knew what I was thinking. My heart was breaking as she spoke. I'd learned to live without her, and seeing her was bringing back the memories I'd struggled to release. She was telling me about her life with someone else—not me. In my heart, I was tormented. *Maybe if the timing had not been wrong, we might still be together—it would be my baby she was carrying.*

She then said, "I understand you're divorced." I paused because this had been a difficult issue between us.

"Yes, it went very well," I responded. She looked away, down at the table. I winced. For a moment, I could feel her regret. That was when it became harder for me. I just felt compassion for her, and my love for her came to the front of my mind.

I was becoming overwhelmed with my emotions. I tried to lean on my stoic lessons, and I was not going to be as responsive as I had been to when we were together. But then I looked at her, into her eyes, and I tried to imagine what she was feeling. I felt like she was subconsciously reaching out, trying to recapture our connection.

I buried all my feelings, engaged her, and let the conversation go where she wanted it to. I wanted to live for this one last moment. She stopped, reached out to hold my hand, and smiled. The touch of her hand had more of an impact than I expected. I felt a tremble in mine, and I didn't know what to say. This was the woman I loved, but it was never going to be for us.

"I saw Springsteen's new video," she said. "It's pretty good!"

I smiled back. "Yes, 'Dancing in the Dark.'"

"Remember when I wanted you to change your belt before we went out? He was wearing that same type of belt I wanted you to get rid of! Now I'm not so sure." I smiled again.

Although I don't recall her saying so, I believed—or at least I wanted to—that she felt that if she had to do it over again, she wouldn't have made the same choices. I thought she was trying to let me know she still had feelings for me, trying to make peace not just with me, but within herself. I was overcome with sadness; there was no going back. I realized I still loved her, and there was nothing I could do.

I pulled it together near the end of our meeting, fearing that may be the last time I'd see her. As we walked toward her car in the parking lot, I stopped because my emotions were taking over. I knew I might never have the chance to share my true feelings with her again.

"I need you to know one thing." We waited in silence for a while, then I finally said, "I'll always love you. I want you to know that'll never change." For a moment, we just stood there, then she touched her cheek. I realized she had shed a tear. I reached out to her, and we embraced. I don't know for how long. I was suspended in time—not thinking, just feeling. I was in a daze; I remember feeling her breath and heartbeat. *If this is heaven, please take me now.* I gently caressed her forehead and then turned toward my car. Reality was quickly returning, and I found my eyes watering as I walked away.

The last I heard from her was almost a year later when she wrote me a letter just to let me know she thought I was a wonderful guy. That I deserved to be happy or something like that. Between the lines, and almost by her omission, I could sense that something was missing, that she wasn't as fulfilled as she wanted to be.

But her last contact set me free from despair, loss, and abandonment. She freed me to remember the good times fondly, and in my memory to love her again. Nancy had heart, and she was who she was, and in her soul, she was the woman I loved. She meant no harm to anyone; she was just struggling to find her way through the challenges she was facing. Many years later, I learned that she had passed away. I was as devastated as I would have been if we'd been together all that time. I remember sobbing like a child. She left behind a husband and a teenage son—a son who she had named Ben.

One Mile at a Time

Tim

The afternoon of July 30, 1986, Tim lost his life in an ultralight aircraft flying accident. His girlfriend called me with the news that day. I was in shock. What a deep, personal loss. She told me he didn't suffer, and that the accident was quick. He had been flying over a lake and playfully buzzing a few friends in a boat. It wasn't hard for me to envision that; Tim loved life and loved having fun. He drove cars the same way.

I sat in my car crying. I drove over to Fremont the next day to see his family. They were grieving. His mom and I talked, and she told me how much he meant to them, and how worried they'd always been because he was truly fearless. She told me how relieved they'd been when they learned he was racing with me because they knew I could keep his wild side in check.

Tim and I became close friends not after the race, but during the race. It's funny. Despite our early bickering, he was calling me out on my own dejected state. Not many people could have read me so well. And he knew I had turned it around after my six-hour run. He also nailed the reason without me saying a word. That's something only a friend can do. He felt good about what I brought out in him. He had confidence in me, and it was mutual. Together, we'd become an unbeatable team, as the world discovered on that third day of June in 1984.

In the months before he died, Tim and I received inquiries from the Baha off-road race organizers to see if we might be interested in participating the next year. We were considering it. Neither of us had raced off-road before.

After Tim's death, I lost interest in racing. I needed to heal from my losses. First, my breakup with Nancy, then the passing of my best friend Tim within two years. To this day, I miss him. We just clicked, and we both fed on life's adventures. We loved the same things; we were both comfortable taking risks. I was just *a measure twice, cut once* kind of guy. One of my favorite memories with him was listening to tunes in the car while driving through New Mexico. We were connected, enjoying the moment, and having fun.

At one of the toughest times in my life, the experiences we shared were also some of the best. We were two different people, with two different styles, who fit together well. I sometimes wonder what other adventures we could have had together. I just know my life would have been richer and there would have been more stories worth telling if our friendship could have continued.

Carlene

I had last seen Carlene in fall 1984 when we filed for divorce and parted ways with no animosity. I applied for an annulment with the Catholic Archdiocese of Chicago. Carlene wrote a letter in support of me. She wrote some truly kind words explaining that the marriage was a way to support her in her time of need.

The last time I received a message from her was after her death. It was 2002. One evening, I got a call from someone I didn't know—a close friend of Carlene's. She told me that Carlene had passed. But the most moving part of the conversation came from the instructions she gave in her will.

I was to be contacted and told how much it meant to her that I had been in her life when she needed me most. Carlene's friend went on to explain that she wanted to reach out at the end of her life to thank me for the gift of being able to experience life, a life she never thought she'd have.

Carlene's friend told me she'd had a good and rewarding life. And occasionally she would recount to her friends how it felt to be given a chance to live fully when all she'd known before was the fear that each day could be her last. She would say that I was an important part of making that happen.

I don't know why we meet the people we do. I look back and ask myself if I should have stayed married to Carlene. Is that what God would have wanted me to do? Did I fail? But I look at where I am now. I've had a chance to be a father to four children, four special human beings who wouldn't be here if I didn't make the choices I did. But the fact that she'd written in her will to contact me made me think about how sometimes we have more of an impact on people than we imagined at the time.

We helped each other focus on what we individually wanted for our futures. It ended in a divorce, and in some ways, it was a happy ending. We both grew as people during our relationship, becoming more aware of who we were, and we found a way to extend her life by twenty years.

In moments of reflection, I feel close to her. Sometimes I get choked up when I think of that call from her friend to tell me her last wishes. Carlene was a deeply religious person; I believe she is in heaven. Thinking of her makes me remember a time when I was a better person than I am now.

But in my heart, I know the journey that we shared was good and right. And the next stages in her life and mine were also right. We each chose our own path after our time together, ones we agreed we couldn't share. We both understood that. When I think of her from time to time, I say a prayer that Carlene is alright.

Epilogue

Winning the Four Ball was a turning point in my life.

Although I would never race again, I've had an adventurous career and a thriving family. I feel fortunate that I got to have a lifetime of adventures by the time I was in my thirties. I benefitted from my grandmother's gift of nurturing advice. I have often thought it was this transfer of wisdom from her that enabled me to perform so well despite my young age. I didn't just have my own experiences, but those of prior generations to call on in times of need. I was set up for success.

Six months after my last meeting with Nancy, I was walking down a street in Chicago's Lincoln Park looking for a brownstone to live in. I had just been introduced to the board of directors at Bell & Howell as the new Vice President of Planning and Development at the education and publishing division. Here I was, 31, just about to turn 32, and an officer of a public company and one of its top-five compensated executives.

In the future, my career continued to evolve. I became the CFO of a startup that went public and became a $6 billion NYSE firm.

Edward M. Rahill

Between positions, I served as Campaign Finance Chairman for Senator Paul Coverdale's 1992 campaign when he won his race in a runoff. Later, I held the position of Program Director for the 1996 Centennial Olympic Park, a centerpiece of Atlanta's 1996 Olympics. The park is a major event center and a tourist draw in what is now Midtown Atlanta. Eventually, I was President and CEO of my own startup. I partnered with a large private equity firm and sold it for cash and assumed debt value of $1 billion in just six years.

Five years after the breakup with Nancy, I met a woman who I would eventually marry. We raised four truly exceptional children. Each child is pursuing their dreams, and they are all protected from any financial collapse that would have derailed their lives if they'd been born at another time. Their education was top-notch, but I made sure that the money in their pockets came up a little short. I saw to it that they had to work. Each child's first job ranged from working at McDonald's to washing dishes at a local restaurant.

The only time they didn't have to work was when they had the opportunity to help others. In the summer, they dropped everything at a phone call to join an emergency relief team in a disaster zone. Their volunteer teams would show up at the disaster site a week before FEMA would get there, making them true first responders. I know they grew in character when they saw the plight of the people in Joplin, Missouri, and Moore, Oklahoma, where people had lost everything when an F5 tornado hit.

For the moment, I'm at peace, for I know I have fulfilled the promise I made to my grandmother—that these would be the first children in a string of generations who did not have to give up their dreams. I fulfilled my promise to be the one who finally broke the chain, the chain of broken dreams.

1893–1984: The End of an Era?

Just as the Great Cowboy race of 1893 marked the end of endurance horse racing, the era of documented and organized cross-continental road racing that started on May 8, 1905, with Dwight Huss and Milford Wigle, may have ended with Ed Rahill and Tim Montgomery on June 3, 1984. It was the end of an era in American culture. In 1986–87, Congress began the process to repeal the 55 mph national speed limit. Aggressive coordinated law enforcement with increased legal consequences for drivers and sponsors of large multiple racecar events meant that such races were no longer safe nor practical. The coordinated national police effort to stop the Four Ball race was unprecedented in the history of the United States.

There have been other events since then, such as One Lap of America. These were large twenty- and thirty-car rallies, sometimes for charity, which included multiple planned stops for evening events with fun side challenges along the way. The events were speed-controlled for travel between events. These rallies were regulated to comply with state traffic laws. For almost forty years, there has been no significant effort to organize a major competitive endurance racing event like the Great Cowboy Race of 1893, the Cannonball, or the Four Ball Rally.

There have been several lone wolf efforts, claiming individual records and seeking publicity. But these were not competitive road races and tended to be viewed as single-car demonstration runs, without any press following the run or at the starting and finish line. For this reason, the racing community is skeptical of them. This is because, in some cases, the only evidence of the event was from those who participated with no independent verification. These events tended to involve one car, as opposed to the races in the 1970s and early '80s with up to fifty cars leaving in three-minute intervals. Without independent journalist documentation or true competition from other racers, the race community today does not believe these events can be categorized as true road races. Three decades later, the C2C Express has come the closest to an organized competitive road race. It was conceived as a fun and adventurous rally but was limited to classic and low-priced used cars.

One final reason the public has lost interest in these types of races is that it's just not so hard to drive fast today. There is a huge difference between racing with a nationwide limit of 55 mph in the 1980s and today, when speed limits out west average 75 to 80 mph, or effectively unlimited. Because 20 mph over the limit is the measure of reckless driving in most states, a driver can run at 94 mph and still only get a speeding ticket. A driver today automatically has a 20 to 25 mph legal advantage over the racers of the past.

A recent *Autoweek* article asks, "Are Modern Cannonball Records Proving Something Different Now?" The article laments the fact that recent events have forgotten what the races had been all about: "They were a form of protest against the new 55-mph speed limit imposed in the wake of the oil crisis." The article argues that recent events seem to lack the purpose they once had: a statement of the right of an individual to live free of arbitrary restrictions set by a government thousands of miles away.

Nothing has evolved to the scope of the Cannonball and Four Ball Rally. Both the Cannonball and the Four Ball Rally ran four times. The Cannonball in 1971, 1972, 1975, and 1979, and the Four Ball Rally in 1981, 1982, 1983, and, finally, 1984, the final year, and the year I won.

When I reflect on what we accomplished, I am humbled and grateful to have had the opportunity to run and win the last true American transcontinental road race. Given the complex nature of our society today, I can't imagine how such races could be held again. But from what I know of our human nature and instinctive desire to pursue adventure and competition, I cannot help but believe that some form of a contest will reemerge. I just don't know when. I believe that humankind will someday produce the opportunity for adventures like the cross-continental road races of the twentieth century. I hope they only temporarily ended with Tim and me winning the Four Ball Rally in 1984. Time will tell.

Edward M. Rahill

Looking back: Feelings about Mexico

That summer, I lived and worked with people from many backgrounds. I came to respect the work ethic of the emerging middle class and the young leadership teams of the up-and-coming private sector. I left Mexico with a belief that the country was about to take a step forward in quality-of-life for its citizens. As time went on and I followed the rise of the drug trade and cartel class, I was deeply saddened as I watched the country fall into the hands of lawlessness and criminal terrorist groups. In the late twentieth century, there was still hope that Mexico would have a bright future. But now without a revolutionary cultural change away from lawlessness, drug cartels, and corruption, it's difficult to stay optimistic.

The tragedy was that the United States could have had a major impact in the 1990s. They could have been part of a comprehensive effort against the Latin American drug cartels and encouraged economic development through incentives to American industries to invest in Mexico and Latin America instead of China. Looking back, I believe it could have been a win-win for Mexico/Latin America and North America/the United States.

Distant memories, Personal Thoughts, Lessons Learned.

As my mind drifts back to the first part of my life, I remember more feelings than events—victories, defeats, including unimaginable joys and unbearable sorrows. I have revisited my decision to share a journey with Carlene, my first wife. Tim was there, too. My most vivid memories of him are not so much of the race itself, but how we got to know each other in the brief time we had together and how we grew close at a time of great emotional stress.

My relationship with Nancy was a cornerstone of that part of my life. Many years later, I found a person who had been close to her. I was finally able to ask what had happened. The friend talked fondly of her, reminding me how vivacious Nancy could be. I learned that Nancy never talked in detail about our breakup, only saying that she was seeking stability. I learned that her son was the apple of her eye. I also learned about the seriousness of her endometriosis that required surgery, preventing her from having any more children. I finally understood how serious this condition was and how it would have affected her decisions. It helped explain why things happened the way they did. She lived a good life with a devoted husband. Her friend told me about her final day—how she had passed suddenly and without pain. Her family took it very hard.

But some fragments of joy filled my heart during this conversation. Her friend said she remembered me and recalled when Nancy would talk about us when we were together. Nancy would tell her how I made her feel, that with me life was an adventure, and that I'd been a bright spot for her. She could never tell what the next day would bring, but she knew it would be something she'd look forward to. I once learned that Nancy's baby sister was a Joe Montana fan. At the time, he was quarterback of the San Francisco 49ers. I was an acquaintance of Joe's from our time together at Notre Dame and asked him to send Nancy's sister an autographed poster. Apparently, she was ecstatic when she got it, and Nancy's sister still has the poster framed in her family room today.

This conversation was a gift, and it brought me closure. Nancy was struggling with her secret fears of never having a family. We were a good fit and wanted the same things, but, sadly, the timing never fell into place.

It is wonderful to experience the emotions of the adventure of pursuing love—including the experience of love lost. She was my first real love. I have grown since then, and perhaps we weren't destined to be a couple. I see that now. But many years later, I feel it was a gift to have felt that deeply, to have loved that much.

Mom once told me she wished she had two lives—one to learn from and one to live. In many ways, she gave me both. I made mistakes and suffered heartbreaks, but from her, I learned how to cope. She taught me how to approach challenges, not to be afraid to take chances, and what it means to go through the joys and sorrows we all experience when we live to the fullest. That is the gift of life.

I have written about my children, and how important it has always been to me that they become the first generation in our legacy to live their dreams, just as Mom had hoped. I want them to truly appreciate this gift. If I could change one thing about their upbringing, I would have taken more time to explain how they got here and their connections to their family's past. They are all gifted and good people, and I believe over time they will come to understand what their great-grandmother was trying to accomplish, especially when they have their own children.

We cannot overstate the value of the gift we all have waiting for us when we are born if we just take the moment to recognize it. Life is that gift. Together with this gift, we were given free will to decide what to do with it. I have come to believe we were born with a choice: to just exist or to take on the mission to learn and evolve into better human beings, beyond what we had when we came into this world.

When I started to write this memoir, I had intended it to be a chronicle of my past—how I grew up, the importance of connections between generations, and a highlight of some of my successes in the face of difficult odds. But time has moved on and as I reflect back, I have come to find that these memories are now entwined with emotions shared with others. It is Mom, Carlene, Nancy, and Tim I think about when I reconstruct these memories. The all left me so early in my life. It is lonely without them; it is a warm feeling to remember them.

Edward M. Rahill

A Few Thoughts on How to Live

At birth, our fate is not predetermined. There will come a time when we will each be faced with a choice. It will be our choice to decide to push beyond our limits, it is how we become a better person. To make the world a better place because we were here. This is how you build your capabilities, character, and self-worth.

When faced with adversity and personal loss, it is important to understand that defeat is not permanent, and it's the will to go on that counts. Resilience comes from who you are—your values, your character. Have faith in it, it will pull you through.

It is also imperative to take moments to experience life, and not allow fear to stop you from chasing your dreams. The emotional joys and heartaches that come from taking chances are all a part of your growth into who you can be and ultimately, who you are.

There is a God. He does not exist in a physical sense. I have no way to even comprehend his existence. From my experience, I just know we can communicate with him when we are not thinking about ourselves.

Finally, as you grow, take the time to learn from and build upon the lives of prior generations who chose to take on the same mission: to make themselves better people, to make the world better in their time and for those generations to come. It is all a part of a divine quest to become individually better humans and to contribute to the foundations of a better human race. If current generations can learn to value the lessons from those who love them and came before them, there is hope for humanity.

Turning the Corner

I have been asked if there is anything I hope to experience in the future. I have taken some time to think about that. Looking back, I have grown, stumbled, recovered, failed, and won. I reflected on the risks I took, and I have lived a richer life than if I hadn't taken those chances at all. I had the chance to experience the ecstasies and the miseries that only love can bring.

But the perspective I keep coming back to that most impacts me now is that life is indeed a relay race. We are each members of a much larger team, our legacy, and our team members ran their leg before us and will run it after us. They momentarily overlap with our lives at the hand-off of the baton, but they live in another time. When it's our turn to take the baton, we receive a gift of their wisdom and experience. I often think about the time Mom spent with me and her desire to share her life's experiences with me. As a child, I didn't understand the gift she was giving me, but now I do. For me, in a very personal way, she was handing off her baton of wisdom to me.

As I find myself about to enter the fourth turn of my quarter mile, I can see the finish line. I can see home. If I could have one more experience, it would be to find myself with my progeny from the next generation standing at the starting line, waiting for me to begin the process of handing off the baton to them. I would begin the same way Mom did for me: "It's time. We need to go for a drive." As we climb into my '68 Shelby Mustang, I will give them the ride of their lives. But most importantly, I will feel at peace if I can pass on some of the things I learned, to help them live their own adventure.

I hope I will have this chance to transfer what I've learned to the next generation, just as it was done for me. No other bucket list item would fulfill me as much. At that moment, I will be able to say: In a small way, the world is a better place because I was here. My life was a life well-lived.

Appendix: News Clippings and Documentation

The New York Times
RECORD SET IN SECRET RACE
JUNE 5, 1984
Two Middle Westerners who raced by car from Boston to San Diego at an average speed of 86 miles an hour said today that they had not received a single speeding ticket. At least six other drivers in the cross-country run were arrested on New York parkways. The Middle Westerners, Ed Rahill and Tim Montgomery, did receive $10,000 for winning the clandestine coast-to-coast race in record time.

The police said the drivers were involved in what one trooper described as a "Cannonball Run type of race," covering a great deal of the distance at more than 100 m.p.h. Officials of the race confirmed a record winning time of 35 hours, 46 minutes. The winners arrived in San Diego shortly after 6 P.M. Sunday, driving an especially adapted 1984 Trans am. Twelve of the 24 starters, in vehicles ranging from Corvettes to Mercedes Benzes, finished the race.

Close Call at the End
"A San Diego police officer got on our tail for running a stoplight, but we weren't about to stop that close to the finish line," said Mr. Montgomery, a 23-year-old mechanic from Fremont, Ohio. "When we got to the Hyatt Islandia Hotel, the policeman saw the stop clock and the flags and knew it was a road race, and he just kept going."

Mr. Montgomery said that the car's odometer had shown a distance of 3,066 miles for the trip but explained that the figure might be off a bit. "We got a ticket in Ohio for failure to use the turn

Edward M. Rahill

signal in changing lanes and we got one in upstate New York for using a police scanner, but we never got a speeding ticket," he said.

His partner, Mr. Rahill, a metals technologist from Barrington, Ill., used the victory to mark his 32nd birthday.

Purpose of the Race

"The whole purpose was to demonstrate that the American interstate highway system, with good drivers respecting the road conditions, is safe at speeds greater than 55 miles per hour, much as the Autobahns are used in Europe," Mr. Rahill said. "We never risked anyone's life. Fast doesn't spell dangerous."

One Mile at a Time

Drivers hit 140 mph on cross-country run

SAN DIEGO (AP) — The drivers zipped across the country at speeds of up to 140 mph, and police handed out tickets when they could, but an illegal cross-country auto race was really "a game on both sides," said one police dispatcher.

The third annual Michael A. Preston Four-Ball Rally ended Sunday when Ed Rahill and Tim Montgomery wheeled into the parking lot of a San Diego hotel less than 36 hours and more than 3,000 miles after the race started in secrecy in Boston.

Almost as soon as the 24 race teams pushed the pedal to the metal on Saturday, state police across the country began scouring the highways for the racers.

"We knew they were coming and they knew that we knew it," Aimee Emerick, a dispatcher with the Ohio State Highway Patrol, said Monday. "I think it was a game on both sides."

Some states did better than others in upholding speed laws. Ohio Trooper Roger Teague singlehandedly stopped four racers.

"It made his day," Emerick said.

ED RAHILL
Averaged 87 mph

They were trying to trick him and he just turned it around on them. He hid behind several semi-trailers and could turn off his radar until he saw them. Then it was too late for them to cut their speed."

Teague stopped Rahill and Montgomery for failing to signal a lane change. Rahill, of Barrington, Ill., and Montgomery, of Fremont, Ohio, finished the race in 35 hours, 40 minutes, a record for the event.

"We averaged 87 mph and did not get one speeding ticket," said Rahill, who clocked the distance at 3,066 miles. "The only way you can cross the United States at those speeds is to do it safely."

However, some authorities disagreed. "They're not proving anything, they're endangering lives," said California Highway Patrol spokesman Jerry Bolver. "It's stupid, and if we ever find them doing that in California, they will be jailed."

Six drivers were arrested on the New York State Thruway near Syracuse on Saturday for driving about 100 mph, New York State Police said.

Sgt. James Fisher of the New Mexico State Police said there were no arrests linked to the rally in his state.

"Personally, I think there are some parts of this state where you could go faster than 55 safely," Fisher said.

Montgomery said he and Rahill drove in four-hour shifts in a 1984 Pontiac Trans Am, clocking speeds of up to 140 mph on Interstate 40 in New Mexico.

"We feel the speed limits should be set according to what is safe," Rahill said. "In a metropolitan area, 55 mph is safe. On the open road, faster speeds are just as safe."

Rahill, 41, and Montgomery, 29, had different partners in last year's rally, when of 50 racers they finished 17th and 21st respectively. Before this year's event, they took a race driving course in Indianapolis.

"We were the defensive drivers out there. We were the ones breaking the law," Montgomery said. "But we never put ourselves or anyone else in danger. Everyone in this was an extremely competent driver."

"There are a lot of people driving out there that I don't trust going 55 mph. I trust these people at 100," Rahill said.

Daily News Miner, Fairbanks, Alaska

Auto racer in a 36-hou[r]

By Dick Mitchell

It was like a Burt Reynolds movie, a daredevil from Barrington and his partner from Ohio driving from Boston to San Diego at 86 m.p.h. to win a $10,000 prize and not even getting a speeding ticket.

Edward Rahill, 32, a Barrington metals technologist, said from his room in San Diego's Hyatt Islandia Hotel that the road race had proved the supremacy of America's interstate highway system and had been quite an adventure.

He and Timothy Montgomery, 32, a mechanic from Fremont, Ohio, had been so dedicated to winning the event that they had gone to the Indianapolis Motor Speedway this spring for a refresher course, one of the last pages in a detailed set of plans for the 3,000-mile auto race.

Their studies paid off when they won the Michael A. Preston Memorial

Edward Rahill of Barrington, Ill., and partner Timothy Montgomery of Fremont, Ohio, stand in San Diego yesterday beside car they used to win the Four-Ball Rallye, a 3,000-mile, cross-country race in which they averaged 86 m.p.h. and won $10,000.

CHICAGO SUN-TIMES, Tuesday, June 5, 1984

cross U.S. sprint

...our-Ball Rallye, reminiscent of the Cannon Ball ...aker Sea-to-Shining Sea ...emorial Trophy Dash of ...e '70s that inspired the ...ovies "The Gumball Ral-..." and "The Cannonball ...un."

Both Rahill and Mont...mery had gone through ...e Skip Barber racing ...hool at the track pre...ously. It prepares drivers ... races such as the In...anapolis 500 and Grand ...ix circuits.

"On the very first day ...ey start drumming into ...u that the hardest thing ... learn is when to go ...w," Rahill said. "We ...nt to the school for a ...resher course, and we ...de a pact: 'When in ...ubt, back down and ...it until the highway ...ars out.'"

...ahill's 1984 TransAm ...me prepared: High...ed windshield wipers, a ... gallon fuel tank con...ned in a fire retardant ...l cell and driving lights ...t project a beam five ...es the distance of those on normal autos.

He and Montgomery spent about $1,000 to make their auto the first American model to outrun the higher-priced foreign competition. Averaging 86 m.p.h. for 35 hours 46 minutes means that sometimes during the race that ended Sunday evening, the Pontiac was traveling well over double the national speed limit.

Rahill and Montgomery avoided a speeding ticket but were charged with having an illegal police scanner in their car. And in Ohio, they received a ticket for making a lane change without signaling. At least six of the 25 drivers in the cross-country run were arrested on New York interstates.

Rahill and Montgomery had bond cards and extra money to pay traffic fines. "You have to be willing to pay the penalty if you knowingly do something wrong. We accept that," Rahill said. "We're citizens of this society and abide by those penalties."

But Rahill emphasized that avoiding speeding tickets was not the object. "We chose to drive in accordance to the conditions," he said. "At times we drove 45 or 50 and at other times, especially in the West, we drove at 130.

"We were able to drive at those speeds and do it safely," he said. "The American interstate highway system is the best in the world. They are designed for much higher speeds and speed limits should be set at what conditions allow and not arbitrarily by someone in Washington."

For their efforts Rahill and Montgomery won "a little less" than $10,000, and achieved personal aims. "We set a world's record and accomplished a goal," Rahill said. "It's not my life's ambition to keep running the race. I may do something else. Something more exotic, perhaps something in Europe."

Chicago Sun-Times of June 5, 1984

Tuesday, June 5,

From Boston to San
in 36 hours — and

SAN DIEGO (AP) — The racing team that won an illegal but thrilling cross-country auto race said yesterday they never placed themselves or anyone else in danger and their lack of speeding tickets proves it.

"There are a lot of people driving out there that I don't trust going 55 miles an hour. I trust these people at 100," said Edward M. Rahill of Barrington, Ill., who finished the 3,066-mile course from Boston to San Diego in 35 hours and 46 minutes from Saturday morning to Sunday night.

Rahill teamed with Tim Montgomery of Fremont, Ohio, for the race, which was kept secret until it began. Both men had participated in the event last year with different partners. Both took a race-driving course to prepare.

"This is basically something that Tim and I have had an interest in for several years. Our appetites were whetted by the first Cannonball Runs in the 1970s. It's the adventure and the love of driving," Rahill said in an interview.

Because state police frown on racing of any kind on public roadways, Rahill, Montgomery and the 23 other teams in the rally kept their plans closely guarded.

"But I heard that as soon as the rally started, there was an all-points bulletin out for us," Rahill said.

Rahill and Montgomery were stopped by police twice on their trek, once in New York for having a police scanner — which is illegal there — and once in Ohio for failing to signal a lane change.

"We averaged 87 miles an hour and did not get one speeding ticket," Rahill said. "The only way you can cross the United States at those speeds is to do it safely."

Rahill of Barrington, Ill., and Tim Montgomery of ...ont, Ohio, cannonballed to victory in '84 Pontiac.

Montgomery said the rally was in part a statement against the uniform 55-mph speed limit, which he said he and Rahill followed where necessary.

"We feel the 55-mile-per-hour limit is ludicrous. But we don't do this because we're angry young men. We do it for the love of driving," said Montgomery, 23, who was competing in his second rally. Last year he raced a 1959 Cadillac limousine.

Added Rahill: "In areas where you go 30 miles without seeing another car, then you can open up your auto the way it was intended. On those stretches of road, we were going 120 and 130 miles an hour."

Rahill and Montgomery clocked their record time in a 1984 Pontiac Trans Am, followed by a Ford LTD and a BMW Alpena. They won $7,000 from a prize pool for their efforts.

Los Angeles Herald Examiner

Another 'Cannon

Police arrest speeding participar

By MEL REISNER
Associated Press

SYRACUSE, N.Y. — Six people driving at around 100 mph were arrested on the New York State Thruway in what state troopers describe as an organized coast-to-coast race.

The six were back on the road after paying fines, but police elsewhere have been warned about the Boston-to-San Diego race.

At least 30 other drivers are believed to be involved in the "Michael A. Preston Memorial Four Ball Rally," Sgt. Sidney Bailey said after Saturday's arrests.

Bailey said he didn't know the significance of the name, reminiscent of the "Cannonball Baker Sea-to-Shining-Sea Memorial Trophy Dash," which ran undercover for five years in the 1970s. That race — from Darien, Conn., to

ll Run'
rganized coast-to-coast rally

o Beach, Calif., — inspired the "The Gumball Rally" and "The ball Run."

J.M. Praskey told the Syracuse American the race began Satur- rning in Boston and that some of ple arrested covered the 175 om the Massachusetts-New York yracuse in 90 minutes — averag- mph.

racers were spaced three to four apart, Bailey said.

ey weren't traveling in a con- e said.

ey said a seventh arrest was ter Saturday by Ohio troopers on te 71 near Ashland, Ohio.

key said the cars were equipped phisticated electronic gear such e radio scanners, radar detectors ar jammers, and one driver had f night-vision glasses which retail at around $1,500.

Ten citations were handed out to the drivers arrested in New York — five speeding citations, three for illegally possessing police radio scanners in a car and two for reckless driving.

All six were arraigned at local town courts and paid fines, he said.

"They paid in cash," Bailey said. "They apparently came equipped for that type of emergency too."

He said the six cars — a Chevrolet Camaro, two Porsches, a 1982 Ford, a 1979 Pontiac and a 1977 Mercedes — were registered in New Hampshire, Massachusetts, Illinois and New York.

Bailey said the race was mentioned in the April 15 issue of "Bflo." magazine, a Buffalo-area regional magazine, and had been described in Boston newspapers.

The Tampa Tribune

The Buffalo News, on the front page of my hometown paper

THE BUFFALO NEWS
EVENING EDITION

Vol. CCVIII—No. 55   MONDAY, JUNE 4, 1984

City Native Wins 'Cannonball,' Leaves Police, Rubber Burning

By MICHAEL BEEBE

A Buffalo native who averaged a record 86 mph over American interstate highways won an illegal coast-to-coast road race this weekend, speeding from Boston to San Diego in 35 hours 46 minutes.

Edward M. Rahill III, 30, a graduate of Bishop Fallon High School and the University of Notre Dame, won the Four Ball Rally, which attracted police attention in dozens of states.

"We set out to make a statement that it is possible to drive safely at a somewhat higher rate of speed than 55 on American highways, a network that is the finest in the world," Mr. Rahill said in an early-morning interview from San Diego.

New York state police would argue with his claim. They say they picked off nine of the racers from Syracuse to Fredonia, some of them traveling at speeds of 100 mph or more.

"They paid in cash," Sgt. J.M. Praskey said of the racers who were fined. "They apparently came equipped for that type of emergency, too."

Mr. Rahill said he preferred to call the race, modeled after the Cannonball runs started by Lockport native and automotive writer Brock Yates, a rally.

Driving a 1984 Pontiac Trans Am with partner Tim Montgomery, 23, of Fremont, Ohio, Mr. Rahill said the team drove according to road conditions.

"When the speed limit went down to 45, we went with it," he said. "But in New Mexico, where we didn't see another car for 45 minutes, we went flat out, which in this case was about 140."

Police along the route said they had been alerted the drivers would be coming sometime in June by newspaper stories in Boston and a magazine article that ran April 15 in Buffalo, the Sunday magazine of The Buffalo News.

Written by Christopher Jensen, an automotive writer for the Cleveland Plain Dealer who was in last year's race, the magazine piece told how the fleet of high powered Porsches, BMWs, Mercedes and the high-performance Ford Panteras more than doubled the speed limit in places.

Mr. Rahill said his winning run marked the first time an American-built car outran the higher-priced foreign models. He said there were 25 cars in this year's race.

He said he was first stopped by police near Syracuse and charged with having an illegal police scanner in his car.

His second arrest came in Ohio, he said, when he was charged with not using his turn signal. He was not charged with speeding throughout the race despite his average 85-mph speed.

Mr. Rahill, who lives in Barrington, Ill., and works for Arco Metals there, said he and his partner each won a few thousand dollars and a trophy for the victory.

"It was about enough to cover expenses," he said.

His aim in flouting the laws in the states along the way, he said, was to draw attention to what he said was the artificially low American speed limit of 55.

His mother, Mary C. Rahill, said she was proud of her son's victory.

"I just never discourage Ed from pursuing any of his interests," she said. "I am glad the race is over. And I'm delighted to have him there in one piece."

Brock Yates, who won the original Cannonball Sea-to-Shining-Sea Memorial Trophy Dash — which spawned a few Burt Reynolds movies — said he no longer runs in them because he considers them dangerous.

Colorado Springs Telegraph

Cross-country auto race 'a game on both sides'

SAN DIEGO (AP) — The drivers zipped across the country at speeds of up to 140 mph, and police handed out tickets when they could, but an illegal cross-country auto race was really "a game on both sides," one police dispatcher said.

The third annual Michael A. Preston Four Ball Rally ended Sunday when Ed Rahill and Tim Montgomery wheeled into the parking lot of a San Diego hotel less than 36 hours and more than 3,000 miles after the race started in secrecy in Boston.

Almost as soon as the 24 race teams pushed the pedal to the metal on Saturday, state police across the country began scouring the highways for the racers.

"We knew they were coming and they knew that we knew it," Aimee Emerick, a dispatcher with the Ohio State Highway Patrol, said Monday. "I think it was a game on both sides."

Some states did better than others in upholding speed laws. Ohio Trooper Roger Teague singlehandedly stopped four racers.

"It made his day," Ms. Emerick said. "They were trying to trick him and he just turned it around on them. He hid behind several semi-trailers and could turn off his radar until he saw them. Then it was too late for them to cut their speed."

Teague stopped Rahill and Montgomery for failing to signal a lane change. Rahill, of Barrington, Ill., and Montgomery, of Fremont, Ohio, finished the race in 35 hours, 46 minutes, a record for the event.

"We averaged 87 mph and did not get one speeding ticket," said Rahill, who clocked the distance at 3,066 miles. "The only way you can cross the United States at those speeds is to do it safely."

However, some authorities disagreed. "They're not proving anything, they're endangering lives," California Highway Patrol spokesman Jerry Bohrer said. "It's stupid, and if we ever find them doing that in California, they will be jailed."

Six drivers were arrested on the New York State Thruway near Syracuse on Saturday for driving about 100 mph, New York State Police said.

X-country racer: We've got great highways

Staff and wire reports
Staff Writer

"America's got the greatest highway system in the world, and we don't take advantage of it," said Timothy Montgomery.

The 23-year-old Ohio resident took advantage of it last weekend, streaking from Boston to San Diego at speeds of up to 150 mph. He and his partner, Edward M. Rahill III of Barrington, Ill., covered the 3,066 miles in 35 hours and 46 minutes, the fastest among 24 cars in the Michael A. Preston Memorial Four Ball Rally.

And that is after they suffered a 1½ hour delay in Syracuse Saturday afternoon, when state troopers arrested them for having a police radio. Their only other arrest was in Ohio, for changing lanes without signaling.

Although their speed averaged 87 mph, they were not once charged with speeding.

"It was a great time, terrific," Montgomery said. He and Rahill, 31, are staying in a hotel in San Diego for a few days.

"We're performance oriented drivers with performance oriented cars," Montgomery said. "We were driving safely. When the conditions called for 55 we drove 55, when it called for in excess of 55, we drive in excess of it."

Some cars and drivers, he said, are not safe at 55. He remembers standing on the Thruway while Rahill went to court to pay the $40 fine and forfeit the $300 police radio.

"In 20 minutes I counted half a dozen cars that were unsafe for the highway at 55," he said.

■ RACE, Page C2

■ RACE,
Continued from Page C1

"The cars were going by with tires going 'thump, thump, thump, thump, thump.' There was a guy shifting back and forth in the lanes because his car wouldn't stay in the lane. Exhaust systems hanging on the ground throwing sparks. They are the maniacs you've got to get off the highway."

He said there has never been an accident in the cross-country rallies that have been held since 1971. This is the third Michael A. Preston rally, named after the murdered son of a Boston family that sponsored the race.

He said he does not advocate everyone driving at the speed they desire.

He and Rahill spent a year preparing themselves and their 1984 Pontiac Trans Am for the race. So for them, Montgomery said, the speeds were safe.

They ate chocolate-covered graham crackers, Reese's peanut butter cups and Hi-C fruit drink and each got about four hours sleep. Each lost almost 10 pounds.

"Your mind uses up that much fuel," Montgomery said. "You have to concentrate so intently. You can't afford to let your brain take a vacation for just one second."

He remembers going about 150 mph along the flat, empty highways of Texas, New Mexico and Arizona.

"When we came up to a car we'd slam

METRO

We've got great highways, racer says

on the brakes, slow down to around 85, pass it, and hammer it on," Montgomery said.

What is a safe speed for the Thruway near Syracuse?

"It depends on the conditions," Montgomery said. "Sometimes it's 100 mph. Sometimes not over 45."

State police near Syracuse ticketed five others. A spokesman said troopers in Buffalo arrested some, as did Ohio police.

Police in New York and California condemned the race as stupid.

"We knew they were coming and they knew that we knew it," Aimee Emerick, a dispatcher with the Ohio State Highway Patrol, said Monday. "I think it was a game on both sides."

Some states did better than others in upholding speed laws. Ohio Trooper Roger Teague singlehandedly stopped four racers.

"It made his day," Ms. Emerick said. "They were trying to trick him and he just turned it around on them. He hid behind several semi-trailers and could turn off his radar until he saw them. Then it was too late for them to cut their speed."

"They're not proving anything, they're endangering lives," said California Highway Patrol spokesman Jerry Bohrer. "It's stupid, and if we ever find them doing that in California, they will be jailed."

Sgt. James Fisher of the New Mexico State Police said there were no arrests linked to the rally in his state.

"Personally, I think there are some parts of this state where you could go faster than 55 safely," Fisher said.

"We feel the speed limits should be set according to what is safe," Rahill said. "In a metropolitan area, 55 mph is safe. On the open road, faster speeds are just as safe."

Rahill, 31, and Montgomery, 23, had different partners in last year's rally, when of 56 racers they finished 17th and 21st respectively. Before this year's event, they took a race driving course in Indianapolis.

"We were the defensive drivers out there. We were the ones breaking the law," Montgomery said. "But we never put ourselves or anyone else in danger. Everyone in this was an extremely competent driver."

Montgomery said the adventure and love of driving led to the rally named for an auto enthusiast who died as an innocent bystander in a holdup.

The victory earned them $7,000 from a prize pool raised by participants.

"We don't do this because we're angry young men," he said.

But both men said the race made a statement about the federally imposed speed law.

"This law has been dictated to the states by Congress," Rahill said. "There has never been a law broken more often since Prohibition."

National

Ed Rahill (left) and Tim Montgomery, with the car they used to win the Four Ball Rally, a cross-country race. They are shown Monday in San Diego, Calif.

Illegal Race Called Game Between Police, Drivers

SAN DIEGO (AP) — The drivers zipped across the country at speeds of up to 140 mph, and police handed out tickets when they could, but an illegal cross-country auto race was really "a game on both sides," said one police dispatcher.

The third annual Michael A. Preston Four Ball Rally ended Sunday when Ed Rahill and Tim Montgomery wheeled into the parking lot of a San Diego hotel less than 36 hours and more than 3,000 miles after the race started in secrecy in Boston.

Almost as soon as the 24 race teams pushed the pedal to the metal on Saturday, state police across the country began scouring the highways for the racers.

"We knew they were coming and they knew that we knew it," Aimee Emerick, a dispatcher with the Ohio State Highway Patrol, said Monday. "I think it was a game on both sides."

Some states did better than others in upholding speed laws. Ohio Trooper Roger Teague singlehandedly stopped four racers.

"It made his day," Ms. Emerick said. "They were trying to trick him and he just turned it around on them. He hid behind several semi-trailers and could turn off his radar until he saw them. Then it was too late for them to cut their speed."

Teague stopped Rahill and Montgomery for failing to signal a lane change. Rahill, of Barrington, Ill., and Montgomery, of Fremont, Ohio, finished the race in 35 hours, 46 minutes, a record for the event.

"We averaged 87 mph and did not get one speeding ticket," said Rahill, who clocked the distance at 3,066 miles. "The only way you can cross the United States at those speeds is to do it safely."

Six drivers were arrested on the New York State Thruway near Syracuse on Saturday for driving about 100 mph, New York State Police said.

Sgt. James Fisher of the New Mexico State Police said there were no arrests linked to the rally in his state.

Winchester Star, Winchester, Virginia, June 5, 1984

The Daily Herald from Barrington. Never thought I'd find myself sharing the front page with the President of the United States.

THE DAILY HERALD
Barrington Edition

Tuesday, June 5, 1984

Barrington man wins in cross country road race

Forsake use of force: president

$1 million in death suit

Medical clinic vote delayed

Tragedy at sea

Letters to the Editor

Numerous letters to editors and newspaper editorials were written around the country as our run ignited a debate on the 55 mph national speed limit. Some were pro-race, others were against it. A sampling is presented below.

Four Ball Rally leaves law in lurch

THIS WEEK'S clandestine auto race called the "Four Ball Rally" was proof the 55-mph maximum speed law doesn't have any kind of enforcement priority among the nation's law officers.

Twenty-four cars entered the race, which started in Boston. Twelve cars reached the finish line last Monday, in San Diego's Mission Bay Park.

And, get this. The winning entry, a Pontiac Trans Am, accomplished the 3,066-mile course in 35 hours and 46 minutes, with an average speed of almost 86 mph. This means that the winner — and probably most of the other contestants — were flashing along in excess of 100 mph some of the time.

Tickets? None for speeding! One team of drivers was ticketed in New York for using an illegal radar scanner and again in Ohio for failure to signal a turn.

The race is a takeoff from three motion pictures with the same plot — an illegal cross-country race. They were "Gumball Rally," "Cannonball," both released in 1976, and "Cannonball Run," released in

1981 and featuring Burt Reynolds and Farrah Fawcett. All three movies were funny, featherweight entertainment. But now life is imitating art. And that can be dangerous.

Purpose of the Four Ball Rally, according to racers, was to demonstrate the nation's highway system is safe at speeds greater than 55 mph.

They would like to see our freeways as free as the autobahns are in Europe — no speed limit, just push your foot through the floorboards.

Since the 55-mph speed limit was enacted, in 1974, highway deaths and accidents have been reduced.

Nevertheless, anyone who drives the freeways these days knows that only one out of 10 motorists still observes the speed law — and that motorist usually is in the fast lane holding up traffic.

We don't know if the Four Ball Rally will have any effect on the speed limit, but it should awaken law enforcement officers. Racing across the country is all right in a movie, but in real life the gross violators must be stopped and ticketed.

Auto Race Serious

To the Editor of The Blade:

As a twice-refused applicant to Brock Yates' original Cannonball Baker Sea-to-Shining-Sea Memorial Trophy Dash, I was appalled by The Blade's editorial entitled "Perilous Road 'Game.'"

You missed the point of the Four-Ball Rally by a nautical mile. Those guys aren't irresponsible juveniles or Walter Mittyish adults. They're serious drivers with a serious point to make.

If the people of western Europe can travel at 100-plus mph on their interstate highways, why can't we? Are we Americans so ham-handed or poorly coordinated that at speeds above 70 mph we lose control of our cars? Or are our cars made so sloppily that they're not safe above 70 mph? Ten years ago I would have said yes to both questions, but I think today the average American is safer in his car than he has ever been.

Any recent national highway safety report on auto-related fatalities will tell you that the most hazardous roads to drive are those in urban and suburban areas where speeds only reach 35 mph to 55 mph. Four-lane interstates are by far the safest roads to drive on, and it's a waste of time (the only irreplaceable commodity) to dawdle on them at 55 mph.

Granted, there's more than enough boyish enthusiasm among the Four-Ball drivers and their ilk, but old barriers would never be broken were it not for the derring-do of a few people.

     VIC OBERHAUS
     381 Maple St.
     Liberty Center, O.

Accident waiting to happen

So Ed Rahill, who with his partner Tim Montgomery and their car won the Four-Ball Rally, a cross-country race, thinks that driving 3,066 miles cross-country at an average speed of 87 m.p.h. including speeds up to 140 m.p.h. was "every bit as safe as driving 10 m.p.h. in a village." Well, he should have his 2-year-old brain examined. He definitely posed a very serious hazard to the thousands of drivers he breezed past on the highway.

At his average speed of 87 m.p.h., he was traveling 128 feet per second and at 140 m.p.h. he was devouring real estate at 205 feet per second. At the estimated three-fourths of a second it takes to move your foot from the gas to the brake pedal, he traveled 96 and 154 feet, respectively. Now add the thousands of feet it takes to brake the car and you find that Rahill is a potential killer looking for a victim.

May I suggest Rahill spend a weekend riding along with a state patrolman investigating highway fatalities and interview the drivers—if they are alive. Most of these drivers will tell him that they were in full control of the car and the accident would not have happened if "the other guy" hadn't done something stupid. After due meditation, most will also tell you they could have avoided the accident if they had been driving slower.

James J. Dubinski, Rolling Meadows

Partial List of Additional Newspapers Carrying the Story

St. Petersburg Independent, St. Petersburg, Florida
The Honolulu Adviser, Honolulu, Hawaii
The Morning Call, Allentown, Pennsylvania
St. Louis Post-Dispatch, St. Louis, Missouri
York Daily Record, York, Pennsylvania
The New Mexican, Santa Fe, New Mexico
Statesman Journal, Salem, Oregon
Alamogordo Daily News, Alamogordo, New Mexico
The Olympian, Olympia, Washington
The Burlington Free Press, Burlington, Vermont
Cleveland Plain Dealer, Cleveland, Ohio
The Daily Herald, Arlington Heights, Illinois
The Post-Star, Glens Falls, New York
Alton Telegraph, Alton, Illinois
The San Bernardino County Sun, San Bernardino, California
Spokane Chronicle, Spokane, Washington
News-Journal, Mansfield, Ohio
The Courier-News, Bridgewater, New Jersey
Southern Illinoisan, Carbondale, Illinois
Aiken Standard, South Carolina
Elyria Chronicle Telegram, Lorain, Ohio
The Marion Star, Marion, Ohio
The Des Moines Register, Des Moines, Iowa
The News-Messenger, Fremont, Ohio
Dover Times, New Philadelphia, Ohio
The Billings Gazette, Billings, Montana
Star Tribune, Minneapolis, Minnesota
Nashua Telegraph, Nashua, New Hampshire
News Herald, Port Clinton, Ohio
St. Cloud Times, Saint Cloud, Minnesota

One Mile at a Time

Winchester Star, Winchester, Virginia
Pittsburgh Post-Gazette, Pittsburgh, Pennsylvania
The Morning Call, Allentown, Pennsylvania
The Vincennes Sun-Commercial, Vincennes, Indiana
Fairfield Ledger, Fairfield, Iowa
The Record, Hackensack, New Jersey
Daily Hampshire Gazette, Northampton, Massachusetts
Garden City Telegram, Garden City, Kansas
The Gazette, Cedar Rapids, Iowa
The Independent-Record, Helena, Montana
Laurel Leader Call, Laurel, Mississippi
Salinas-Californian, Salinas, California
Corpus-Christi Times, Corpus Christi, Texas

Wikipedia, Michael A. Preston Four Ball Rally 1981–1984
(as of September 2022)

The Four Ball Rally was a quasi-legal race from Boston to San Diego. It was run from 1981 to 1984 and stands as the last of the true competitive cross-continent road races held in the twentieth century. The rally's official name was the Michael A. Preston Memorial Four Ball Rally (FBR) in commemoration of its founder who passed away prior to the first event. The FBR was conceived to be the longest practical distance race between two major cities in the continental United States. The rally had multiple route options determined real time by the driving teams and generally exceed 3100 miles. On average the race was 250 to 300 miles longer than the Original Sea to Shining Sea rallies of the 1970s. Up to 50 entries, including international teams, were selected to participate. The event was invitation only, and generally was restricted to professional drivers and others with documented driving experience.

On June 3, 1984, the team of Edward M. Rahill, of Barrington, Ill., and Timothy Montgomery, of Fremont, OH, driving a performance and range enhanced Pontiac Trans Am, won the race in a record time of 35:46, despite several hours of delays due to two arrests and mechanical issues during the race. This time still stands today as the fastest documented time for a race crossing the continental United States between Boston and San Diego. A significant point reference was that Rahill and Montgomery were believed to be out of the race after their two arrests and mechanical breakdown in Illinois. Race records indicated the team were able to reach an average speed between St. Louis to San Diego, including stops, exceeding 104 miles an hour.

An interesting development coming out of the race was the near celebrity status of Ohio State Trooper Sargent Rodger Teague who apprehended four participants including Rahill and Montgomery, the eventual winners of the event. Sargent Teague was awarded the 1984 Super Trooper Award by the FBR races sponsors and attended the winner's banquet with his wife to receive his recognition.

One Mile at a Time

The 1984 Four Ball Rally received coverage from National and International News sources such the AP, UPI, *New York Times, Chicago Sun Times,* Paul Harvey's June 5, 1984, broadcast and 73 other newspaper organizations on June 4th and 5th. The level of police enforcement was so intense, of the twenty-seven cars that had planned to leave Boston that day, only eleven where to finish. The New York State Police alone arrest seven participants. The level of coordinated national police effort to stop the race was unprecedented in American history and led to its discontinuation as the increase in national publicity and added attention from law enforcement made running the event untenable.

SUMMARY OF THE FINANCIAL CRISIS IN LATIN AMERICA

The United States and the Crisis in Mexico

Summary: The crisis of the 1980s, which appeared to threaten the longstanding stability After the economic crisis of 1982–83, Mexico lost much of its influence in Central America. 530 foreign creditors reached an accord with Mexico and in 1984 re-instated the agreement originally negotiated in 1982. (U.S. Library of Congress, "The United States and the Crisis in Mexico" in http://countrystudies.us > Mexico)

A bank advisory group [including ARCO personnel] representing 530 foreign creditors reached an accord with Mexico in 1984. The rescheduling agreement allowed Mexico to repay its foreign debt over a term of fourteen years at interest rates lower than those originally contracted. United States Federal Reserve Board Chairman Paul A. Volcker, among others, had pushed for the interest rate reduction, in part as recognition of Mexico's having instituted difficult austerity measures and needing some fiscal relief to restore economic growth.

The Mexican debt crisis and the World Bank

4 August 2020 by Eric Toussaint Series: 1944-2020, 75 years of interference from the World Bank and the IMF (Part 18) Table 3. WB loans to Mexico and repayments (in million dollars)

	1978	1979	1980	1981	1982	1983	1984	1985	1986	1987	Total
WB loans	167	326	422	460	408	360	682	840	1,016	983	5,664
Repayments	184	220	255	283	328	399	485	597	819	1,072	4,642
Net transfer	-17	106	167	177	80	-39	197	243	197	-89	1,022

Source: World Bank, *Global Development Finance*, 2005

Table 3 shows the evolution of World Bank loans to Mexico. We note a sharp increase from 1978 to 1981. The WB was then frantically competing with private banks. In 1982 and 1983 we note a moderate decrease. Loans increased again from 1984 on as Private Banks developed their own recovery plan. The World Bank behaved as a last resort lender. Loans were conditioned on the Mexican state repaying private banks, a majority of which were North American. Net transfer remained positive because Mexico did use WB loans to repay private banks.

Table 1. Foreign banks' loans without any state guarantee and repayments to the banks (in million dollars) Table shows by 1984 a dramatic increase in new loans to Mexico as the nation's cash flow started to show signs of increasing in accordance with projections. [In 1983, the banks agreed, in advance of the recovery, to provide the working capital to Mexico's manufacturing sector in 1984.] This was after no new loans from commercial banks were provided in 1983.

	1978	1979	1980	1981	1982	1983	1984	1985	1986	1987	Total
Loans from the banks	931	1,565	2,450	3,690	590	0	2,144	1,115	1,700	247	14,432
Repayments	860	1,390	1,450	2,090	2,890	1,546	4,630	3,882	3,490	2,453	24,681
Net transfer	71	175	1,000	1,600	-2,300	-1,546	-2,486	-2,767	-1,790	-2,206	-10,249

Memorable Quotes

"Are you having fun yet?"

"Life isn't fair; get used to it."

"Life's odds are that everyone will get one opportunity to pursue their dreams sometime in their lives; the challenge is recognizing it when you see it."

"When you get that chance, take it. If you have a dream, chase it. The opportunity might only last for a moment and never present itself again."

"Your toe is too far away from your head to hurt that much."

"Laugh and the world laughs with you, cry and you're going to cry alone."

"There are two types of people in the world: people where life happens to them and people who make things happen in life. It's your choice what type of person you want to be."

"Sometimes a lost cause is the only one worth fighting for."

"Maybe, just maybe, Don Quixote in pursuing his seemingly impossible Quest was not crazy."

"You will be measured not by the outcome of the struggle, but by your courage and how well you handle it."

"Success is not final. Defeat is not fatal. It is the courage to continue that counts."

"Resilience is an ability. The ability to recover and try again. It is the will to bounce back, the persistence to keep going after something bad happens to you. It will help you find the courage to dig deep inside and fight through those emotions of defeat that will haunt you."

"God helps those who help themselves."

"Pray as if everything depends on God, but try as if everything depends on you."

"When faced with another's plight, and you have the ability and the opportunity to do something about it, God will leave the decision up to you, because he wants you, not him, to make the choice...to make a difference."

"You see, God does not make miracles happen in life, He works through people who do."

"But with these gifts will come a burden and a responsibility."

"When you make choices and are not sure what to do, just ask yourself: by following this path, will I be able to say in the end the world is a better place because I was here?"

"Engage the mind, bury the emotions."

"The more hopeless the situation, the more important the response."

"One moment at a time, one stride at a time, one runner at a time."

"Improbable does not mean impossible."

"A man's character is his destiny."

"The more we surrender our responsibilities to another person, a society, or a government, the less of a complete person we become.

"Reason and Logic are your friends in this situation. Perfect is the Enemy of Good."

Edward M. Rahill

I was going to let my heart set the direction I was to travel, and my head was going to get me there. I Just needed to make sure I let my heart talk to my soul."

"Do not give up in the face of setbacks, do not go against your values in the face of adversity."

"It is not how far you fall that is a measure of your worth, it is your will to find your inner strength and recover that is a measure of a man."

"Driving in traffic can make us zombies: don't think, just do what the traffic signs tell us to do. Driving competitively is the law of the jungle."

"You need to experience speed to understand speed. You need to understand speed to be able to handle speed."

"God, if this is what heaven is like, please take me now."

"A man was not meant to live his life alone. Only the love of a woman and the sense of belonging she brings him, can truly complete him."

"Discuss your thoughts to the group as if you're speaking to just one person."

"It is simple to get things done if it's not about you, it's about the people you surround yourself with that makes it all work."

"Love hurts? Not true. It's the loss of love that hurts."

"God, it must really piss you off that we only think of you when our lives suck."

"Winners have a commitment to do everything right, and if it's not right, do it over again until it is done right."

"Every battle is won or lost before it is ever fought."

"Remember where you came from...draw on the foundations of your character. It is there you will find the courage to reengage life...It will help you recover from the emotions that are crippling you; it will set you on the path back to who you are."

"Maybe this is what it's all about. Life isn't so bad when you're living for the moment. In this state of mind, it seemed that the demons of the past and my fears of the future were fading away."

"One moment at a time, one vehicle at a time, one mile at a time."

"Sometimes it seems like society expects men to take the emotional blow, to suck it up like we can't be hurt, to act like it doesn't matter—but it does."

"Fear kills more dreams than failure ever will."

"We can strive to understand spacetime, whether the past and future are real at this moment. But the past is what has happened."

"We cannot overstate the value of the gift we all have waiting for us when we are born, if we just take the moment to recognize it."

"Life is that gift, together with this gift we were given free will to decide what to do with it."

"We are born with a choice; a choice to just exist or take on the mission to learn and evolve into better Human Beings beyond what capabilities we had when we came into this world."

"Life is indeed a relay race. We are but members of a much larger team, team members who ran their leg before us and will run their leg after us."

"They momentarily overlap our lives at the hand-off of the baton, but they live in another time. When it is our turn to receive the baton, it is a gift of their wisdom and experience."

About the Author

Ed Rahill's love of endurance road racing was born when he was a boy listening to the 1966 24 hours of Le Mans. Raised in Western New York and a graduate of the University of Notre Dame, Rahill spent his successful career in the energy business, as CFO of ITC Holdings, then as Founder, President, and CEO of GridLiance, a Blackstone Company sold in 2021. True to his philosophy of life, at the completion of this book, he is planning to pursue a new venture this year.

Ed Rahill remains the cross-continental endurance road race record holder, with the fastest time in a competitive road race crossing the United States from Boston to San Diego. With the publication of One Mile at a Time, he chronicles the journey to honor his commitment to his grandmother that his children's generation would finally break the chain of broken dreams, has finally come to fruition.

Ed Rahill resides in Atlanta, Georgia, and is the father of four adult children.

https://edwardrahill.com

Printed in the USA
CPSIA information can be obtained
at www.ICGtesting.com
LVHW091631110624
782910LV00001B/43